On, Immortals

On, Immortals

Christopher Shipman

E. L. Marker
Salt Lake City

E.L. Marker, an imprint of WiDo Publishing
Salt Lake City, Utah
widopublishing.com

Cover design by Steven Novak
Book design by Marny K. Parkin

ISBN 978-1-947966-64-2

The Mustering

WE KNOW WE died before because we all remember it: the pain, the fear, the slipping from our skins. We have only a vague memory of what came between then and now; a dreamless slumber in the dark. Yet somehow, we have come back from the grave. And where we were once scattered across place and time, we now suddenly find ourselves together in an ancient house with twenty-three floors.

Like wind-scoured idols, the oldest of us have been made almost unrecognizable by the millennia, and yet their stormy, sea-colored eyes shine like stars through the distant past from which they emerged. We regard each other and smile. We share the same knowing glance and the visceral, unspoken understanding that this house was crafted just for us. We soon discover that each of us has a warmly lit room without walls where we can relive our fondest moments or review our most foolish misdeeds.

We explore our new forms and surroundings with the fascination of children. We ebb into the past, to the places we have been. We stand at the tops of snowy mountains and in the depths of chasms, and in between, we stroll through the bustling villages and cities where we played our part in history. Each one of us need only blink to return home.

Some of us ask why we have been brought together. It is the oldest ones who finally answer. They say there is one who sees us and needs us. They say there is one who will change everything.

Chapter 1

NOAH BATSON WAS finally jarred from his trance by the sharp metallic sound of loose gravel pelting the underside of his car. Because he knew well the rural, twisting byway that took him home, it was not necessary for him to see through the featureless night to know with grave certainty that he had drifted onto the narrow shoulder and was about to crash into dense forest that socked the road in on both sides like cliff faces. Noah turned the wheel quickly to the left, but only enough to nudge the car back onto the blacktop without overcorrecting.

Though Noah understood that he should have been thankful for avoiding an accident and that he should now be using all of his wits to anticipate dangers that might lurk beyond the reach of his headlights in the fast-approaching distance, he found that he could not help himself.

He glanced expectantly at the cell phone on the seat next to him, desperately willing it to light up. He finally grabbed it and swiped the screen. He scrolled through a list of recent calls. Still nothing. Nothing since this morning when she had told him to forget about her. Noah, on the other hand, had called her more than a dozen times since then. He shook his head. It just did not make any sense.

Noah steeled himself, then hit the call button yet again. A computer-generated voice told him to leave a message. He let out a long sigh, then hung up before the tone. What could he say that he had not said before? What difference would it make? Noah tossed the phone back onto the seat and put both hands on the wheel. Though Noah stared straight through the windshield, he put his mind to the past.

They had met while they were standing in line at Starbucks. Noah had locked on to her deep emerald eyes, the kind that were unnaturally transfixing because you could see yourself clearly in them, though you were somehow diminished in comparison to their natural beauty. They were the type of eyes that reflected your faults and made you want the person behind them to make up for everything that you lacked. And Noah lacked much (he had remembered thinking that that day), not the least of which was his self-confidence, which took a gut shot the moment he had failed out of law school three years ago. Admittedly, he had been out of sorts since then, acting rashly—even recklessly—to his almost constant detriment, but the moment he had seen her, he was convinced he was due for a win, and he believed his temerity might actually pay off.

Noah swallowed hard and then held out his hand: "I'm Noah, and I would like to buy your coffee if you'll let me."

The woman's eyes narrowed for several seconds as she tried to figure him out. Finally, her lips made a curious smile that told Noah he was in.

"I'm Violet," she said as she shook Noah's hand. "But not coffee. Chai tea for me."

Noah nodded, then showed her to an empty table by the door. He soon struck up a conversation, and she smiled sincerely and often, as if there were no other place that she would rather be. They talked until they melted into each other.

It was not long before she was spending so much time at Noah's place that he had to make room for some of her things. The last time he saw her, she was in the kitchen making coffee, wrapped only in a blanket, her sleep-tousled hair resting on her naked shoulders. When she caught Noah staring, she flashed him a provocative smile. If Noah had not already been late for work, he would have carried her right back to bed. Instead, he gave her a peck on the cheek and hurried down the hall.

But just as Noah opened the front door, he stopped dead in his tracks. Something made him turn around and look at her once more. What he could only describe as a soft, almost imperceptible voice inside his head told him to savor that moment because it would never come again. Though Noah had thought little of it at the time, the voice was spot on.

She was tired or busy every time he wanted to see her after that, and their conversations became increasingly infrequent. When Noah had finally gotten up the nerve to ask what was really going on, he had been met by maddening silence. Eventually, she flatly said that she was just not herself anymore. When Noah had asked what that meant, she said she had to go and hung up.

Noah had decided to make what he thought would be one last call for his own sake, so he could check the failed relationship box once and for all and get on with grieving. He had told her that he knew it was over, but he at least deserved a reason why. He could hear her quietly sobbing on the other end of the line.

"I'm not even here anymore," she said cryptically. "I don't know what else to say except that you should forget you even knew me."

But that was no answer at all. Noah had begged for a coup de grâce, yet she would not put him out of his misery. He even told her that in the last several messages he left. Now, he was calling but not leaving any messages. Now, he was just a creep.

Noah looked down to his phone once more. He wanted to call her a thousand more times, but he found some resolve and resisted the urge. It was time to put it all to an end, he decided. It was time to let it go. He rolled the window down. The cool night air rushed in and filled the car with cricket song. To his own great surprise, Noah snatched the phone and flung it into the blackness. He could briefly hear it clattering on the road. Noah instantly realized his expensive mistake and looked over his shoulder to try and mark where the phone would have come to rest so he could go back for it. Just when he got his head around to the front once more, something instantly materialized in the darkness.

At first, Noah caught only two or perhaps three startled pairs of red eyes, and he was certain it was a herd of deer crossing the road. It was not unusual to spot them in the dense wilderness, especially after nightfall. Normally, Noah would just slow and let them pass, but he had not been paying attention and had lost precious reaction time. Still, he saw a way around; if he feathered the brakes and swerved into the opposing lane, he could just skirt them and avoid impact. But as he got within just a few car lengths, they began to fill up his windshield. Noah gasped, and his blood ran ice-cold.

They were not deer at all, but people. *People!* In the middle of the night in the middle of nowhere, skittish, hunched-over figures in dark clothing were dashing across the road. Some had backpacks or duffel bags, which they flung aside in their haste to get out of the way. In the milliseconds before Noah had to act, he could make out their terrified expressions.

Noah slammed on the breaks and yanked the wheel hard. The car careened to the left and broke loose into a spin. Noah heard a loud thump. Finally, after what seemed like an eternity, his car stopped and stalled out in a dusty cloud off the wrong side of the road, the head-lights showing sturdy trees just inches from his bumper. The horrible sound was echoing in his head. Noah could picture the broken, bloody body. He could hear the death rattle.

Noah emerged from the car slowly, trying to prepare himself for what he might encounter. Once he got a sense of direction, he shuffled tentatively back to the scene of the crime, having to feel his way in the darkness.

"Is there anyone there?" he finally said in a halting voice. "Is anyone hurt?"

Hearing nothing, Noah began to walk in ever widening circles, both hoping and dreading in equal measure that he would find *something.* Just then, his foot got tangled, and he stumbled to the ground. He reached back. His hands found fabric; it was a duffle bag. Noah discovered that it was torn open, its contents disgorged onto the road. He gave silent thanks and took a long, deep breath. This had to be what he struck when he lost control of the car.

He called out once more: "Does anyone need help?"

Noah held perfectly still for a moment—still no response. He began to sort through items from the bag. Although he could not see clearly, he was pretty sure it was some type of food. Then he felt something hard. It was a flashlight. He found the button and shined the light on the road. He was right. They were silver pouches of dehydrated camping food: lots of them.

Noah found his feet and swept the beam of the flashlight up and down the road, then he walked to either side and aimed the light into the woods. There was absolutely no sign that anyone had been that way, let alone any carnage. He collected the pouches of food and stuffed them back in the shredded bag as best he could. He set it gently alongside the highway in case someone came looking for it.

"I'm sorry," he said loudly to the dark.

Noah climbed back into the car. With a trembling hand, he turned the key. The engine spit and sputtered, but it soon turned over. He made a K-turn and pointed the nose toward home. This time, Noah drove slowly, scanning the night intensely for any sign of movement. He imagined people would soon be popping out of every shadow.

For the life of him, Noah could not think of a good reason anyone would want to camp out there. As far as he knew, there were no trails, no scenic vistas, and no water sources nearby. And why were they moving around at night and wearing clothing that made them almost invisible? It was as if they were running from something.

Noah thought that perhaps there was some news he had missed that might provide an explanation, but when he reached for the radio, he saw that his hand was shaking badly, and he could not find the buttons. Then he realized his whole body was quivering, as if he were naked in a blizzard. Soon, he felt a pressure in his head that was expanding against his temples. Though painless at first, it very quickly blossomed into a four-alarm migraine. Noah winced and moaned under his breath as the agony set in.

Noah tried to keep driving safely, but his eyes became so sensitive that the dashboard lights, even the glow of his headlights on the pavement, blinded him. He had to squint, which gave him only a hazy, gun slot view of the road. He thought about stopping and waiting it out in the car, but he was so close to home now. He pressed the accelerator hard.

But once more, something blocked his way.

Two small blue orbs shone directly ahead, seeming to hover just above the road. Noah's first thought was that his addled mind was playing tricks on him. But, as the two orbs hurtled toward his windshield, they grew larger and more defined, like ghostly cannonballs.

Instinctively, Noah switched into the other lane to avoid the strange bullets, but they matched his move. Just before they hit, Noah's car dropped out from beneath him, and he was briefly as weightless as air. In an odd moment of clarity, Noah understood what had happened: he had driven straight through a high-banked turn and had launched himself into the stratosphere.

An instant later, light and dark were furiously tumbling together like a pin wheel in a tornado, set to a soundtrack of breaking glass and screeching metal. When everything finally stopped, it was so quiet that Noah could hear his own shallow, labored breaths. He found himself hanging upside down by his seat belt. A tree branch as thick as Noah's arm had gone through the windshield like a spear and had buried itself in the passenger seat. One headlight still worked but pointed directly into the ground. Noah tried to move, but his limbs would not budge. They felt strangely numb and wooden, as if they belonged to a discarded marionette. His head, on the other hand, was pounding like a jackhammer.

Then, the spectral blue orbs reappeared, twinkling in the distance. But they were now in the middle of the forest. As shattered as he was, Noah still had the presence of mind to understand that that was simply not possible. Anything that far away would be obscured by the trees. Still, the lights were there, and they were shooting toward him again.

Noah closed his eyes and held them shut for a moment. *They were still there!* They were on the backs of his eyelids, like smudges on a pair of glasses that'd been mistaken for objects in the distance. *They only appear to be far away!* Whatever these things were, they were in Noah's head. No wonder he could not escape them.

As they got "closer," Noah realized that they were not just points of light, but a pair of pale blue eyes set in a man's deeply shadowed, disembodied face. The eyes seemed to be searching for someone. Though

Noah did not recognize the man, he was somehow so familiar. The man's expression suggested that he had something very important he wanted to say, perhaps some secret to be revealed, but only to the right person. The man spoke slowly, deliberately, to be sure he was understood.

"Tell Miranda that you . . . *see* me."

As Noah tried to put a name to the face, he recalled the brittle black-and-white photos of a long-dead man he had once found in his father's dresser drawer. The man with pale blue eyes was Edward Batson, Noah's grandfather, who had passed away long before Noah was born. The man was only a vague memory even to Noah's father, who had been just six years old when Edward Batson died.

"This is most crucial," Edward Batson added. "You must tell her."

If the man wanted some response from Noah, it was already too late. Noah was falling fast down a deep well where lights and eyes and even thoughts could not find him.

Chapter 2

NOAH WAS WOKEN from his nap by a light touch on his skin. He found a withered, trembling hand resting on his right shoulder. His eyes followed along the wrist to an arm, then to a wrinkled face worn thin and translucent by almost ninety-two years of life. Her concerned smile was barely discernible from the many deep creases on her face.

For a very long time, Noah realized, Miranda Batson was little more than a potted plant living in a nursing home. It was there, in a small, sterile room with a bed on wheels that Noah had last visited her. Her tiny body had been hunched over in a wheelchair by a window, and she'd been staring vacuously into the dark.

"How are you doing, Grams?" he remembered asking as he walked in and plopped down on her bed.

No response.

"Grams, I asked, 'how are you doing?'"

She cocked her head toward Noah. "A little down today."

Noah nodded. He knew what she meant even if she refused to say it. She was lonely because she had only memories for friends, and, with the exception of Noah, even her own family did not come to see her much anymore.

"How about Scrabble, Grams? This time, I won't let you win; we'll play for real. What do you think?"

She only shook her head.

But today was different. Her milk chocolate eyes tracked Noah's every move with some single-minded purpose.

"I am so glad you called, my boy," she said presently. "I came as soon as I could."

Noah studied her for a moment while he got his bearings. Finally, the light bulb went off, and he remembered the secret he had shared with her.

"You didn't say anything to Mom and Dad about what I told you, right?"

She gave Noah an annoyed look. "Of course not. I just told them I wanted to come to the hospital to see you . . . alone. And your father said he had to run some errands anyway, so he dropped me off. He said he would be back in an hour or so."

"Good," Noah said, "I just don't want them knowing. I feel like they're disappointed in me already. I don't want them to think I'm crazy, too."

Miranda Batson leaned close, scanning Noah's face strenuously. "I know you're not crazy. Now, please," she pleaded quietly, "tell me about Edward. What do you mean you *saw* him?"

Noah told her just about everything he could remember about the events leading up to the crash. Of course, he left out the part about him being a stalker.

"Then," Noah said, "I saw these strange blue lights; they forced me off the road. Then, they somehow became eyes in a face, your husband's face. He told me to tell you that I saw him. And he said that last part slowly; he said it was important." Noah shrugged. "I mean, I shouldn't remember any of this considering how banged up I was." Noah lifted the sheet to reveal the pins sticking out just above the knee of his discolored left leg and the fiberglass cast on his left arm. "I'm sure Mom and Dad told you about my broken arm and that my leg was a jigsaw puzzle. I had a bad concussion, too. As it turns out, some anonymous person, using my own phone if you can believe it, saw the whole thing and made the call to 911. I bet it was one of the people that I almost hit. Anyway, I don't know for sure what I saw that night, maybe it was a pain-induced hallucination. Either way, real or imagined, it really stuck with me."

Miranda gripped his good arm with unexpected strength. Noah winced. "What color were his eyes?"

"I told you: they were blue."

"That doesn't tell me much, boy. There are all kinds of blue. You have to give me more than that. Were they blue like yours? Were they light or dark?"

Noah stroked his chin while he thought about it. "His eyes were lighter, paler than mine or Dad's. They were kind of unusual." Noah gestured toward the window in his room with a nod. "A lot like the sky is right now."

"Oh my," Miranda Batson whispered, trying to contain her excitement. "It *was* your grandfather! I never had any color pictures of him, so it was the eyes that would tell, and you got it exactly right. There's no way you could have known their color unless you met him. Even your father wouldn't have known that they were like the top of the sky on a clear fall day. He was too young to remember that."

She leaned back and settled into her wheelchair. "He was a great man," she added. "Never a harsh word for anybody. And so handsome and well dressed; he was something out of a Hollywood movie. When I first saw him, he looked at me, and I mean he stared at *me* if you can you believe it—the daughter of a poor trolley conductor!" She shivered and exhaled slowly. "But we just didn't have enough time together."

Noah had heard the story a thousand times before—it was legend in his family: Edward Batson was forty years old when he had arrived on the train from parts unknown, apparently on his way to New York City. But when he had laid eyes on Miranda, who was barely twenty, his plans had changed. He was handsome and rich enough that Miranda's parents approved the match without question, but he died from a heart attack seven years later, when Noah's father was only six years old. However, Edward had left his wife a sizeable fortune.

Despite the fact that she lacked much in the way of a formal education, Miranda Batson fancied herself to be an intellectual and great patron of the arts. Noah's father said that she had often disappeared for days at a time when he was a child, leaving him in the care of servants, so she could attend parties as far away as New York and Philadelphia, where she claimed to have rubbed elbows with famous artists and actors of the day like Jackson Pollock and Alec Guinness.

Apparently, at least back then, Miranda Batson said what she felt whenever she felt it, to the point where many people, including Noah's father, confused her honesty for cruelty. She had the brash personality of one accustomed to great wealth, he had explained, one who could buy the affections of anyone she happened to offend—that was until she frittered the money away and was forced to take a humble job as a cashier in a women's clothing store so she could put food on the table. It was there, his father had said, that Miranda Batson discovered that she had an eye for fashion, which helped her eventually land a high-paying job as head purchaser for an international department store.

Though quite begrudgingly, Noah's father even held Miranda Batson up as a shining example when the situation called for it.

About a year ago, Noah's parents had moved away to an old farmhouse with a couple of acres, something to keep them busy after his father's imminent retirement. Once they were settled, Noah had made the hour-long drive to have dinner with them and get a tour of the place. He had found his father in the kitchen reading the newspaper. Maybe it was because Noah's thirtieth birthday was a few days away and he had nothing to mark off in the achievements category, but to his astonishment, he suddenly found himself gushing with self-pity.

🔑

"What do I do now, Dad?" Noah remembered saying. "You know what I do for a living? I'm an account manager for a trucking company, which means I'm mostly just a glorified dispatcher. I come home every day to a dark, empty house. I feel nothing most of the time because there really isn't anything that I am passionate about. Is this the way it is going to be for the rest of my life?"

Noah's father stared at him over the top of the newspaper for a long moment. He opened his mouth to speak, but Noah cut him off.

"Don't tell me that I'm intelligent and that I can do anything I want. I don't want to hear it. That's easy for you to say anyway. You're a veterinarian, you were mayor of that shitty little town for God knows how long. You and Mom have fed me that crap my whole life. Anyway, you think every kid who participates should get a trophy, too, right? Washing out of law school—that showed me the cruel truth. I'm talentless and only smart enough to see how truly intelligent some other people are."

Noah's father slowly and deliberately lowered the newspaper to the table, as if trying to contain his emotions. He cleared his throat. "Is it my turn now?" Noah folded his arms across his chest and nodded.

"I have never told you anything that I did not believe was true," he began. "But even if you are not the smartest person in the world, so what? The point is that intelligence is only one part of the recipe for success. Probably the smallest part, too. Talent is part of it for sure, but by far the biggest piece of the pie is hard work. As for me, I was lucky enough to know what I wanted since I was a kid. It's no coincidence that I had a talent for it, too. People tend to feel passionate about things they are good at. Then came the hard work: all the years of school, then working twelve hours a day, seven days a week. That's what brought my dream to life.

"As far as law school goes—okay, it didn't work out. I'm not sure why you pinned all your hopes on that anyway. But that doesn't mean you're not smart. Since then though, it's like you've lost your way. Some of the things you've done, some of the stunts you've pulled lately, I just don't understand. It seems like you have a big hole inside you that you're trying to fill with . . . nonsense."

"Really, you're going there? I thought we already talked about that stuff."

"No, we did not. That's exactly why I'm bringing it up. And how could I not? You're my son, and I'm worried about you. So, let's review: First, you intervened in a bar fight that was none of your business, and you got your ass kicked in the process by the way. Then you let a homeless guy stay with you for a few days to get back on his feet, and he ends up robbing you blind. And, of course, on a whim, you drove halfway across the country to see a girl you met online only to find out she was married with three children. And those are only the things I know about! God knows what else you've been up to that I haven't gotten wind of yet!"

Noah hung his head. "I don't know why, Dad," he mumbled. "I guess I just wanted to accomplish . . . *something*."

His father frowned. "You don't have anything to prove, Noah—at least not to your mom and me. You have to get back on track, to find that one thing you're good at, that one thing you want to do. I know you feel like a failure, and that breaks my heart, but I'm pleading with you: You have to get past it, you have to stop beating yourself up all the time. I have no doubt you will find your part to play, as long as you don't kill yourself in the meantime."

Noah finally looked up. "But Dad, I'm getting too old now to make any real changes, even if I am able to figure out my *purpose*.

His father shook his head. "Not so. Take your grandmother, for instance. She was, unfortunately, not very good at being my mother, but she managed to finally find something she could do well, something she loved and was meant to do. And that was not until she was in her early forties. Believe me, if she can reinvent herself, so can you."

Someone was patting Noah's cheek. "Earth to Noah."

A shadow of confusion passed over Noah's face. "Sorry, Grams. I just wandered off there for a moment. The meds make me loopy sometimes."

"I don't mean to be a pain," she said, "but my time on this rock is coming to a close." She winked at Noah. "Some, meaning your father, would think it's way past due. That means we better get to the bottom of this—now. What I was asking was if you remembered anything more, about what he said, I mean. I just want to make sure."

"He said I should tell you about it, that I saw him . . . nothing else."

Miranda Batson clapped her hands softly. "That's enough; I've heard enough to know it's true." She rummaged through her purse. "I have something for you." She handed him a small plain key. Noah turned it over in his fingers. Other than being tarnished and worn, it had no markings of any kind.

"What's this?"

Miranda Batson tilted her head sardonically. "Well, plainly it's a key that I have had a long time, since your grandfather gave it to me on our wedding night seventy-plus years ago."

Noah rolled his eyes. "I get that it's a key, but what's it for, I mean? What does it open?"

She threw up her hands. "I have no idea, but Lord knows I did my best to find out. I tried every door in our house, then every lock in every place I ever was. Can you imagine how silly I must have looked? People would have thought I was crazy or took me for a robber. If I went to someone's house, when they weren't looking, I would try it in any door that happened to be close to me. As strange as it sounds, I even tried it in the doors at the nursing home when I had a chance. I used to sneak out of my room at night, when they only have one nurse on duty. I was just so curious. After all, your grandfather liked to keep his secrets."

Noah looked incredulous. "Why are you giving it to me then?"

"He told me that it should go to the person who *sees* him. And I don't mean that in a literal way, because I asked him that. I told him that by that direction, I should give it to the next person that happened to lay eyes on him. He laughed at that. He said I would know when the time comes and that it would most likely happen after he was dead and gone. He said that he was working on something, that he was close to an answer, and that if he didn't finish, someone else special would. I tried to get more out of him, but he never said another word about it." She shrugged. "He died seven years later and left me with a six-year-old son and this blasted key."

Noah contemplated the key in his hand once more. She said it should go to someone "special." But there was nothing about the key that was special, and there was certainly nothing about him that was special. He sighed aloud because that was the sad reality. Still, he did not have the heart to tell her that he was not the one she wanted and that the key was only worth the shiny memories it symbolized. Noah decided he would play along though, if for no other reason than he had never before seen his grandmother so animated and happy.

"I will need some clues, of course. So, Grams, where did Edward Batson come from? How did he make all that money?"

"Where he was from? Well, I never got a straight answer to that, except he said he was from somewhere out West. As to money, he never said too much about that either, except that it was family money. He said he was the last of his line and it had all come to him. I loved all the mystery, so I never bothered him too much about what came before."

Noah waited for more, but there was only silence.

"Well, that's not very much to go on."

Miranda Batson shook her head. "Didn't I tell you that he liked to keep his secrets?"

Noah slowly pulled himself up, then stuffed a pillow behind his back.

"If he didn't have to work, what did he do all day? What were his hobbies? What was he good at?"

Miranda Batson squinted while she thought. "He spent a lot of time in libraries; he liked to read and research—whatever interested him. And he liked history, I can tell you that, especially things about his ancestors. He always had a story about so and so, who came from such and such a place, who did something remarkable. I asked him how he could know so much about people he never met, but I never really got an answer. Or maybe he had given me one, and I just don't remember it anymore. Anyway, I always felt a little lost when he talked about things that happened so long ago. Looking back, I probably should have taken more interest in it, or at least written all that down, but I was young and in love, and I thought I had forever in front of me."

Miranda Batson gazed into a shadow-draped corner of the room and reminisced with the ghost of her husband. "And I never understood how you could be so good at so many things." She turned back to Noah. "You know, there was virtually nothing that man could not do. He could shoe a horse just as easily as he could fix a car. And once, I told him we should have a garden, and he went right out and did just that. He grew everything from sunflowers to melons, the biggest and tastiest around. And it wasn't just that he was good with his hands. When he walked into a room full of people, it wasn't long before they were gathered around him, hanging on his every word." She turned to the emptiness of Noah's room once more and wagged a crooked finger in the air. "And the ladies loved you the most; they stared and fanned their faces when you were around. It always made me so jealous." Then she laughed quietly to herself.

Noah put the key in the drawer of the nightstand next to his bed. He examined it once more for a moment before he shut the drawer. He yawned. "Do you have anything of his—any papers, pictures, anything he may have had that had something to do with this key?"

Miranda chewed on her lip while she contemplated the question. "I know he kept a lot of papers. He had them in a file cabinet in the den. But it was always locked. After he died, all I could find were his legal documents: ledgers and insurance policies and the like. Maybe he moved some things before that; I just don't know. I couldn't find anything unusual anywhere in the house."

Noah could hardly keep his eyes open. The conversation and meds had finally taken their toll. His grandmother rested the back of her hand against Noah's forehead for a moment, as if gauging his temperature, then she gently pushed back a lock of hair that had fallen across his brow.

"You remember what I said Noah: he meant for you to have the key—I know it."

Noah was almost out, but he managed a smile. "We'll talk more, Grams," he whispered. "I just need a little sleep right now. We'll figure it out tomorrow."

Miranda Batson nodded understandingly. "I'm tired, too. This took a lot out of me." She turned her eyes upward and smiled. "I've done my part."

But Noah did not hear her last words because he had already plunged into a warm pool of opiate-induced unconsciousness swirling with vivid dreams.

8——▼

Noah was standing on a veranda looking down on a silent crowd of people who seemed to be waiting impatiently, as if gathered on a busy street corner and anticipating the signal to move across the intersection. Suddenly, they turned toward Noah. He scanned their faces, but there were so many that he could not figure out whether he knew any of them. He felt naked and alone, even with so many pairs of eyes focused on him.

Noah broke the silence. "Are you here for me?"

"Yes," they responded collectively.

"Why?"

They turned to each other and exchanged hushed words. One of them, a man, stepped forward, his faced disguised somehow, mottled by soft light and gray shadows. "That's our job, of course!" The man happily announced.

The scene instantly changed. Noah realized he was now sitting alone in a movie theater, popcorn scattered on the floor at his feet. Faces appeared on the screen, one after the other in increasingly rapid succession. Hundreds, perhaps thousands of faces flickered by with such speed that they all seemed to melt together to form one blurry, yet familiar portrait. Noah craned his neck and leaned forward for a better look. A name was on the tip of his tongue. He closed his eyes and bent all his thought on it, but it was like trying to find his shadow in a dimly lit room. It was right there, but he just could not see it.

Chapter 3

NOAH WOKE EARLY and lay still in his bed, staring at the red oak tree outside his bedroom window. Though a late winter frost clung desperately to its branches in some places, tiny red leaves still began to sprout from swollen buds. In years past, Noah thought they resembled candle flames lighting the way for spring. But now, he decided, they looked more like blood droplets spattered on the yellow backdrop of dawn. It made him think of death and funerals, especially his grandmother's. She passed away not quite a week after she had dropped the key in his lap. Noah was then still too frail to attend and he had spent the day in his hospital bed with his back to the door, clutching the key and pretending to be asleep.

Ever since he had arrived home, quality rest proved frustrating and elusive, as if he were being punished for having mocked the gods of sleep that day. The faces showed up night after night, looking up at him, silently waiting for him to say or realize something. But like always, he could offer them nothing. He woke some mornings in twisted sheets, more exhausted than he had been when he had gone to bed the night before. Whatever faith the faces had in him was entirely misplaced.

Noah rubbed his eyes, then started his morning ritual. He began to move one part of his body at a time: first his neck, then his fingers, then his arms, and then he worked his way down through his stiff legs and feet, trying to assess his recovery. Was he better than yesterday? Hard to tell. Was he better than last week? Perhaps. Was he better than last month? Almost certainly. Although it was slow going, at least he could say that he was always getting better, even if that only really meant that he was not in quite as much pain as before.

Noah swung his feet onto the floor. He tested his weight on his legs before he reached for the cane. His head throbbed, and his legs wobbled for a moment, but he stood slowly, using the cane to ease himself forward. He paused and opened the nightstand drawer. In the back, beneath some tissues and a magazine, Noah's fingers found the key. From time to time, he examined it closely, remembering everything his grandmother had told him in the hospital. If Noah had known that that was the last time he would see her, he might have asked more questions, maybe gotten some more information to go on. It was all so important to her, as if she had given him a piece of her very soul, and Noah wanted to honor that. But it all seemed so far away, now that she was gone, like it had happened in a book that he had read a long time ago. However, even if Noah could not experience that moment freshly in his mind, he could never forget it either. Not just because he had the key, but because the day she gave it to him was the day the faces first appeared, and he had the feeling that they would never leave his dreams until he figured out what they wanted.

Noah shambled into the bathroom. He caught a fleeting glimpse of his gaunt face in the mirror, and it startled him. He knew he had lost weight; after all, the pain had a way of making food taste like dirt and ashes. He had to do something about that, he thought. Maybe he could force a couple of Big Macs down his throat every day. But picturing the greasy burgers made his stomach turn. He would stick to the nutrition shakes his doctor recommended until his appetite was back.

Noah shed his underwear and T-shirt, carefully avoiding the mirror this time, then slowly climbed into the shower. He sat on the stool and waited until the hot water awakened his senses. He had no place to go; he could just sit around the house all day in his pajamas. There was no reason to pretend otherwise. But this was all part of his therapy, he thought—do the things that other people take for granted, and he would continue to improve. So, he kept the routine no matter how sour and low he felt: get up, take a shower, get dressed, and find something to do outside of the house, even if it is only a slow, unsteady walk to the end of the block.

After he gently patted himself dry, Noah dressed in a pair of now very baggy jeans, a button-down shirt, and sneakers. He put on a pot of coffee and lowered himself to a chair at the kitchen table. He had ignored the mail since he got home, and it was piled high in front of him. He grudgingly began to sort through it, throwing the junk into the garbage. Only the bills remained, and they were all past due, way past due.

Any inspiration Noah might have found in his improved physical condition was stamped out by the crushing realization that he was running out of money. If being haunted, in pain, and out of work was not reason enough to feel entirely defeated, the threat of foreclosure should certainly seal the deal. Noah buried his head in his hands. Worst case scenarios flooded his brain. He imagined himself living in a refrigerator box, or worse yet, with his parents.

Noah turned back toward his bedroom. His thoughts drifted back to the tiny key and the faces that visited him at night. They came together, and they were linked together. As foolish and desperate as it may have seemed, Noah felt a spark of excitement when he thought about unraveling the mystery one day. In a strange way, it gave him purpose and a reason, though perhaps a pathetic one, to keep getting up every day.

Noah stood up and leaned against the counter. He pulled a mug from the cabinet. But as he reached for the coffee pot, he suddenly remembered that he was standing in the exact same spot Violet had been in the last time he had ever laid eyes on her. Yet it was not like before the accident, when the mere thought of her turned him into oatmeal. Now, the image of her conjured up a feeling more like nostalgia, as if she had taken her proper place in his glossed-over history.

Noah supposed that the passage of time coupled with earth shattering events had a way of naturally sorting out one's priorities. Still, he could not help but think that there was something important he should have learned from the relationship. Perhaps he was just not far enough removed from the turmoil to understand what that was.

As he poured his coffee, Noah glanced out the tiny window above the sink. Except for a fat gray cat walking a tightrope on top of his fence, the neighborhood framed in the glass was still and quiet; most everyone was gone to work or school or whatever other place they were expected at.

After several sips, Noah decided the coffee tasted like crap, and he dumped it in the sink. He grabbed his cane and shuffled falteringly down the hall. After he put on a fleece jacket and wool hat, he opened the front door. He stepped outside and immediately felt the warm sun on his face. Noah closed his eyes and took a deep breath.

"Hey kid," someone called out. "I heard about what happened. It's good to see you out and about."

Noah turned toward the voice. His long-time neighbor, Rick Hallman, was just emerging from his house. He was wearing a wrinkled shirt, and his tie was too short. It also appeared that he had forgotten to shave. Noah glanced at his watch. Rick was usually off to work at least an hour before now.

Seeing him reminded Noah that things could be far worse. After twenty-five years of marriage, Rick's wife had inexplicably packed up her stuff and taken off. Though Rick rarely talked about it, he had once mentioned that his kids blamed him for some reason and that they had barely spoken to him since it happened.

"For sure," Noah said. He pointed to the sky. "Especially on a day like this."

Noah started to walk toward him, but Rick held up a hand to stop him. He made his way across the grass to Noah instead.

"I'll come to you," he said, slightly out of breath. "I don't want you to catch a foot and fall on my account."

Noah took his outstretched hand. He detected the faint odor of booze. Noah suddenly felt deeply ashamed for not making contact with him sooner.

"How have you been, Rick? I meant to get by to see you one of these days, . . . to see how things were going with you. I've been dealing with my own shit, but that's no excuse." He paused for a moment. "Anyway, you need anything?"

Rick forced a weak smile and waved Noah off. "No, not really. I'm pretty much used to it now, . . . being a bachelor again, I mean.

"Glad to hear it," Noah said, although it was clear from his shabby state that Rick was lying.

"I want to ask you something though," Rick said. "Now that it's getting warm maybe we can grill out back one of these days, like normal people do. You bring the beer, okay?"

Noah nodded several times. "Of course, of course; it's a plan."

"Great." Rick did his best to fake a smile once more. Then he turned around. "I'll see you soon," he said over his shoulder as he walked to his car. A moment later, he drove off.

Noah focused once more on the task at hand. He decided he felt well enough to walk two blocks. As he moved slowly down the sidewalk, he noticed his already modest house was sorely in need of a new coat of paint. He could also see some loose slate tiles on the roof. He might have tried to do these repairs himself if his body were sound, but they would have to wait until he was better, or he would have to pay someone to do it—yet another bill to give him tunnel vision in the morning. When Noah heard the distant rumble of an approaching motorcycle, he welcomed the distraction.

The pounding black and chrome machine was loudly accelerating down the street in front of his house. Noah stopped for a moment. He raised his hand to the rider and a helmeted head nodded as the motorcycle roared by and chopped up the stillness. Noah watched until the bike turned at the end of the block and disappeared around the corner.

Noah leaned back, found his balance once again, and moved on, one foot in front of the other, careful to avoid cracks or seams that might trip him up. Noah was pleasantly surprised. He was walking more fluidly and had less pain than usual. Inspired once more, he picked up the pace, using the cane only when he felt as if he might get too far ahead of his feet.

A moment later, Noah heard the high-pitched squeal of tires skidding, and his heart stopped. He froze where he stood, waiting for the other shoe to drop. Then it happened: the metallic smack of vehicles colliding. Noah unconsciously dropped his cane and limped to where he had last seen the motorcycle, oblivious to the wave of crippling pain that warned him against such sudden movements. He turned the corner and followed the smoking patches of rubber to ground zero.

Noah knew instantly what had happened. Someone had backed out of a driveway, directly into the path of the motorcycle. The driver of the car, a young woman, was glued to her seat, her hands still clutching the steering wheel. The twisted motorcycle rested on one side of the car while the rider lay in a heap of leather and denim in the roadway about fifteen feet away on the far side of the car.

Noah finally got to the unconscious rider. He leaned down for a closer look and felt something spritzing his face. The rider's leg was badly broken: a fragment of bone was sticking out just below his right knee. It must have cut an artery because blood was spraying from the wound in a fast-thumping rhythm. Noah patted his pockets and discovered that he had not brought his phone. He turned back to the car and yelled for the woman to call 911, but she was still a mannequin. He screamed at the top of his lungs, hoping someone might be within earshot. Noah suddenly felt lightheaded. He tried to cry out for help once more, but the words never reached his lips.

The world around him began to fade away to a pinpoint of light at the wrong end of a telescope. Everything swirled and twirled and then went completely black. He saw the faces in the dark. The strange film rolled by, the images always just enough out of focus to prevent any reliable identification. The movie reel stopped, and one picture, one face, came into view. It was rippling and distorted, as if it were a reflection in the water. The only way Noah could describe what happened next was that a door was flung open somewhere deep in his mind. Somebody—or something—stepped inside.

Chapter 4

The Healer

THE SUN WAS just beginning to rise over the hills and reveal their thick, green cover when I got to the stream. Just atop the next rise was my destination. But I was early, and my pack was heavy, so I stopped to rest and quench my thirst. I squatted down where the trickling water backed up against a tumble of stones and formed a deep, cold pool. As I leaned out to drink, I found my undulating reflection staring back. My skin was dark brown, bronzed by the summer sun, and my beard and my black, curly hair were long and wild. I did my best to tame both with the ivory comb that my mother had insisted on giving me when I left home so long ago. I was more boy than man then, and I could not yet understand what place it might have among the sharp and deadly gear of a Roman soldier. But then, I met Ravenwing, and I gave silent thanks for the wisdom of my mother who knew I would one day fall under the spell of a woman.

After I combed and washed and once more checked my supplies, I jumped across the stream and climbed the slippery, moss-covered path that snaked to the top of the hill. When I arrived at the clearing, I found more of them than usual. Some were sitting, others were still arriving on litters, too sick or too old to make it on their own. And there, the last to arrive, her glossy black hair taken up by the wind, was Ravenwing. When she saw me, the deep concern on her face faded, and she smiled. I waved, and she came to me and brought heaven with her.

She bowed her head slightly. "Abreus, the Healer," she said with a tone of respectful familiarity. "There are so many who need your care."

Her Latin, though a bit choppy, was improving. She must have been practicing the lessons I had taught her during our meetings on this ancient spine of the land. I bowed my head to return the courtesy. Then our gazes locked, and we regarded each other silently. Her eyes were deep and as black as the night. Yet, there was a soft light somewhere inside that was felt more than seen, like the glow of a morning sun that had not yet crowned the horizon. She was aptly named, I thought, as it was said that she had been born in the darkness under the watchful eye of a raven that took flight only after she took her first breath. Her beauty was known throughout the land.

"As always, it is my honor to serve your proud people," I said loud enough to be heard by all present. Even if they could not understand the words, the tone of my voice would help to allay any lingering suspicions.

After all, Ravenwing and her companions were long-boned Silures, and their ferociousness and distrust toward outsiders was legendary. It was said that they had arrived in Brittany after a long voyage centuries ago. Their dark complexion suggested they came from Spain or North Africa, but their histories claim that they were born directly from the mouths of their mighty gods and commanded to go forth. What cannot be disputed is that they subjugated the small tribes they encountered in Brittany and ruled their land in relative peace, . . . until the Second Legion marched into their midst.

Rome quickly discovered that it was not welcome and that the Silures would not be easily pacified. They would accept no gift or bribe or promise of freedom; only their deaths in battle would silence them. And so, for almost one hundred years, the Second Legion fought them bitterly. I had heard stories about the bloodshed and the wretched battle cry of the Silures—a horrendous shriek that many times caused the Roman soldiers to break ranks. But inevitably, the Silures could not replace their fallen warriors quickly enough to defeat an army that could draw men from a thousand nations across the earth.

By the time I arrived in Brittany, stationed at Isca, the Silure hill forts had long been empty and crumbling. Still, they had not entirely learned to bear the yoke of foreign rule. It was not unusual for deadly skirmishes to break out over some perceived insult cast by a Roman soldier. And the Silures rarely adopted any Roman manner or idea, still preferring their ancient, mystical ways to the accumulated, practical knowledge of Rome.

The scene before me now was the epitome of their pride and stubbornness. They had left their villages only under cover of darkness to seek me out, claiming the false pretense of a pilgrimage. Although, as Ravenwing had told me, everyone already knew where they were going. In this way, my presence was tolerated. After all, I was not an armored death dealer. I was a Roman army medic, schooled in the capital itself and trained in the field. My knowledge and skill had been compiled from a thousand years of the trial-and-error experiences of those that came before me.

I had been recruited into the ranks of the Roman army from my island home of Cos in Greece, the birthplace of the great physician Hippocrates. Naturally, I had gravitated toward the medical arts advanced by my fellow countryman, and I was sent to Rome where I had earned my commission as a medic. Then I was sent to the battlefield to practice and ultimately hone my skills. From the burning sands of North Africa to the fog-shrouded land of Brittany, I proudly served the soldiers who served Rome. I treated their wounds, and when I could not, I held their heads and ushered them off to dwell with their gods. But in times of peace, it was not unusual for medics to employ their skills to help Rome's former enemies. In fact, it was encouraged so that Rome could win their loyalty. But I did not do it for Rome. I did it because I was skilled in healing and because I enjoyed helping others. And now, I took even greater pleasure in my tasks outside the fort because I could be with Ravenwing, if only for a while.

I set down my pack and nodded to her. She knew what to do. While I carefully laid out my instruments, herbs and supplies, she started a fire. Next, she fetched water from the stream, filled a cauldron, and hung it on a tripod over the flames. Once the water was brought to a strong boil, she dropped in my instruments. Then, together, we visited each patient in turn, beginning with those most in need.

The first, just a boy of ten or eleven, had suffered a deep stab wound to his left thigh. He was pressing his palm against it to stem the bleeding. I knew immediately that it was from the sting of a sword, a straight thrust it seemed. I glanced at Ravenwing.

"Has there been some fighting?"

"Their warrior spirit is still strong," she said proudly, "and they sometimes forget themselves during their sword games." Then she stared at the frightened youth. "But this one will now never forget that swords are not for games and that sticks might be better suited for their fun."

"The herbs, my suture kit, a probe, . . . and a clamp, in case the artery is damaged," I said.

Even though I knew the boy could not understand the words, I spoke calmly to him until Ravenwing returned. She gently placed a leather wrapped stick in his mouth and explained softly in her native tongue what I was about to do. He closed his eyes and clenched his teeth. Ravenwing leaned close and watched with wide, curious eyes. I pulled the boy's hand away from the diamond-shaped wound. The blood did not spray out but seeped forth slowly—a good sign meaning that the artery had likely not been pierced. But I had to explore the wound to be sure.

Ravenwing handed me a thin bronze probe, still quite hot, and I inserted it into the cut slowly to determine its extent. Though the wound was not severe enough to cause any serious injury, it was still too deep to close with sutures. I turned once more to Ravenwing, but she had anticipated my instruction, and she was already mixing the herbs and honey. I could not help but smile. She had learned much from our time together and was now quite skilled in her own right.

She handed me the salve, and I pushed it gently into the wound. The boy cried, but Ravenwing stroked his hair and steadied him. The salve would stop the bleeding and heal the wound from the inside out to keep it from rotting. Ravenwing took the stick from the boy's mouth, and he began to sob. Then he said something. Ravenwing looked at me and whispered in the boy's ear.

"He asked me if he was going to die," she translated, once more anticipating the question I was about to ask.

"What did you tell him?"

She reached out and touched my hand. "I told him you would not allow it because you are death's master."

I blushed at the compliment. "But I only wish that were true."

"For this boy, it is true because he will be strong once again—and far wiser."

I looked around at the others, then back to Ravenwing. "I hope I do as well for them."

Next, I found a young Silure woman soon to give birth. The strain was beginning to crease her brow, yet she bore the pain with the indifference that a boulder shows the wind. But the baby was in breach position, and soon, the agony would be more than even a warrior maiden could stand. This presented a dilemma because I knew she would not allow any man, even a medic, to place his hands inside her, so I instructed Ravenwing about what she must do to turn the child. I watched over her as she worked. When it was done, she washed her trembling hands, and I placed my instruments back into the steaming cauldron.

While Ravenwing reorganized and replenished my supplies, I examined a middle-aged man who was grimacing with pain. His forearm was splinted and bound with cloth strips to stabilize a fracture. I gently removed the wrappings and found that only one of the bones in his arm was broken. However, about a hand's width above the wrist, the fracture was displaced and would not mend properly unless the bone was aligned. I slowly pulled his arm toward me. I placed one hand around his wrist and the other beneath his forearm. I looked at him seriously, and he immediately understood what I intended to do. He closed his eyes and held his breath. I quickly rotated his forearm until I could feel the bone snap back into place. He reared his head back, but not a sound escaped his lips. I replaced the splint and tied the cloth strips firmly. Then I fashioned a sling from a piece of my cloak and rested his arm inside so that it was held very close to his body. Ravenwing brewed some bitter tea and urged the man to drink it because it would blunt the pain.

Another young woman had dislocated her shoulder when she had apparently fallen from a tree. Ravenwing told her to brace herself just before I shoved her arm back into the joint. Ravenwing told her to be more careful in the future because she would be prone to more easily injuring herself again since the fibers in the joint would now always be a bit weakened.

We turned our attention next to the remaining three patients, all elderly men suffering from the nagging symptoms of their advanced age. Ravenwing prepared warm ointments for their aching bones, and

I brewed more bitter teas to stifle their pains. If there was a remedy that Ravenwing was unfamiliar with, she watched me carefully as I worked on it. Once I demonstrated my technique, however, Ravenwing duplicated it perfectly and never forgot it.

Now relieved of their discomfort, at least temporarily, each old warrior bowed unsteadily to show me gratitude. Ravenwing then spoke for me so they could understand. When she had finished, they glanced at each other and nodded with apparent approval. When I asked Ravenwing what she had told them, she said she had explained that although Romans and Silures are peoples from different sides of the horizon, my work was offered as a token of Roman good will to unite them in peace,

"As always, Ravenwing," I said, "your beauty and wisdom prove more powerful than any medicine I could craft."

It took all of my strength to resist the urge to take her into my arms. But I was afraid that she had learned enough to serve her people without me, and I was stricken low by the realization that our time together was coming to an end. I stared into the darkening sky and imagined her face among the stars, always out of my reach.

"You have done well," I finally managed to say, trying not to betray my sadness. "Soon, you will not need me any longer. You will be a healer famous throughout the villages."

Ravenwing caressed my cheek with the back of her hand. "Do you not know by now, after all the moments we have passed together, that there will *always* be something that I need to know, so that I must *always* be at your side so that you can teach me?" Now she reached up and gently cradled my face with her hands. "If you will not speak of it, then I will. . . . Why should we not be together? Word of your work has spread across the countryside. You stand high among my people. If you should take a wife, should it not be me, the one who has shared your work, your passion?

I pulled Ravenwing close to me on the top of the hill, and I kissed her. No more words were necessary. That moment was etched forever in my mind such that even when I was old and broken, I could recall every word, every detail of her face.

Chapter 5

IT WAS NOT uncommon for Roman soldiers to take foreign wives, so my commander granted permission for me to wed and live outside of the fort so long as I was nearby and attended sufficiently to my duties.

After a lengthy and sometimes heated debate among the Silure elders of Ravenwing's village, they eventually consented to our union. This, I believe, was due not only to the fact that I was able to provide a valuable service, but I suspected it was also because my physical appearance resembled their own. I was told that I was the first "Roman" in recent memory to be permitted such a privilege.

The night before my wedding, I sat on my bunk and wrote a letter to my parents. I had heard nothing from them in several years, and I wondered if they were even still alive. I did my best to describe how I felt about Ravenwing and the work we did together. I poured my heart into the letter because I had to explain why I would likely never return to my island home again and why I would never see them again.

As was the Silure custom, we were married under a harvest moon at midnight, witnessed by many curious villagers, in a brief ceremony. Ravenwing explained to me that it occurred over the edge of night and into day to symbolize the transition into married life.

Soon, Ravenwing was pregnant. With the help of soldiers and villagers alike, we constructed a proper home of stone and mortar, with a sturdy thatched roof and a large hearth. I built a post-and-rail enclosure for the animals, and Ravenwing tilled and planted an immense and colorful garden for both food and healing herbs. The work was completed just in time for Ravenwing to deliver the first of three sons into the world. And when my black hair had just begun to frost with grey, Ravenwing gave me the last of our children, a daughter with pale sky blue eyes like my own.

My sons became tall and broad-shouldered, and they also served with the Second Legion when their time came. They returned from the north with stories of their bravery in battle against strange painted people. In fact, many Silures served with honor and distinction in the Second Legion and were eventually revered for their ability to both heal and to hack, if need be, with unimaginable fury. I, of course, encouraged my sons to be healers first and soldiers second, as the power to heal, I believed, proved to be far more formidable.

My beautiful daughter was born with the first rays of the morning sun, so we named her Daybreak, or *Diluculo* in Latin. She was all the more coveted by us when our sons left for their own adventures. As I was by that time retired from service, and because Daybreak remained at home (as there were not many opportunities for either Roman or Silure women to strike out on their own until they were married), she became the sole focus of our attention. When she fell in love with the soldier son of a wealthy Roman general, Ravenwing and I had heavy hearts because we knew Daybreak would soon be whisked away from us. After her marriage, she traveled with her husband to Ostia, a bustling port on the Tiber River near Rome. Although we never made the journey to visit Daybreak in her new home, due mostly to our considerable age, we wrote to each other several times a year.

Ravenwing died quietly one night while I slept next to her. My turn came just a year later. I remember my sons and others gathered around my bed while I explained to them how to make the elixirs that would settle me and ease my pain. I can still see their worried expressions and hear their tender reassurances. It is difficult to describe what happened next, except to say that I was swept from this world back to the place from whence I came, just as a beached puddle is reclaimed by the sea when the tide returns.

Yet now, I have been remade. I do not have to ask why. I spring into action with the passion and vigor of my youth.

Chapter 6

NOAH WAS JUST about home when he suddenly noticed that he was winded and that his body ached all over, as if he had just pulled up from a sprint. He stopped and leaned on his cane with both hands while he sorted things out.

"That's . . . weird," he said between breaths.

Noah turned his head back in the direction he had come from as he retraced his steps in his mind, searching for an explanation in the same way he might look for a dropped wallet or set of keys. He had left the house for a walk, and now he was back. But what about in between? Noah thought hard on it, but it was blacked out, as if someone colored over that memory with permanent marker. A moment later, a figure emerged on the corner at the far end of the block. A man, a police officer, stopped and looked around. He soon zeroed in on Noah and walked toward him briskly enough that the officer had to use both hands to secure the various items hanging from his duty belt.

"Sir," he said as he closed in, "I need to talk to you for a minute. Did you see what happened back there? The accident with the motorcycle, I mean?"

Accident? Motorcycle? The words kicked off an almost dizzying sense of déjà vu, as if Noah should know exactly what the officer meant because Noah had been there and seen the whole thing. But that was all it was—just a feeling. The blanks were still blank.

"I'm sorry," Noah eventually said, "but I can't say that I did."

The policeman screwed up his face in a befuddled expression. "May I ask what you were doing out here?"

Noah tilted his head toward his house. "I live there; I was just out for a walk, and I'm headed home."

The officer pointed over his shoulder. "Well, it happened right around the corner. You had to have passed it—you must have seen something!"

Noah shook his head. "Again, I'm sorry I can't help."

The policeman appeared unconvinced. "Look, no one is in trouble. The ambulance just got here, and they're loading the guy on it now, but the paramedic has some questions for the person that helped the guy, that's all."

"Helped? What does that mean?"

The cop looked annoyed. "*Someone* put a tourniquet on the guy with his belt. *Someone* set the bones in his leg and splinted it with a stick and strips of cloth torn from the guy's shirt. The paramedic said it was better than what most surgeons could do." The officer shook his head with disbelief. "I mean, that guy would be dead right now; he would have bled out or died from shock. There's no one else here. So, you tell me: if it wasn't you, who was it?"

Before Noah could tell the cop that he was talking to the wrong guy—he couldn't even peel the wrapper off a Band-Aid without getting the whole thing stuck together—Noah looked down and noticed the dried blood under his fingernails, and he suddenly lost the ability to speak.

A shout in the distance broke the silence. Noah and the officer both looked up at the paramedic walking toward them and waving his arms to get the officer's attention.

"I said he's ready, but we have to go now! Can you help clear the way?"

The cop nodded, then turned back to Noah once more.

"Can I get your cell, just in case I have a few more questions?"

Noah rattled it off while the officer scribbled in a small notebook. Then the cop joined the paramedic, and they jogged to the end of the block before disappearing back around the corner. A few seconds later, the police car and ambulance sped off with lights and sirens blazing.

Once Noah was back inside his house, he closed the blinds and collapsed on the couch. *What just happened? Is it possible? Could I have done all those things? Could I have saved the motorcycle rider?* Perhaps it was something like sleepwalking? No, he decided, because first of all, as far as he could remember, he had not fallen asleep, and second, he had never learned even basic first aid. He could not have done something unconsciously that he never knew how to do in the first place!

Noah pressed his fingers against his temples, as if that might somehow help him fill in the picture. He remembered leaving the house and walking down the block. Then what? He searched his mind. There was something there, some *experience*—for lack of a better word—that he could not pin down. Finally, a few grainy, water-stained images materialized. A man lay still on the ground. Blurred hands worked furiously and decisively around him. *My hands?* Noah concentrated, but the image had already faded and vanished like a wisp of smoke in the night. The only rational thing he could think of was that someone else must have stopped to help and then left before the ambulance arrived.

Noah looked at his hands once more. But if he were not there on the scene working some sort of medical magic, how else could he explain the blood? Noah could feel the rush of thumping panic in his chest gaining momentum, so he stood up and staggered into the bathroom. He leaned on the sink and took a long, dreaded look at himself.

He immediately gasped. There was another man staring back at him. Despite his shock, Noah didn't look away from him. The man was a bit younger perhaps, with unkempt black hair and a patchy beard, but Noah somehow recognized the blue-gray eyes, which were very much like his own. The glass moved and shimmered, like still water. Noah reached out, expecting his fingers to plunge into a cold pool, but the moment his hand touched the mirror, he saw only his own drawn, worn face gazing back in disbelief.

Noah quickly found his painkillers and popped two pills. He scrubbed his hands, then crawled into his bed and waited for the numbness to wash over him and make him forget. Strange dreams, blacking out, hallucinations in the mirror—was this all a result of his accident? But then he thought of his grandmother's cursed key, still secured in his nightstand drawer. Did it have some role to play in all this? That was silly and superstitious. Still, if he had had the energy, he would have flushed it down the toilet just to be sure. But the drugs had already begun to wash him out, and he drifted off before he could do any harm.

Chapter 7

O N A SWELTERING day in July, Noah assessed his well-being as he
stood in the mirror and dressed for work in a polo shirt and kha-
kis. He noticed his pants were a bit more snug since the last time he had
worn them. That was good, he thought. It seemed he had finally put on
enough weight so that people stopped asking him whether everything
was okay. This had also coincided with renewed physical strength,
enough that he could even jog short distances now.

Noah's mood, he considered, had also improved. Though there were
still occasions when he was overcome by malaise because he realized
that the most he could achieve was a return to his insignificant life,
Noah recognized that there was something satisfying, if not a bit joyful,
about mounting a comeback that had nothing to do with the status one
was actually coming back to.

Noah was convinced that his all-around recovery had mostly to do
with his grandmother's key or, stated another way, not thinking about
or looking at his grandmother's key. It remained where he had last put
it, under a layer of crap at the back of his nightstand drawer.

Since he had been able to ignore the key, even the dreams of the
faces had stopped. Although Noah had received several messages on
his phone asking whether he was the Good Samaritan who had tended
to the motorcycle rider, he had, with great effort, avoided giving the
bizarre incident much thought. The key and the faces and the broken
rider seemed to have slipped off into the deep washes of his mind.

With a long-absent bounce in his step, Noah grabbed his wallet and
keys then headed for the door. Just as he got to his car, he got a text
from work. His heart sank a little.

Noah was told to go directly to a grocery store warehouse just outside of Philadelphia to determine whether his trucking company was

at fault for two dozen pallets of damaged watermelons. Although this was a task usually above Noah's pay grade, his boss, the fleet manager, was conveniently out sick, and so the job fell to Noah. Great, Noah thought as he climbed in and started the car, *I guess I'll be the whipping boy today.* Noah knew there was no way to win in a situation like that. If he took responsibility, his company would likely have to pay out, and somehow it would be held against Noah. If he denied all responsibility, his company would likely lose a customer and possibly get sued, and, once again, Noah would be blamed.

After arriving at the warehouse, Noah was escorted to the loading dock by a perturbed manager. He threw open the door to a trailer.

"Well," he growled, "what do you have to say now?"

Noah immediately saw that the watermelons had been loaded properly but were now bruised and jumbled about the trailer, as if a giant had picked it up and shaken it. He quickly snapped a few photos. Though Noah said nothing to the manager, there was no doubt something had happened during transport, and thus there was no getting around the fact that his company was at fault, a conclusion he would be forced to include in his report. His boss would not be happy to hear that.

While Noah drove home on the turnpike, he unbuttoned his collar and turned up the air conditioner, which seemed to work only half-heartedly against the blasting heat. He caught himself thinking about a cold beer and his quiet house. Noah began to wonder why his ambitions were not greater. He wanted to want more, to be bolder and to be fascinated by bigger questions, but all these aspirations eluded him. It seemed he preferred to sulk and count his shortcomings rather than take action to improve himself. Pathetic, he thought. He was a coward, and that was that. Suddenly furious, he pounded the steering wheel. He screamed and swore he would do *something* to change his life. But just when he found his composure once more, Noah found himself among a sea of brake lights as the churning rush hour traffic ground to a halt.

For two hours, Noah's car and a thousand others sputtered and idled in place while their drivers were slowly poisoned by a cloud of peppery-scented exhaust fumes. Occasionally, Noah lowered his window for a sense of space in spite of the eye-watering heat and smog that greeted him. It was all he could do to keep from just leaving his car and walking home. Finally, just as the sun descended over the jagged urban skyline, the traffic began to break ranks and move forward. Noah gunned the engine, passing cars carelessly, trying to make the city and his half of a life disappear in the rear-view mirror. But the ordeal had already taken its toll. Noah could barely keep his eyes open as darkness fell.

A sign said a roadside plaza was ahead. Though Noah was only twenty miles from home, he decided he could go no further without at least a few minutes of shut-eye. He drifted off the exit and parked his car in the spot furthest from the pale artificial light that marked a cluster of fast-food restaurants and a gas station. He cracked his windows and tilted his seat back as far as it would go. The cool evening air and rhythm of the distant traffic found its way in and lulled Noah to sleep.

Noah began dreaming of a cheese steak of all things. It was on a plate in front of him, piled high with fried onions and molten cheese. He reached for it, his mouth watering. He was about to take a bite that promised a nirvana of salty goodness when a deafening hiss distracted him. The cheese steak turned into a fat brown snake. Noah recoiled. The sandwich-turned-serpent looked up at him with dead, black eyes.

"Shut up," the snake whispered, "shut up. Shut up, shut up!"

Noah opened his eyes. He was staring at the dome light on the roof of his car. For a few seconds, still in the weakening grasp of sleep, he could not understand where he was or what was happening. Soon, the weight of reality returned, and he glanced around and realized he was in his car, still shackled to his stunted life. But he could still hear the snake hissing exclamations in the dark. Then he heard something else: a high-pitched yet stifled cry, like a scream into a pillow. Noah stayed perfectly still, waiting for the vestiges of his dream to finally evaporate. He heard the scuffling of shoes on the pavement right outside his car door. Noah's heart jumped in his chest. There could be no doubt—a struggle was underway. He raised his head just enough to see.

Two men had their backs to him. One was bald, and the other was wearing a dirty baseball cap. The bald one was holding a woman against a shiny new Mercedes parked about ten feet away from Noah. She must have pulled in while he was sleeping. The bald man had his right forearm across her throat, and he was covering her mouth with his left hand. The one with the hat was rifling through her purse.

"I got 'em," he said, holding up a set of keys.

"The wallet, too," the bald one growled. "With a car like this, you know she's got money in there." The woman cried out once more. The bald one pressed harder. "If you don't shut up, you're gonna get hurt, so shut the fuck up!"

"There's nothin' in it, just credit cards," the one with the hat said.

"C'mon," said the bald one incredulously. "No money?" The other one just shook his head. The bald one leaned close to her. "I bet you got it in your house, right? I bet you got a whole bunch of stuff there in a safe behind a picture or somethin' like that. And I know right where that is because we got your license now."

The woman stopped struggling and went perfectly still.

Although Noah could not make out any details in the woman's face, he could imagine the paralyzing realization that must have struck her like a freight train at that moment. She no doubt understood the implications. Getting mugged for your car or cash in a parking lot was one thing, but if these men got into her house, where they were out of sight of prying eyes and had all the time in world, there was no telling what horrors they might inflict upon her and anyone else they found.

The woman turned her head ever so slightly toward Noah and stared in his direction. It was clear that she had seen him there, cowering like a whipped dog in his car.

Noah dropped back down out of sight. Every part of his body was shaking violently. He could hear the blood pulsing in his ears. He thought about using his cell phone, but then realized he had left it in his briefcase in the trunk. There was no way to get it from the inside of the car. He raised his head quickly and looked out once more. She was still looking at him, silently pleading for help. Beyond her car, maybe only a hundred feet away, people came and went under the lights, completely unaware that hell had opened up in the very shadows behind them. Noah thought about screaming for their attention, but he doubted anyone would summon the courage to venture over until well after the lady had been gutted.

Noah tried to envision some plan of attack, but he was no fighter, and the roiling cauldron of panic in his mind shut out any other rational thought of action. Finally, instinct decided for him: he would jump in anyway, . . . with both middle fingers in the air. If they slaughtered him, so be it. At least maybe he could buy the lady time enough time to get away. Better that than to have to explain to the cops why he had stood by and done nothing. He took a deep breath and reached for the handle. But just as he began to push the door open, expecting to be swamped by fists and feet and knives, something else happened. His vision quickly grew fuzzy on the edges, and he felt heavy, like weights were strapped to his back. Blackness suddenly enveloped him. The faces appeared in rapid succession. Another pair of eyes met Noah's astonished, inward gaze. Once more, a door formed in the dark. Everything shook as the man forced his way in. And swift death came with him.

Chapter 8

The Warrior

JUST AFTER THE rain slowed to a light drizzle, we took up our positions. I forgot about the cold and my growling hunger when I glanced across the field and saw the French frantically forming their lines. The call rose behind us.

"Archers up!"

At once, 5,000 men strained to bend and hook strings to longbows that were taller than most of the archers wielding them. We all stood behind rows of sharpened stakes we had placed in the ground and pointed toward our enemy. I examined my arrow points, all iron-tipped bodkins that could even pierce plate armor at close ranges. I gently pushed forty arrows into the soft ground next me, tip first. I practiced reaching for them quickly to be sure I was in the right position.

Unlike most of the archers on the field, I was also skilled in the sword and grappling, and I had been called to serve as a man-at-arms when my lord required it. In fact, that very day I had been instructed to don my chain mail and take my place in the battle line after my arrows were spent.

Our army arrived in France in August of 1415 with nearly 13,000 men. It was now late October, and sickness, siege, and skirmishing had thinned our ranks to 8,000. And because the French had harried us at every turn and laid waste to the land before us, those of us left were slowly starving to death. Without relief, we would perish before the New Year. But King Henry rode with us and shared our fate. So, the men found their strength each day when they saw him sit high atop his charger, seemingly assured of victory no matter that his forces had withered.

Even now, I could see him in the saddle gesturing wildly and barking out orders to his knights, who were riding off in mud-flinging haste to be sure his will was done.

Agincourt. That is what our king called this wretched field where only days before farmers had turned the rich black soil.

While we waited, I kneeled and glanced into a puddle of dirty water that now seeped into the ground where I had slept, wet and shivering, the night before. My face, my beard, and my lord's colors on my tunic were all smeared with mud, rendering me unrecognizable and barely visible against the dark clouds that hovered just above me. Only my blue eyes colored the drab scene and reminded me that the strange face staring back was my own. I whispered my name, just to be certain of it.

"Allard Davey."

Like all commoners, I was given my first bow when I was just six years old. This was the only manner in which one could be trained to wield the feared English longbow in war. Every year, I was given another slightly longer bow until finally I had acquired the strength to pull back the string of the six-foot bow that I now held. Because I excelled in this task, I came to the attention of my lord, who saw that I was trained in all weapons and arts of war. He had even given me a fine long sword, helm, and mail so that I might serve him as both an archer and a man-at-arms, a rare privilege indeed.

Though I had my duties in the fields—I was a poor farmer—I never refused the opportunity to train and spar instead of plow, which was, thankfully, quite often. I had bested many men in tournaments, and I had killed men in skirmishes, but this was my first war. When my lord was called by King Henry to fight in France, I did not lament but brimmed with desire for adventure and fortune. So, I signed my name to the pay rolls, took up my Lord's colors, and crossed the Channel with him. Though our campaign had faltered at times, as I looked once more across the field that would soon be painted red, I believed we could win.

I glanced around and noticed that many of the men were nervously muttering prayers and fingering locks of hair or strange charms for comfort. But there was no fear in me, just excitement. In my mind and in my heart, I was ironclad, and I was sure that no man could defeat me in battle.

Another order was passed along. We were to continue to wait, to let them come to us. I examined our position and immediately understood the wisdom of this strategy. I could see the battle taking place in my mind, springing from the seeds of our formations and the lay of the land. Our knights and men-at-arms were packed tightly in several rows and flanked by the archers, who, in turn, were shielded by thick forest on either side. This meant that the archers could not be outflanked by the French cavalry.

I stepped forward and tested the field. The mud was thick and quite deep, unsuitable for heavy horses and armored men who might sink up to the calf or, perhaps, even to the knee. Though the French outnumbered us two to one, they would thus be slow to make their way across the field and would be exposed for a great length of time to a hail of arrows. If somehow the French made it to our lines, they would be exhausted and in no condition to fight. I thought our enemies might realize these dangers as well, but I could see they had organized their cavalry for a charge. Perhaps they did not know of their peril, or perhaps they did but were confident in their numbers. Nevertheless, they began to move forward.

As they closed to within about 300 yards, the order was given. All the archers knocked an arrow, bent their mighty bows, and aimed to the heavens. Five thousand bowmen held their breath. Then came the signal as a shout broke the tense silence.

"Loose!"

The sharp stingers fluttered high then began to rain death on the French. Although the arrows could not pierce armor at that distance, they could kill or wound horses, and soon the French were in complete disarray as bucking horses threw riders and bolted for home. Undeterred, the French knights and men-at-arms dismounted and once more started across the field. But they were quickly bogged down in the mortar-thick mud and could hardly keep their balance, let alone make a forceful charge. We unleashed wave after wave of arrows as they emerged from the gray distance. Some French soldiers fell when arrows found uncovered faces, so the rest lowered their visors and bore the storm of the battering bolts. But they traded visibility and unrestricted breath for this protection, and, already exhausted, they slowed even more as they struggled for air.

Our battle cries began to rise as the French stumbled forward. At twenty-five yards, I could pick my targets, and my arrows pierced all but the most well-forged suits of armor. One after the other, we felled them until they became a wall of writhing, moaning bodies that those behind were forced to climb. The weight of the pile was so great that those on the bottom sank into the thick slurry and drowned in their helms.

After I spent my last arrow, I unstrung my bow, took up my sword, helmet, and mail shirt and joined the men-at-arms. We moved forward from beneath the waning fire of arrows. This time, it was our turn to climb over the dead to meet the enemy. This obstacle forced us to break formation, and somehow, in the confusion that followed, I found myself alone on the edge of the field. Very quickly, two French knights turned toward me, one slightly behind the other.

As was my way, when I was in combat, I could slow the world to a crawl. In between blows, I could feel the wind on my sweating neck. I could see plump and glistening raindrops as they fell, one by one. In one tournament, I remember I could count the notches on a sword blade aimed for my head before I knocked it away—seven. And in the flash of time it took my French opponents to act that day, I had already determined how the entire exchange would end.

I knew instantly from the way the first knight moved that, in his haste to strike me down, he would not allow sufficient time to pull his feet from the sucking mud, causing him to trip and clumsily lurch toward me. Before he could recover, I would trap his sword and use his momentum to throw him over my hip and take him off his feet. Once on his back, I would stun him with a fist blow to his armored head, and before he could find his senses, I would lift his visor and plunge my sword through his face. While I was killing the first knight, the second would already be charging with his sword raised. So, I would block his strike with my sword from a kneeling position and while locked together, I would draw my dagger with my left hand and thrust it into his unprotected groin. Although the blow was not immediately fatal, he would nonetheless crumple and bleed to death before he could ever manage the strength to attack me again.

In those breathless, bloody seconds, I lashed out quickly according to plan, and both men were soon dead. I stood and nodded to myself in approval, yet I noted where I could improve the swiftness and brutality of my kills in the next contest. However, I did not enjoy the violence; it was simply a means to an end. Combat was a game of death, and I had to be better than anyone else in order to survive and claim my prize.

I found a discarded shield and quickly waded back into the melee. Amid the screams and clanging of steel, I hacked and slashed, and we pushed the French back, stepping over their dead and dying as we pressed forward. Soon the rest fled, and a cheer rose from our ranks. At our feet lay the flower of French nobility, and their bodies were already being stripped of their priceless armor as spoils of war. Those noblemen that were not mortally struck down were taken to command a price from their king. The rest of the wounded and captured got a dagger through the eye for good measure, since we could not care for any but the most valuable prisoners in a foreign land, especially when we had not enough grain even to feed our own men and horses.

While I sipped sour wine from a flagon I had found among the dead, I heard shouts and followed the noise to a commotion. One brave French knight still stood unharmed in the midst of our men. He challenged the king in single combat, but most of the men, now drunk on victory, only teased him.

"Knock him on his head and take him," a voice cried out. "This one would bring ransom enough for the lot of us!"

"No," another voice rose up, "fill this proud peacock with so many arrows that he looks more like a porcupine!" This made the men howl and hoot.

Despite their banter, I knew none would dare move against the knight, for once a challenge was issued, it was for our king alone to decide the man's fate. And word must have spread quickly, for a moment later, King Henry, still mounted, sauntered into our midst. As soon as the men caught sight of him, they fell silent and put their eyes to the ground.

"Who would be my champion today?" he bellowed. Then he pulled a heavy purse filled with coin from his saddle bag and held it up for all to see. "Two years wages to the man who would meet this noble in chivalrous combat."

The knight wore expertly made plate armor and stood at the ready with his blood-stained sword. Certainly, most of us were weary and grateful to have survived, so it came as no surprise when only a few raised their voices to volunteer for yet another deadly task. However, I threw both hands high and shouted the loudest. With two full years of pay added to what was already owed for my service, I could acquire my own small parcel of land and perhaps pay others to tend the crops. I kneeled as the king rode to me.

"Stand up, man! Today we all bask in equal glory before God. What is your name?"

"Allard Davey, archer and man-at-arms, my King."

"You are a Welshman, no doubt?"

"Yes, my King."

"Who is your lord?"

"I am in the service of Lord Marlton."

"And in this matter, you are directly in my service. Only a nobleman should face another in single combat, but I have lost many knights in this campaign, and I will not chance to lose yet another when we have already broken their backs today," he explained.

The king shouted over the crowd to the knight. "Will you not yield and be ransomed? Will you not spare yourself and the suffering of your family?"

"I will not," he answered. "I will be victorious, and you will leave the field, or I will die with my brothers. It is my right to demand this."

"Let all be witnesses," the king commanded as he stood in his saddle. "Allard Davey shall be my champion."

Then he turned to me once more. "Choose your weapon."

"Hammer," I said.

A moment later, a steel war hammer was passed through the eager crowd and placed in my hands. Although extremely heavy, and thus difficult to wield, it bore both a hammer head and a curved spike, either of which could deliver a devastating blow, even to the hardest armor. I had extensive training with the war hammer; however, I had never used one in combat. Nevertheless, the knight's armor had few gaps where a sword might bite, so I chose a weapon that could crush steel and break bones no matter where it fell. But I would need all my faculties to use it, so I cast aside my helmet, much to the astonishment of some near me.

The men formed a wide circle around us and fell silent. The knight lowered his visor and bowed. I returned the gesture. From the way he held his sword, I could see he was right-handed. And while he was clad in virtually impenetrable heavy armor, I wore only a mail shirt and was vulnerable to a sword attack. All this meant that he would swing his weapon from right to left, favoring his dominant hand so as to end the contest with one powerful blow aimed at my unprotected head and neck. However, I would step back to avoid being struck, and I would land a crushing blow to his right shoulder, instantly incapacitating him. In that moment, I would recover, turn the hammer over, and land the spike on the top of his helmet, killing him quickly.

I watched his feet as the attack began. He moved lightly, avoiding getting stuck in the mud, and swung the hissing blade at my head. I leaned back as the point flashed, narrowly missing my face. As I brought the heavy hammer down, however, the knight quickly moved to his left, and I missed. I knew he would immediately swing again, so I allowed the momentum of my strike to carry me forward. I tucked and rolled, and the knight missed once more. He was extremely skilled, and the superb, made-to-measure armor allowed him to move almost effortlessly.

I knew then that the combination of his skill, speed, and armor would best me in a duel of weapons, especially since mine was so awkward and ill-balanced. I had to get him onto his back as quickly as possible to gain an advantage, so I charged him and closed the distance. Before he could raise his sword once more, I dropped the hammer at my feet and wrapped both my arms around him, pinning the knight's arms to his sides. At the same time, I twined my right leg around him so he could not step back, then I threw all my weight against him. He fell with a muffled smack into the mud. With my added bulk, he sunk in deeply. While he tried to raise his head and wrest his sword free, I reached back and retrieved my war hammer. I straddled his straining body, and with all my strength, I brought the hammer down—spike first—onto the top of his head. The fine steel yielded easily and might as well have been worn linen, for there was almost nothing that could resist a flush blow from the deadly spike. The knight's body shuddered and shook, then went completely still. A shout rose from the men as they crowded around me, and a bag of coins found its way into my hand. I glanced over my shoulder: the king nodded, then rode off.

I should have fallen to my knees, thrown my arms to the sky, and moaned a thankful prayer, but I felt only regret for destroying such a fine and honorable warrior. Otherwise, emotion never overcame me. The truth was that I was as cold as winter frost, a fact that did not escape the men. But this was the way of life in these times, to ignore hope and fear and lay low anyone my king and my lord put before me.

The fires blazed that night in the camp, and the air was filled with songs of home, love, and death. The men patted me on the back and called me the Sower of Swords for all those men that I had put into the ground that day.

Chapter 9

OUR ARMY ROLLED slowly back to the coast. We were weary, yet we savored our victory. Even I allowed myself to be prideful, since what we had done would not soon be forgotten. Still, we remained vigilant because we heard rumors that French reinforcements would soon arrive. Though we could see men spying us from distant hills and tree lines, no one dared to engage us again. Finally, we found the fleet, and I boarded one of the crowded ships bound for England.

As soon as my vessel docked, I collected my pay, bought a good horse and, laden with a small fortune, made my way south toward home. More than once, hooded characters loomed near the road, intent on waylaying me, but once I lifted my cloak to reveal my armor and the hilt of a fine sword, they melted away to find easier prey.

As I plodded along and considered my new-found wealth, I began to feel an urgent need to bind myself to a woman. I was already twenty-six, well past the age when most marry. I had devoted myself to the sword and had never before given more than a passing thought to hearth and home, wife and child. Perhaps it was the security of the gold in my pocket, but every time I came upon a woman of age, strangely, I found myself bowing and forcing a smile. So, I turned my horse down a different path, determined to settle the matter at the hands of one who knew far more about such things than I.

As I approached Lord Marlton's castle, I found that news of my deeds at Agincourt had already preceded me.

"The King's Champion," they said, or "the Sower of Swords," they shouted as I passed, and I dropped coins into their outstretched hands.

Finally, I stood before the gray and corpulent Lord Marlton, who greeted me warmly and offered a chair at his table for the feast that evening. He asked whether I was well and whether there was anything he could offer me for the glory I had brought to his house and the king. I thought for a moment and then said that I found my body no worse for wear, except that my heart was heavy because I had decided to take a wife and I knew not how to undertake such a task. This drew a collective uproar from all present. Lord Marlton scowled at his company then took me aside and whispered that I should return tomorrow, and I would find my bride waiting for me.

The next morning, I rose before the sun, scrubbed my body, trimmed my beard and hair as best I could by candlelight, then made my way back to the castle. I was escorted inside by a servant boy and found Lord Marlton seated at the head of his table. Next to him stood a tall sandy-haired woman who looked several years younger than myself. She stared nervously at the floor and would not meet my gaze.

"This is Katherine White," Lord Marlton announced as he rose from his chair. "Her husband, a blacksmith, died of fever after only two weeks of marriage, which happened while you were serving in France. Like you, her parents have also died, and so, she is without means. But she comes from sturdy stock, and she will give you strong sons that will bear your name."

Lord Marlton took her by the hand. "This is a good man, my child, the King's Champion at Agincourt. He will provide for you and restore your honor. Then he turned to me. "Come forward, Allard Davey, so that you may be properly joined."

I walked to her and bowed, then reached out my hand, which she gently received in her own. Her eyes finally met mine, and her lips formed a quivering smile.

I cleared my throat, and some words found me: "I am not handsome, . . . but I am strong." I paused for a moment. "And I can read; this I can teach you, . . . and I will protect our home and never harm you. I have seen my share of war, and I would always have peace between us."

Katherine White spoke: "That is more than enough . . . for one such as I. And I will give you children and take my place at your side."

Lord Marlton stepped forward and laid his hand on ours. "So then it shall be under the eyes of God! May you both go forth with my blessing, and may this union serve my house and the crown. Long live the king!"

Lord Marlton was kind enough to let us remain his guests, if only in the stables, until I managed to acquire a windswept swath of land with a small cottage in the shadow of an ancient Roman fort. Often, I gazed upon the moss-covered ruins, and I wondered what manner of men they were, what gods and what purposes they served, to have come so far and built such things.

Katherine and I, driven as are those who are free and have a stake in everything, worked well into the starlit nights to make the land obedient. Neither of us were much for conversation, but we had found our purpose and were content at least to build our lives together. She knew more about crops and animals than I did, but I could move the trees and boulders that blocked our way. We never felt passion for each other in the way we had heard about in the old tales, where even the harvest moon could not force lovers to look away from each other. But we both kept the promises that we had made on our wedding day, and we served each other with loyalty and gentleness because we knew of the hopelessness and violence of the world beyond our home.

Although I never made war again, I practiced my skills in tournaments until the young men began to defeat me. Then, I taught my children how to fight, even my daughters. They showed eagerness and skill in their martial lessons. Some said it was wrong for women to know such things, that they should merely cook and wait upon their husbands. But I told them that when the arguments of kings inevitably came to war, there was no use for doting.

I was still a sturdy bull, even in those years when muscles turn soft and shoulders slump forward from the weight of time and experience. Though I no longer worked the fields, I hauled our crops to the markets. On one such journey, as it should have been, I died as I had lived.

As I passed the silent Roman halls where the ghosts of long-dead soldiers kept watch, highwaymen with hooded faces once more blocked my way. This time, though, they did not yield to my mail and the fine sword at my side; they mistook my age for weakness, which they seemed certain made me an easy mark. However, they learned otherwise when I wrested their souls from them, one by one. But when I stood victorious this one last time, I noticed the blood—one of them had plunged his dagger home. I did not cry out, but I settled down next to the ruins while awareness faded and limbs grew heavy. Better this than become a useless, wrinkled old fool, I thought. Katherine would understand.

Yet, death has apparently not relieved me of my duties. I tower once more over a field of combat. My Fathers silently urge me forward to fulfill my purpose.

Chapter 10

IT SEEMED TO Noah that a sad, common theme played out to varying degrees in all of his dreams of late; complete helplessness in the face of adversity. Some of these were were simply tedious and only mildly frustrating, like when he fumbled about in a dark room, frantically searching for something that he desperately needed that was never where it should be. Other times, Noah endured more terrifying nightmares in which pale monsters emerged from the fog behind him. No matter how fast he ran, they were always close behind, their claws reaching for him. At their worst, the cursed faces found him in the night, daring Noah to solve a riddle that his mediocre intellect simply could not fathom.

This dream, however, was entirely different.

Noah slowly emerged from his car. He loomed over the scene like an ancient battler at the peak of his powers. All the muscles in his body felt like coiled snakes, ready to strike on command. His mind was transformed, too, and was now infused with the experience of hundreds of duels, to the point that he welcomed the imminent violence like an old friend. His senses were open wide to anything in his surroundings, no matter how subtle, that he could turn to his advantage in a fight. The breeze, the shadows, the oily blacktop—he inexplicably knew how to play them all in his favor. It was as if he had somehow climbed into the skull of a forgotten gladiator who had learned the secret to surviving mortal combat: it was simply a task to be done.

The woman's pleading eyes fixed onto Noah. After a moment, the men followed her intense gaze and suddenly became aware of Noah's presence. The bald one turned to the one with the hat, and they exchanged a nervous look. Then the bald one gave a sharp nod. They would attack together.

When the bald one flashed a knife and lunged, it seemed so feral and clumsy that Noah chuckled to himself. He could have taken a nap in the time it took before he was forced to react. In this eternity, Noah considered and disregarded many possible counter measures, but he finally decided on a course of action that would quickly and efficiently place him in the best position to deal with his other enemy, who was still just beginning to move.

With a practiced swiftness, Noah stepped to his left to avoid the wild thrust, and with both hands, he simultaneously grasped the knife-wielding arm near the wrist. Then he directed the assailant's momentum in a wide arc away from him and toward the other conspirator. In one fluid motion, he forced one assailant to stab the other through his neck. Before the bald one had even realized what had occurred, Noah pulverized his nose with a well-placed headbutt, then flipped around behind him and locked him in a choke hold that even a crowbar could not loosen. When the stunned man lost consciousness, Noah dropped his body to the pavement. He brought the heel of his shoe down on the assailant's neck with full force and crushed his windpipe, which gave way with a sharp crack. Both men were soon dead, their unblinking, bulging eyes fixed on some invisible point in the sky. But Noah was not flustered—emotion was something he just could not find in his new skin. And he understood why: killing the others meant that he lived, and nothing more need be said. However, when Noah found no other enemies, he felt himself being yanked from the head of his glorious battle wagon. The scene of his war quickly grew to a pinpoint in the distance, as if Noah had been snapped back by a rope to a far-off hilltop where people and buildings resembled a diorama.

When awareness returned, Noah found himself standing outside of his car. The woman's car roared to life, and Noah turned just in time to see it speed away into the night. Then he glanced down to his feet. Two lifeless figures were splayed on the ground in his shadow; a glistening pool of blood was spreading out slowly around them. Noah's chest tightened, and once more, icy fingers climbed his spine.

Noah covered his mouth and looked to the sky. *Wake up now!* He screamed in his mind over and over again. He was sure that in a moment, he would find himself lying on his couch, and this hallucination would soon evaporate like the morning dew. But when he looked once more, the only thing that changed was that the fat fingers of blood had worked their way closer to his car.

Noah climbed in and buried his head in his hands. He could not have done this, he decided. It simply was not possible. He had no such skill or strength, no such iron will. To believe otherwise, he would have to suspend belief entirely. For anyone to think that Noah was a human wrecking ball, there would have to be a place of opposites where the weakest were the strongest, where sheep rose up and killed wolves. He had only fantasized that he was a cool and casual killing machine to make up for everything that he lacked. Yet, the bodies were there, crumpled and absolutely still, like small islands in a black sea that only time could eradicate. Someone else must have come along to help, just like when the motorcycle rider was injured. Another angel on his shoulder, perhaps. Noah must have heard the action and incorporated it into his bizarre dream.

Noah thought about waiting for the police, but what could he really tell them? He was catatonic when some hero that he did not see came and did what he could not do? All Noah could offer was a statement to his own cowardice, and there seemed no point in that. The woman would tell the story, maybe she saw the brave man who saved her. There was no crime anyway, Noah thought. Two bad men who wanted to murder people and bathe in their blood were dead. End of story.

Noah suddenly felt the sting of bile in the back of his throat, and he leaned over and threw up on the passenger seat. He wiped his mouth with the back of his shirt sleeve and started the car. He drove home in a daze, as if he were looking at the world through warped, dirty glass.

Chapter 11

A FINGER OF DUSTY sunshine found its way through the curtains where Noah had not pulled them together at the top. The light gradually lengthened until it fell across Noah's eyes and forced him awake. He yawned, then casually checked the time on the digital clock next to his bed. It was just after one in the afternoon. He sat bolt upright. Noah was gut punched by the realization that he was not just late for work, but he had missed half the day already! As he grabbed his clothes, he tried to think of some excuse that would save him from immediate termination. Perhaps he could just call in sick, maybe even forge a doctor's signature. Then it dawned on him: it was Saturday! His pants still around his ankles, Noah fell back on the bed and sighed blissfully.

However, Noah's relief gave way to confusion as he stared at the ceiling and began to wonder how he could have slept so late. He was by no means an early riser, especially on the weekends, but he could not remember the last time he slept into the afternoon. Had he been up late? There was a black hole where his memory should have been. Noah racked his brain to put together a timeline. He had worked yesterday; he was certain of that. Then what? He thought harder. *Right, you were stuck in traffic, then you stopped and had a nap. You were dreaming about food.* But there was . . . something else.

A silent movie clip shot from a first-person perspective played out in Noah's mind. Though it was fuzzy around the edges and some details were blurred, the action was unmistakable: two men had been violently cut down, murdered by an unseen actor. Panic once more snatched the air out of Noah because he knew he had been behind the camera. He could feel it in his bones. Noah cradled his head and screamed for it all to go away. He clamped his eyes shut so tightly that he began to see stars. He was sure it would not be long before police got to him. The SWAT team was probably outside his house right now, gearing up in the back of a van. But he would not wait for them to break down his door. He was determined to go out and meet them with his hands in the air. He would tell them anything they wanted to know.

Noah sat up, quickly pulled up his pants, and stumbled over to the window. But where he expected to see a hundred guns pointed at him and helicopters in the air, he found emptiness. The only things moving were the shimmering currents of hot air rising from the quiet, sun-baked street.

Soon, the tightness in his chest eased, and his breaths grew deeper. He could still see the horrible scene playing repeatedly on the backs of his eyelids every time he blinked, but it was moving away and becoming increasingly obscure, drained of its life and color a little more each time. Sailing off with it was Noah's certainty that anything strange had actually occurred. Noah smiled to himself. He decided he was fool. It was just trickery—a dream within a dream.

Noah suddenly felt free and full of energy. He stripped down and jumped into the shower. Today, he thought, was the perfect opportunity to fulfill his promise.

Chapter 12

NOAH KNOCKED SOFTLY. He waited a few moments, but no one answered. This time, he hit the door hard several times with the side of his fist.

"Hey, Rick, you in there?" Noah asked through a cupped hand to amplify his voice. "It's Noah. Thought I would see if you're around, take you up on that offer to grill me something." Noah held up the six pack he was carrying, although it was unlikely anyone in the house could see it. "Like I promised, I brought the beer."

Noah could hear the lock being turned. The door opened slowly to reveal a dark interior. Rick's face appeared, still bearing the impression of what appeared to be a pillow. His hand shaded bleary eyes against the sun.

"Geez, Noah," he finally said. "It's a little early, isn't it?"

Although he already knew the time, Noah checked his watch for dramatic effect. "It's almost two . . . *in the afternoon.* And I thought *I* had gotten up late. I'm a train wreck; what's your excuse?"

Rick backed away from the door and motioned for Noah to come inside with a casual sweep of his hand. "Don't judge me on the mess. The cleaning staff has the day off," he said sarcastically.

Once Noah's eyes adjusted to the darkness, he found himself in the living room, which appeared to be, quite literally, the place where Rick lived out every aspect of his existence. There was a long couch along the wall with a pillow and blankets. On either side of it, newspapers and magazines were piled high on the floor. Dirty dishes, utensils, and empty microwave meal boxes rested on the coffee table along with a half-empty bottle of vodka. There were two laundry baskets in the middle of the floor; both seemed to be filled with dirty clothes. The local news was playing at a whisper's level on the television, which hung on the opposite wall. Noah wanted to say something about it needing a woman's touch, but he swallowed the words.

"It's just easier to stay here," Rick said, as if reading Noah's thoughts. "I got the kitchen right there, and there is a shower in the bathroom down the hall. The rest of the house is spic and span."

Noah tore his eyes away and turned to face Rick. He was wearing a pair of shorts but was shirtless. Rick usually carried a pot belly, but now, Noah could see the vaguest outline of some muscles.

"It looks like I'm not the only one who lost some weight," Noah said while he gestured to Rick's midsection with his free hand.

Rick looked down and smacked his stomach with both hands. "Yeah," he said. "Maybe that's the only good thing to come out of all this. She was always saying I was too heavy. Ironic, isn't it? She leaves, and then I lose the gut."

Noah pointed to the beer. "What do you have to go with this?"

"I have some steaks in the freezer, some potatoes too. Sound good?"

Noah nodded. "How about a drink first?"

"Let me get some clothes on," Rick said. "Then we can go on the deck. I'll meet you out there."

A few minutes later, they were both settled into aluminum chairs under an umbrella on a small, concrete pad behind Rick's house. Noah twisted the cap off a beer and handed it to Rick, then he opened one for himself. They clicked the bottles together in a toast.

"To getting through . . . stuff," Rick said with a shrug.

Noah smiled. "That sounds about right. I'll say yes to that."

They sipped beer and talked about work, sports, and home improvements, just about anything that had nothing to do with their personal tragedies. Eventually, however, once the alcohol greased Rick's tongue, the conversation took a turn.

Rick set his bottle on the table and leaned back in his chair. He tilted his head back and took a deep breath.

"I feel bad for not warning you before," he said, "but you being here, with me, is like social suicide in this neighborhood."

Noah stared at him blankly. "What are you talking about?"

"I told you that Jean left me and that my kids hate me, right?"

"Sure. That was right before I crashed."

"What I'm pretty sure you don't know, because it happened while you were in the hospital, is that the cops questioned me a bunch about it. It seems that no one, including either one of my kids, has heard from Jean since she left." Rick abruptly grabbed his beer and drained it, as if trying to work up the courage to continue. "What I'm trying to tell you," he said as he wiped his mouth with the back of his hand, "is that the cops accused me of making her disappear. Everyone thinks I'm a murderer. You don't want to be seen with me."

"Well, is it true?" Noah found himself asking.

Rick leaned forward and looked him straight in the eye. "No," he said seriously. "Just like I told the police."

Noah nodded, then handed Rick another bottle of beer. "That's good enough for me," he said, even though he was not certain he meant it.

Rick settled back in his chair and took a swig. "She left a note," he offered matter-of-factly. "I gave it to the police. I think that's the only reason they did not arrest me."

Noah raised his eyebrows. "A note?"

"That's right, even signed it and dated it, as if she knew it would be a get-out-jail-free card. Makes me so mad though to think that she knew the hell she would put me through, yet she decided to go AWOL regardless."

"Can you tell me what it said?"

Rick shrugged. "I don't see why not. The cops never said I had to keep it a secret." He cleared his throat. "It was only a few scribbled lines, as if she was in such a hurry that she didn't have time to write more. Anyway, it said: 'There is nothing else you could have done. I have everything I need, so please don't look for me. I know I should be sorry, but *I'm not here anymore.*'"

The blood drained from Noah's face. Each of those four words hit him with the force of a sledgehammer, jarring loose his own memories. Noah knew at once that Rick was telling the truth.

"You okay, Noah? You look like you've seen a ghost."

Noah ignored the question in favor of his own. "What do you think it meant, what she put in the note?"

"Well, about doing all I could, that's easy. You see about a year or so before, Jean was acting strange. She said she was sick a lot, nausea mostly. And she said her ears were ringing all the time. We went to a few doctors, had a bunch of tests, but no diagnosis. She got so sensitive to *everything*. She started sleeping in the spare bedroom. No light, no clocks, no sound. She hated being in the car, let alone driving it. She had to take a ton of Xanax just so I could get her to her appointments. Finally, one of the doctors thought it might be a mental illness. She went to a shrink a few times, and he gave her more meds. Still, she just kept getting worse. Eventually, I just ran up the white flag. I told her I didn't know what else to do. A few days after that, she left."

"What about the 'not here anymore' part?"

Rick threw up his arms. "I really don't know. I told the cops she may have meant she was emotionally gone, especially considering all the problems she was having. But they had a different take. They say it could mean she was dead now. They said it could mean she killed herself or, as was more likely, I made it look that way. They were keen on that explanation because she did not take much with her except some clothes and her toiletries. Everything else, she left behind: her cell phone, credit cards, and family photographs. She may have taken some money, but it's hard for me to tell since she kept the books. If she did, it was not enough that I would notice. The cops were really on me about that, too. The detective said he did not believe she would leave a twenty-five-year marriage and not take what she was entitled to. I had to agree with him. It did not make any sense."

"I'm sorry." Noah absentmindedly peeled the label off his beer bottle. "I really am." When Noah finally looked up, he could see Rick's eyes were welling with tears.

"I don't know whether I want her back or I want her to stay gone." Rick shook his head. "Don't get me wrong; I love her, but the way she left . . . she really screwed things up. My kids, our friends, no one talks to me anymore. People at work give me a strange look, too. It won't be long for me there; I can tell. I just need to make it another six months, then I can retire. I can get out of here, make a fresh start."

Noah held out his beer. "To fresh starts then; we both need them."

Rick dabbed his eyes with his shirt sleeve, then tapped Noah's bottle with his own. "Right you are," he said as he forced a smile.

When the beer was gone, they drank screwdrivers. When the vodka was gone, and Noah could barely stand, he declared loudly that he had had enough. Before he stumbled home, Noah gave Rick an awkward hug and told him that he had at least one friend.

Chapter 13

NOAH WAS STARING out of his living room window and contemplating the change of seasons once more. It was mid-September, usually Noah's favorite time of year. The days were often still warm enough that he could work in the yard without a jacket, yet at night, cool, crisp air laced with the smells of wood smoke settled him into sleep. It had been raining for days though, shutting him inside and preventing him from doing any chores outside the house, including raking up the leaves, which now formed slimy mats in his yard. The fact that the weekend had arrived and that he was still socked in only deepened his melancholy. But there was more going on than just his bad mood.

If Noah's every waking moment was not occupied by at least some menial task, the strange incidents, especially the one at the rest stop, crept into his mind and tortured him until he prayed for a lobotomy. Although he had for the moment held off those thoughts, he was afraid that it would not be long before they found him idle and again took hold. If that happened, it would be a sleepless night or two before he got himself squared away once more.

And Noah still felt a deep restlessness, or perhaps a craving, though the object of his desire was not certain. As of late, he had been able to quench it with the trappings of the daily grind. But Noah could not escape a belief that only big deeds could ever fill him up and give him life, the kind that had ironically left him injured, broke, and unloved—the kind that had made him ashamed before his father.

Noah walked to his couch, plopped down, and loosed a frustrated sigh. He thought about calling Rick for some company, but then remembered he was out of town on business for few days. He found the newspaper and perused the headlines. No wonder he had not bothered with it before—so much terrible news across the board. He was trying to understand an article about increased tensions in the Middle East, but he was distracted by the pitter-patter of the rain outside that seemed to increase in intensity with each passing minute. Finally, he threw the paper on the floor and once more took up his station at the window.

The wind had picked up, and the rain was now falling angrily in thick gray sheets. The ground was already saturated. Noah thought his yard would soon resemble a shallow moat. He glanced down the street, where a torrent of foaming water backed up against a storm sewer. Noah knew that the water was being dumped into a nearby stream, the Bushkill, which—even in the driest of times—was filled almost to capacity by runoff created by new box stores that sprung up farther north.

Noah flipped through the channels on the television until he found the local news station. There was talk of severe flooding along the Delaware River and all its tributaries, including the Bushkill. Another nor'easter could bring a hundred-year flood (even though it was the second time in the past ten years). The screen flashed, and the ear-piercing warning of the Emergency Broadcast System filled the air. Noah winced, and he fumbled for the mute button on the remote. A list scrolled by of waterways where flooding was imminent. The Bushkill was near the top, followed by a bold-lettered caution that people living within two miles should seek higher ground because the creek would likely crest its banks within the next four to six hours. Noah was at least eight miles from the Bushkill, so there was no need to panic.

Like everyone else though, Noah was fascinated by the raw, angry power of nature that, at least until recently, had so rarely showed itself in his lazy countryside setting. He remembered where there was a pedestrian bridge that spanned the Bushkill as part of a newly restored biking trail. It would be a front row seat to the show if he was so inclined. Noah thought about it for a moment and decided he was.

He grabbed a pair of boots and a yellow rain jacket, climbed into his car, and set off for the bridge.

The deserted streets had been turned into rivers. There was so much water falling that his windshield wipers, even on their fastest setting, could only manage to make his view of the road opaque at best.

Sometimes Noah rolled down his window and stuck his head out for a better view of what lay ahead. And though he drove slowly, his car threw up a wall of water onto the sidewalk. He slowed for a blinking traffic light in town and then drove straight through the intersection.

Noah soon found himself on a narrow two-lane road that eventually ran parallel to the Bushkill. He wound along the creek, but he could only catch fleeting glimpses of the roiling brown water through the thick trees that anchored its banks. He finally found a gap in the foliage that marked the trailhead. There was a small parking lot on the other side of the road where Noah was surprised to find several vehicles. One of them had a kayak strapped to its roof.

Noah zipped his rain jacket to the top then pulled the hood up. He walked quickly across the road to the pedestrian bridge and made his way toward the middle. Normally, the water would be flowing gently at least thirty feet below, but today, the creek was so swollen that if Noah hung down from the bottom of the bridge, his feet would have gotten wet.

It was not simply the sheer volume of water that left him speechless. It came with terrible force, like a perpetually cresting tidal wave driven in sheer terror toward the sea. And perhaps it was a misnomer to call it water at all. Certainly it contained water, but it was filled with so much mud and detritus that it more resembled a liquefied garbage dump than a creek. Noah watched an entire tree, perhaps two stories tall, complete with dangling roots, flash by at breakneck speed. A shopping cart was trapped in its branches. The mighty tree was tossed about like a child's toy, powerless against the force. Occasionally, Noah could make out large humps in the water that rolled by, like the arched backs of a great serpents, which concealed the passing of huge objects in the depths below. Noah thought that if he had the misfortune to fall in, he would probably be bludgeoned to death by the freight train of solid waste well before he could drown.

Just then, Noah noticed two people, a man and a woman, both draped in green ponchos, step onto the bridge from the other side.

"Hello!" the man yelled to be heard over the thunderous torrent and pelting rain. Noah nodded. The man, maybe in his sixties, walked closer while the woman remained near the bank, ready to flee it seemed. "You know this is dangerous," he said. "It's already washed out the bridge at Stewartsville, and it's about to jump its banks at the bend up there. It'll happen in the blink of an eye. This bridge is a lot smaller; one good clip and this thing will crumble."

Noah thought about it for a moment. Already the bridge seemed to rhythmically twist and roll slightly under his feet as the water surged against the banks.

The man pointed to the side of the bridge where he had come from. "If you can see it, the bank is starting to wash away where the bridge is moored. It may come down even if nothing hits it. You should get off. You won't even see it coming."

Noah suddenly realized his peril. He had been so entranced by the spectacle that he had not even anticipated that his perch might collapse beneath him without warning.

Noah cupped his hand and called out. "I guess I was too caught up in the sight of it. I wasn't thinking about it. . . . I mean, it really is something to see."

The man shrugged. "They weren't thinking about it in Stewartsville either. Now the water is almost at their doorsteps."

Noah glanced down at the water, then back toward the man. "Did they get out?"

"I heard on the scanner that some did. But there are a lot of retired folks up there. They were either too old or too stubborn to go. The National Guard dropped off food and water and a bunch of sandbags, but they couldn't stick around. Apparently, they have bigger problems."

"Who is helping them now?"

"They're on their own I guess, at least until the Guard gets back. But they may be underwater by then." Then the man paused and glanced over the rail, once more reminded of their precarious position. "Hey, look," he said with urgency, his eyes fixed on the wild water. "You better get going." The man turned and began to walk quickly back toward his companion, who was now motioning frantically for him to get off the bridge. He yelled something to her then turned back. "Good luck," he bellowed. "You will need it if you don't get out of here, . . . and I mean now."

Noah pried his eyes away and walked back to his car. He started the engine and sat there, listening to the gusting rain.

He began to think on what the man had said about Stewartsville. It was nothing but a small collection of ten or fifteen low-lying, simple houses built by a long-defunct concrete company in the early 1900s for its employees. They were clustered along a narrow road and a gravel railroad bed that had long since been stripped of its tracks.

Noah recalled images of peeling paint and yards cluttered with rusting cars and broken swing sets. Noah used to run on the soft railroad path, that is, until one day when a mangy dog slithered from underneath a fence and chased him, snarling at his heels. Noah escaped only by climbing a tree and waiting until the dog lost interest and wandered off.

He remembered that the village sat on the outside of a sharp turn in the creek. It made sense that this was where the water would first find its way over its banks. The force of momentum would naturally push it up and over the bend, across the railroad bed and road, and directly into the dilapidated town.

Usually, disasters in other places took the form of urgent news flashes that only momentarily concerned him. If it did not impact him directly, then he would not lose any sleep over it. It was not that Noah did not care about the tragedies suffered by other people, but what could one broken man do about it? Still, Noah kept thinking about the grim folk of Stewartsville and their junkyard dogs, all left stranded because just about everyone and everything else was more important. Maybe it was because he shared their insignificance, or maybe it was nothing more than his need to carve another big thrill notch on his ego, but Noah thought he should and *could* do something about it. So, he pointed his car toward the rising waters in Stewartsville with absolutely no plan about what he was going to do once he got there.

About a quarter of a mile from the town, orange barricades took shape in the roadway, warning that the street was closed. Noah stopped the car and got out, searching for a way through. But the barricades were secured by heavy sandbags, and they extended along the entire two-lane road and the narrow dirt shoulder on either side. He decided to pull his car off the road and walk the rest of the way. He found a small flashlight in the center console and slid it into the front pocket of his rain jacket.

Because the wind drove the rain horizontally at times, Noah's pants were already soaked through to the skin. And he found it difficult to move quickly because he was shielding his face against the stinging drops while at the same time trying to avoid fallen branches that were strewn about. Eventually, he rounded a curve and caught a glimpse of gray roof lines in the distance. Though already exhausted, Noah pushed on, sometimes walking backward for a brief respite from the whipping wind and rain.

He soon found himself in the shadow of a small home with dented aluminum siding. Water, perhaps six inches deep, was already beginning to lap at the foundation. The windows were dark. Noah glanced around: black holes for windows everywhere. The power lines were down, too. He circled the house, moving across the now-submerged road and railroad bed toward the creek. Water was churning by in the channel, but the creek was so swollen that it was beginning to top its banks at the sharp curve, just as he had suspected, and send a silent cascade of water into town. And with the crest of the flood still hours away, the water would soon come higher and suddenly turn houses into coffins.

Noah remembered what the man on the bridge told him about the sandbags. He slogged back to the road and began to walk toward the other end of town. Sure enough, he found about two dozen pallets of sheet-wrapped sandbags sitting off to the side of the road, just north of the last house in town. He took a closer look. The pallets were stacked about four to five feet high. He lifted a sandbag from the top of one of the pallets and guessed that it weighed about twenty-five pounds. Noah was certainly no engineer, but it seemed as though there were far too few bags to build a dike the entire length of the hamlet.

After a moment, Noah reasoned that if the bags could be placed just where the water would jump the bend, it might be enough to deflect the bulk of it away from the houses. But how was he going to do that? These people had already been warned by people in uniforms, and they had still refused to go. How could he prompt them to come out into the rain and help him? Noah knew that he had about as much charisma as a concrete block. And the low growl of the surging creek reminded him that time was running out. As if on cue, the rain picked up, and it seemed like the sky was hammering nails into the ground.

Then he felt that sensation coming on again. Everything glistened, then at the same time, his vision began to darken from the outside in. He leaned against a tree to steady himself. Like the other times, the sensation happened when he found himself isolated and powerless. And despite knowing better, he had blown his cover and walked himself right into it. "Fuck!" he screamed out loud. So, if he knew that, why did he come? Why did he invite the madness to find him? Some part of him, he realized, had betrayed him. Some part of him wanted it to happen again, perhaps out of sheer curiosity or a desire for control. But even Noah's rage could not stop it now.

Noah started to wobble on his feet, so he sat down on the grass and leaned back against one of the pallets. Blackness crept in until it shut out all light. Sound became muffled, and then everything was quiet, as if he had been sealed alive in a tomb. For a moment, panic seized him in the darkness of his mind, and he bucked and shuddered.

The images instantly materialized and flitted by, backlit by an unseen source of soft light. As usual, the faces were hazy, as if the movie reel were being played on a tattered old screen. When it stopped, ancient, soulful eyes were gazing back at him.

She was smiling.

This time, the door opened slowly. Soft, warm light spilled in.

Chapter 14

The Leader

THE NAME *GENOA* suggests nothing of my ancient city's true nature. Even "Lady of the Sea," as she is known to the sailors of the many ships moored at her shores, only manages to capture her alluring beauty, the face she shows the world. However, such few words could never truly describe her many rich layers or her moods that change as often and as swiftly as the winds.

Genoa cascades down a steep mountain face to the sea. At the very top, the wealthy occupy grand villas with sweeping views that direct one's gaze to the bustling ports far below. Nestled deeply into the shadow in between is Old Town, a disorienting labyrinth of dark, narrow alleys called carrugi, some of which cannot accommodate even two people walking abreast. In this forest of shabby, jumbled tenements can be found everything needed to serve the sea-faring traffic that never seems to halt, even in times of war. From the street vendors hawking exotic wares to the drunken shouts from crowded lodging houses to the kitchen smoke that tickles your nose with the scent of fresh bread and pies, Old Town has everything a weary and homesick sailor from any land could desire. And for those whose tastes are outside of the law, Old Town is even more accommodating. Countless games of chance abound, as do sultry women who beckon from the shadows. But these vices are found in the deepest, darkest corners of the carrugi, where cutthroats and criminals are always in audience. On account of many disappearances, it was said that Old Town swallows people whole. For the unwary traveler, this was oftentimes true.

And if the elite, high up in their sprawling estates, are the scheming mind of the city, and if the many harbors are her clutching fingers, then Old Town is her beating heart from which all her lifeblood flows. And this is the only home I have ever known.

It was dusk, and as I often did, I found my way from Old Town to the very tip of a narrow, weatherworn pier, which was lesser used because it was one of the oldest and sorely in need of repair. It was one of the few places where I could escape and steal a solitary moment away from my many duties, a place where I had an uninterrupted view of the sun and sea. Here, I let my normally disciplined mind wander and spread out across the undulating water.

My mother was an orphan raised on the docks, then taken in by stern nuns. Though she was a housekeeper by trade, she had faithfully nursed an old tailor, who on his death bed willed to her his only possession: a modest two-story brick home with black shutters along one of the few alleys in Old Town warmed by direct sunlight twice a day. But the cost of keeping the house was daunting, so in order to make ends meet, she rented the first floor to travelers and forbidden lovers from the heights searching for anonymity. After a full day of tending to other people's houses, she came home only to cook and clean for the lodgers downstairs well into the night.

Though I had never met my father, in the few quiet moments my mother spent with me before bed, she told me he had come south from Britain on a ship bound for Virginia, an English colony in the New World. His vessel had lost a main mast during a terrible storm, and it had been forced into Genoa for repairs. She had to catch her breath when she spoke of him. She said he was a mason by trade and that his hands were rough and strong. She told me that my eyes were like his—slate gray and deep and luxurious, like fine cloth. And when I was little, my mother would hold her hand high above her head to show how tall he was. I always imagined he was a lumbering giant that had to duck his head to avoid hitting the shop signs in the street.

They had met when my father took a room in her house for the several weeks it took to make his ship seaworthy again. She practiced her English with him by candlelight, and he learned a little Italian, at least enough to know the way to melt my mother's heart. Before he left, he promised he would send for her when he was settled. But he was never heard from again. However, my mother was not angry—even though she always told me that promises were words written in stone and meant to be kept—because they had been young and neither of them had known I was growing inside her. Besides, it was best not to dwell on the past, she'd say, because we only have so few days before we are claimed by eternal sleep. Still, there were times when I crawled out of bed in the middle of the night and found her sitting by a window and staring down into the alley below, as if waiting for the familiar shadow of a giant to darken her door.

When I was twelve, a strange and deadly fever brought by the ships swept through Old Town like a tidal wave. Even in the best of times, the authorities were indifferent to the struggles of the people in Old Town, but once word of the epidemic reached their ears, they locked us away from the rest of the city under pain of death to any who tried to escape. Armed troops maintained a constant and menacing presence on the docks and the outskirts of Old Town. My mother fell ill, and seven days later, she was dead. She had fallen into such a wretched state, delirious as she was, that there was no time for any final words. There was only responsibility that had been heaped like a mountain on top of me. And during the quarantine, Old Town had become so lawless and friendless that I dared not mention to anyone that my mother was gone for fear that my home would be soon overrun by squatters and that I would be put to the street or the quiet knife. So, when I finished crying, I dressed my mother and dragged her to the garden. I dug a deep hole in the corner, then I folded her arms across her chest and placed her gently in the ground.

Even amid the chaos, some noticed my mother's absence, but I put them off with an explanation that my mother was confined to her room due to a painful episode of gout. I assured the few lodgers who sought her services that I could carry on in her place until she felt well enough again. By the time anyone knew that my mother had succumbed, the disease had passed, and a skittish normalcy had returned to Old Town.

I carried on in my mother's work. Though in the beginning, I only earned just enough to keep a roof over my head. In time, I mastered the garden and the ability to negotiate a favorable price for rooms. Although I was already an accomplished cook, since I had done so much of it at my mother's side, I had honed my skills to the point where travelers and citizens alike sought me out for a taste of my fresh pesto dishes. And for those with the means, I demanded proper payment. Eventually, I was able to hire others to help me, which afforded me precious time to think and wonder. I even taught myself to read, and I managed to acquire a modest library.

"Francesca?" a distant voice beckoned, drawing my mind back from the horizon. Still, I could not tear my eyes away from the frightening vastness that had swallowed my father. "Francesca Avaldi!" the voice at last demanded, albeit playfully. "It is difficult enough to gather such manner of people in the same place. I can only imagine what they will do to each other if you keep them waiting and are not there to chide them!"

"Can I not have one moment to myself, Marco?" I pleaded as I turned to face him. "Can I not have anything that does not also belong to everyone else?"

Marco was nineteen years old, only a few years younger than myself, and, like me, he was eager and showed the iron purpose it takes to keep Old Town sane. He was a dyer's apprentice and would soon be well established in the guilds. It was to him that the mantle of leadership would pass.

He smiled, then bowed curtly. "Unfortunately, you may not, my lady. The city would tear itself apart without you."

"Well, one day soon it will have to, and then it will fall upon you to carry on," I warned as I walked toward him. Sadness swept over his face. He fell silently in stride next to me as we made our way back.

Chapter 15

THE CONVERSATIONS TRAILED off as soon as Marco and I arrived. I surveyed the small crowd gathered in the alley just outside my door and found the occupations of Old Town well represented. There were assorted prostitutes, gamblers, inn keepers, shop owners, beggars, and merchants—those who were not counted among the ranks of civilized society. I knew most of them by their Christian names, but they just called me *Lady*, a title they apparently chose out of respect. For in the old days, violence ruled the dark alleys and made it difficult for any person to ply their trade. But I had forged a peace in Old Town that gave way to prosperity for all. So, when I asked them for an audience, they put aside their squabbling and came without question.

But, when I stood before them this one last time, I could not find the words that had always come to me so easily. My eyes began to well with tears when I thought about how far we had all come, so I excused myself for a few moments and retired to my garden. I cried alone at the grave of my mother.

When I was sixteen, I left Old Town for the first time and found my way out of the shadows for a peek of the Via Garibaldi, a broad sunbaked avenue created to display the wealth of Genoa to the world. The pristine street was lined by stately homes, some belonging to the premier families of the city, which were tended by small armies of busy servants. Finely dressed men and women walked arm in arm and nodded to the sturdy policemen who lazily patrolled, no doubt just to ensure that none like me would spoil the gleaming portrait.

I was struck by the peace and rigid order of things there, where everyone cooperated and dutifully played their part, as if it had all been painted by design. At the same time, I suddenly became aware of my own sad state: my dingy dress, my worn stockings, and the dirt under my fingernails. Although my hardscrabble existence had made me wise beyond my years, I was infinitely naive about the intricacies of "civilized" society. Nevertheless, I decided at that moment that even I could live in a place where people smiled at least some of the time and spoke kindly to one another. And the only way to accomplish that, I knew, was to make the carrugi safer.

The very next day, I visited the shops and the inns, and I spoke with the prostitutes and the shabby peddlers. I asked them all what they thought should be done. As for the ones who shooed me away, sometimes at the point of a knife, I went back day after day until, exhausted, they finally relented. And they confirmed my suspicions. No one who lived in Old Town could feel truly safe until the thieves and robbers were cleansed from their black dens.

As cutthroats mostly roamed at night, or in places otherwise hidden from daylight, I decided to banish the shadows from the alleys entirely. I convinced my immediate neighbors to make a small contribution to my effort, and I made up the rest of the money needed from my own meager savings. I purchased oil lanterns that I placed high along one notorious alley where only one month before, a prostitute named Squinting Mary had been found strangled to death. Though some of the lanterns were stolen, the result was a resounding success. The criminals moved on to blacker pastures. Soon, there was a beaten path to my door. The people of Old Town, feeling safer, came with small sums, or in some cases, fine things that could be traded. Lights soon blazed along many alleys. The people could work in relative safety, and that meant increased profits.

I became known as the "Lady of Old Town," and nothing happened of which I was not instantly apprised. Thus, all the wretched became my responsibility. When disease struck, I arranged for physicians. When violence spilled blood in the streets, I rooted out the scoundrels using a network of spies to whom no place in Old Town was unknown.

Soon, it was the criminals whose bloated bodies were pulled from the waters rather than their victims. My efforts did not go unnoticed high above in the villas of Genoa, and I was often privately consulted by finely dressed messengers when wealthy, debauched sons found their way to Old Town for wine-soaked adventure. I made sure they returned home unmolested (though with much lighter pockets of course) and was handsomely rewarded for their safekeeping. Though most of the money I received I used to feed and protect the citizens of Old Town, I managed to accumulate a respectable sum for myself—for I had long harbored a dream of seeing the New World, where a person was limited only by their talents, where my father had disappeared into a legend that only I now kept from oblivion.

⚷

Once I had finally composed myself, I left my mother's grave and returned to find everyone silent and still waiting. I cleared my throat.

"Marco already knows of what I am to speak," I began, acknowledging him with a slight nod, "but I tell you now that I will soon leave this place, and I cannot say if I will ever return."

I paused, waiting for this to sink in. And it was not long before I was met with wide eyes and slack jaws that told me they understood me perfectly. They were no doubt struggling to find words to express what they perceived as a stinging betrayal. But there was a purpose in the way I shocked them with these few blunt words without any preface. First, they were a simple and (for the most part) honest people who distrusted eloquence because it was associated with the high citizens of Genoa who promised reform but who so often abandoned Old Town. Second, by initially stripping them completely of hope, if I restored even a measure of it with the remainder of my words, they would be grateful and more readily accepting of this drastic change.

I turned to Marco as I spoke. "You will look to Marco now. You all know him. He will carry on in my place. I have taught him all that I know. He will keep the order we have made here, our city within a city."

"But what of you?" a voice demanded. "What could mean so much that you would leave us? Have you found a home above the docks, perhaps in the company of those perfumed villains?"

Antonio Selestro was an old cobbler with gnarled fingers and a drooping face that seemed to embody his downtrodden existence. He was always the voice of skepticism. As well he should be, for he had suffered through more dark years in Old Town than most.

"And yes," I said, "you deserve to know more, for as much as I have been your Lady, I have always been your friend." I cleared my throat once more to buy time to gather myself. "I have taken no husband, nor have I had children of my own, and I have given most all that I have to Old Town. In fact, I will give my home to Marco, and to all citizens of Old Town, so that you will always have a symbol of our cooperation in the hope that it will continue. Even if I am not here, some part of me always will be. But I have already purchased passage to Virginia in the New World, and I will leave in one month. I have been told that there are Italians there already, and I will find a place among them. Thus, to answer your question, I leave you not for some loftier position, but only for a different place where I am certain to endure far more hardship than I know now. I am determined to follow my heart, and I will seek my father, or at least what became of him, so that I can honor my mother's memory. And since I am not getting any younger, I will seek a husband. In the New World, I hear that a strong woman has no lack of fine suitors."

Some cried, others shook their heads in disbelief, but they mostly held their tongues. To further ease the transition, I deferred all matters to Marco, whom I publicly served as confidant and advisor, until my departure. I educated him as to all my practices and methods of leadership until I was confident I had left Old Town in capable hands. Each night, I packed, repacked, and checked my things with growing anticipation of the day when I, too, would disappear over the horizon.

But when the time finally came and I set eyes on the creaking ship that would bear me, my will began to falter, and I lamented my uncertain fate. Once more, I found myself a whimpering orphan with only memories for company. However, I had at least anticipated this circumstance, and because I did not wish to cry in front of the others, I told only Marco of the exact time of my departure. I handed him the keys to my house and the strong box where I kept the money. But I reminded him that this was mostly symbolic since the value of these things paled in comparison to the responsibility that would now be his constant bedfellow. As we slipped from the harbor, I stared back until Genoa sunk beneath gray waves in the distance.

Chapter 16

DESPITE HAILING FROM one of the greatest port cities in world, I took poorly to the sea. I was violently ill for a good portion of the crossing, which nevertheless served as a welcome distraction from the frightening vastness that stretched endlessly in all directions and was so at odds with my narrow confines in Old Town. When my wobbly feet finally met the ground in Jamestown, Virginia, I collapsed and sobbed both with relief and sorrow.

Although it was a world away, I instantly found a measure of comfort as I made my way through the bustling town. Although only a village by comparison in size, like Genoa, Jamestown depended on sea trade, and many languages were spoken by citizens and sailors alike. It was not long before I followed the welcome sound of my native tongue to a dusty barrel shop where a master was barking out orders to his young apprentice.

I soon secured a place on a wagon bound for the Italian enclave founded by Philp Mazzei, a wealthy nobleman from Tuscany who was attempting to bring to root some of the first vineyards in the New World. Though I was warmly welcomed, I was quickly put to work in the fields and kitchens of my hosts, from which there was little respite until well after the sun set. Whenever I could escape my duties, I made inquiries with the local authorities as to the fate of my father, Robert Davey.

As it happened, the British were meticulous record keepers, to the point where it could be determined, to the exact date and time, when any person or cargo set down upon the king's soil. And so it was with my father, whom I learned had disembarked a ship twenty-two years before, though his current location, or even whether he was alive or dead, remained a mystery. A census noted that he was last a resident of Jamestown fourteen years ago, employed as a stone mason. A clerk claimed to have known of him, but that last he heard, my father had set off alone to the north, probably Philadelphia, because there was much new construction that required skilled labor.

Though I continued to search for news of my father to the point where I found myself tilting my head toward any conversation in the hope I might catch even a just a whisper of his name, in the two years following my arrival in Virginia, I played my own part on life's stage with as much fortitude as God afforded me. Though I took no real opinion of myself with the exception that I was mostly optimistic and not wholly unattractive, I became known for hardiness, leadership, and charisma, qualities in a woman that could only be truly appreciated on the tenuous cliff edge of civilization.

I was eventually charged with the duties of domestic manager at the vineyards, which meant that I was responsible for overseeing the kitchen and laundry staff, as well as tending the vast gardens that produced herbs and vegetables sold to support the cost of maintaining the currently unproductive grape vines.

During this time, many young men sought my affections. Some of them I could have loved, but I remained aloof. I would marry only for advantage, which meant not simply wealth, but deference to my will and desires that would not be satisfied until I either met my father or stood over his grave. And the truth was that I certainly did not need a husband, for I had earned enough money to serve my own needs, even enough to get to Philadelphia. Though what I would do after that, I did not know.

And the fates would see me have my way.

After a welcome rain shower on one hot summer afternoon, I found a thoroughly soaked-though, well-dressed gentleman at the gate, who had apparently lost his way. By this time, I was fluent enough in English that I could carry on a limited conversation with most anyone I met. The man removed his hat and introduced himself as William Coddington, a tobacco merchant from Pennsylvania who was searching for a small plantation nearby. He was about thirty years old, neither tall nor short, though he stood a few inches higher than I did. He had long black hair and large dark eyes that gave me the impression of intelligence and quiet shelter. As unremarkable as I must have appeared to him in my worn skirt and tattered scarf wrapped about my head, he spoke nervously in my presence, even apologizing for any inconvenience he may have caused me. This was not someone entitled to wealth, I decided, for such a man neither needed nor cared for the company of common folk.

I led him back toward the road then directed him to his destination, which was no more than half a mile away. He thanked me and mounted his horse. Though just before he made off, he turned, and our eyes locked tightly for a slow, light-bending moment in which we silently acknowledged that our paths would now be intertwined.

Two days later, I was summoned to the gate, where I found William Coddington with hat in hand once more. He asked if I would walk with him and we immediately fell into conversation that was unforced and natural, as if we were childhood friends catching up after a long absence. He was from Easton, Pennsylvania, a small city due north of Philadelphia. His father and only brother had died of consumption, and he had taken the helm of his family's tobacco business there. He explained that he procured tobacco at its source in Virginia for a cheaper price and then sold it in Pennsylvania for a tidy profit. His duties often called for him to travel, which he described as an exhausting endeavor, but which gave him the chance to see much of the colonies. His work sometimes took him to Philadelphia, which he said was practically in a state of open rebellion against England. I took his enthusiasm in this regard to mean that he supported a revolution. He said that he did, though he believed it could be accomplished peacefully.

William was very curious about my life in Genoa, and I explained as much as I could in my adopted tongue. I showed him through the vineyards and the gardens, which he found exotic and fascinating. We met on several more occasions, since William had found various excuses to extend his business in Virginia. Though soon, all pretenses fell away, and on one afternoon, we spoke frankly to each other. William wanted me for his wife. I told him that if I were to wed, there could be no finer match. But the truth of it was, I explained, that I could not devote myself to home and family until I retraced my father's footsteps. William said that as he was quite familiar with Philadelphia and as there were a great many buildings being constructed, many masons were needed and had found work there. He promised to return in the spring with any word of my father he could acquire. I, in turn, promised that I would wait for his return, and if he was successful, I would be his.

Though I had prepared myself for news of my father's death, I found myself weeping uncontrollably when William finally returned and quietly explained that he had found a marked grave for a man of the same name as my father, hailing from Staffordshire, England in the same year as my father, who had died only a few months before I arrived in Virginia. By all accounts, William reassured me, he was a man of honor and had acquitted himself well in his trade. I asked him how he could know these things, and he said that he had met some masons who claimed to have made his acquaintance.

Though I did not doubt William's word concerning my father, at my insistence, he brought me to the outskirts of Philadelphia, where a small church cemetery was being carved in half by a babbling creek. There, I cried aloud once more because I knew that my father lay just below, as close as he ever was to me, yet farther away than any distance that could be measured.

William proved to be a kind and attentive husband, always willing to listen to my advice concerning his affairs. And together, we proved a remarkable team. I bore him three healthy children, and, despite my domestic obligations, I helped manage his business with the same resolve that had served me so well in Genoa, a resolve that increased our wealth at least twofold. During this time, I witnessed the birth of my new nation as well, albeit by the violence of a terrible war that left virtually no family unmolested.

Even during those times when every moment was occupied by the needs of my family, there was not a day that passed that I did not think of Genoa and my mother's grave in the garden. I wondered what had become of my house and beloved Old Town. Had it returned to the shadows, or had it become a painted place that finally made people smile? I was never to know, for it was the fourth child that doomed me.

I could see the doctor's weary face just before he turned away to deliver the news to my husband that neither I nor my baby had much time to live. I tried to tell my husband all the things he should know about our children, but the words faded away into my last, shallow breaths.

I now find myself once more in the light. It was my turn, they proudly exclaimed, and they urged me on.

Chapter 17

ROBERT VOLKNER, WRAPPED in a blanket, sat in his chair. He stared out of a window toward the churning water. When darkness fell, he would not even be able to see it coming, he thought. No heat, no electricity, and no help.

"Goddamn National Guard," he whispered.

He used to be in the army himself, at the tail end of Vietnam. The irony was not lost on him, since he had been abandoned here by his own, as he saw it. He turned toward the hallway that led to the back bedroom that his wife now occupied on a full-time basis while she recovered from hip surgery. She certainly wasn't going anywhere, he thought, so neither was he.

"You still all right, Doris?" he asked, loudly enough to be heard through the flimsy walls. He would have just walked back to her room to talk to her, but he was afraid to leave the grim scene, as if the moment he averted his eyes, a wave might carry his house away downstream.

"You just asked me that," she answered. "Now I'm beginning to think *you* might not be all right."

Robert said nothing. He didn't want to worry her. There was nothing they could do about it anyway, at least until someone came to evacuate them or build a dike.

"What's going on out there?" She asked. "Is the water still up?"

"It's fine, no worries. We just have to sit it out."

"Did you go next door? You should check on Bill. If we have no power, then nobody else does either. He's got a lot of pills to take; maybe he needs some light. Maybe you can bring some candles."

Robert got up and walked to the window. The water was climbing the concrete steps to his front door. It was already about a foot deep.

It was getting worse by the minute. Another foot or so, and the water would be inside. He walked to another window that had a direct view of his neighbor's house. He could see the beam of a flashlight bouncing around inside.

"He's got a light; I can see it. . . . I don't want to bother him. It's all under control."

Once more, the truth was far more frightening. Robert knew now that they should have left when they had the chance. They had been warned. Even if he could somehow get his wife out of the house, then what? His truck would likely get washed out in the road, and they would be trapped. And what about everyone else? Would he leave and forget about them? He shook his head. He was sure the storm would have passed already, or, at the very least, the army would have been back for them by now. He was a fool, and some of the others had followed his foolish advice.

Robert sat back down in his chair once more to continue his vigil. He jumped when he heard someone pounding on his door. *Thank God! The troops had arrived at last!* He let out a sigh of relief as he stood and walked toward the front door. Suddenly, the chaos outside seemed distant and hardly cause for concern. There was never really any need to panic, he assured himself. After all, what was a few inches of water compared to a thundering convoy of heavy machines packed with strong men and supplies?

"I thought we were goners," he said as he cracked the door. But instead of chiseled faces and broad shoulders bearing lifesaving equipment, Robert was greeted by a thin, water-logged figure that appeared far more in need of saving than himself, like a stray dog looking for a way out of the rain.

"Who are you?" Robert asked incredulously.

"We can stop the water," the man said, "but I need your help."

Only then did Robert notice the man's eyes, which glowed softly like two blue coals from underneath the hood of his raincoat. They conveyed both wisdom and kindness, as if they had seen many ages.

Robert poked his head outside and looked around. "You're just one man? You can't make no difference. Unless you got an army behind you,

you're gonna be stuck here just like we are. The National Guard is on its way; we just have to wait."

. The man shook his head. "They won't be here in time. In just a few hours, it will all be washed away. Besides, we have an army here already." The man tilted his head in the direction of the other homes down the road. "I have a plan. Get everyone together who can walk. We have to get started right now!"

Robert had so many questions, so many doubts. But there was something about the stranger, an almost supernatural confidence that virtually compelled Robert to follow him. He soon found himself knocking on doors, relaying what the man had told him. Most of them, like Robert, were long past youth and were hindered by some chronic condition or the other. Eighteen men, including Robert, and one woman, a visiting nurse, answered the call. Huddling together under umbrellas, they stood near the pallets of sandbags, where the stranger began addressing them.

He said there was no need to build a dike along the entire length of town. All they had to do was get the sandbags piled up at the bend in the creek, where the water would crash over first, and that would be enough to keep the houses from getting completely flooded. He said it would at least keep everyone alive until help arrived or the storm blew itself out.

However, the sandbags were far away, and most of them were ill or had trouble walking or hadn't exercised in a long time. The stranger said he had a way to minimize the work any one person had to do: they needed to create a human chain to carry one bag at a time from the pallets to the creek. He said they may not have to use them all to get the job done. Besides, the man warned, if they did not take action, they would soon be overwhelmed and drowned, so while he understood their limitations, they had to work together nonetheless if they wanted to make it through.

Robert cut the plastic wrap and passed the first sandbag. Very quickly, they had a rhythm going, and he moved one after the other until the first pallet was empty. Every so often, he glanced down to the end of the line, where the stranger took each bag and created a wide base, which he narrowed a bit with each rising layer. Sometimes the stranger paused, examined the rising waters, and once more urged them to work faster because time was running out. They complied as much as their aching and tired bodies would allow. The roar of the water was gradually notched back to loud static as the barrier took shape. And as the wall eclipsed their view of the water, their anxiety seemed to flow out on their labored breaths.

Finally, the stranger raised his hand and told them to rest. Robert collapsed on ground where he stood. He felt like a knife was being twisted in his back. It had been about two hours, and he wondered where he had found the strength. The others fell off the line, too, their heads between their knees. The stranger inspected the work, even climbing on top of the pile and peering down into the churning abyss.

"We're good," he yelled, holding both thumbs up. "It's stable. All it has to do is redirect the water beyond the houses. It doesn't have to hold it back."

The stranger walked along and congratulated each wheezing member of the motley sandbag brigade. When he got to Robert, he helped him up and took him by the arm, out of earshot of the others.

"We still have to keep an eye on it," he warned. "It was the best we could do with the time and materials we had, but maybe it just isn't enough. I don't want them to know that though. If the water breaks through, we've got to get people onto their rooftops. I know that's not much, but the higher you are, the better off you are. I'm going to need your help if it gets to that."

Robert's eyes widened. "But my wife, she can't get out of bed. Some of them, too; no way they could get onto a roof!"

The stranger smiled casually, confidently, as if he were a giant troubled as much by a raging ocean as Robert was by a puddle. He rested a hand on Robert's shoulder.

"If that happens," he declared, "I'll take care of it. I'll stick around to make sure. Just follow my lead, okay?"

Robert nodded. The stranger had a way of making him feel that he was mighty and that even nature was a slow, dumb beast that could easily be outwitted. Robert decided the stranger was the rare sort of man that took up far more space than his body, the kind that projected his will like the beam from a sturdy lighthouse.

The stranger squinted, then suddenly cocked his head toward something. He smiled.

"Ah! I think help has arrived. Look!" he said, pointing into the drab distance.

Robert turned. He concentrated for a moment. He could just make out the clattering noise of large diesel engines. Soon, the soft twinkle of headlights fought through the deluge. The convoy had just about arrived.

"Like I said, Robert, everything is and will be fine."

Robert put his hands on his knees and let out a long breath. "Boy, oh boy, that was close!"

The stranger nodded in agreement.

"What about you?" Robert asked. "You going to catch a ride with us?"

"No," the man said as he pointed over his shoulder. "My car is parked back there, off the road, outside of town."

"Well, I guess that's it then; I'm glad for your help."

The stranger gave him a genial smile then shook his hand.

"By the way, it just occurred to me that I never got your name."

The stranger stared at the sky for a long moment before he spoke.

"It's a funny thing," he whispered, "but just now, I'm not sure."

Then the man turned and disappeared into the storm.

⚷

With each step, Noah's body gradually became his own once more. When he was sure he was out of sight, he sat on a tree stump along the road so he could take stock. He felt his scruffy face, then examined his hands carefully. He rubbed them together, then balled them into fists, just to be certain he was once more in charge. He cleared his throat and said his name. Why was that so hard?

He was there this time, awake and aware, when it happened. It was as if he were peering just over his own shoulder as some sort of invisible passenger. He could feel himself speak, though he had no thought of the words he said before they came out of his mouth. He could feel himself move, but he had no inkling of where his body was taking him.

But, oddly enough, Noah thought, this was a step in the right direction, because it seemed to prove his theory correct. It was stress that brought it on, whatever *it* was. That meant that if he avoided extreme situations, he could maintain control and prevent it from happening again. But he still had to figure out precisely the nature of his condition. Perhaps it was dissociative identity disorder caused by the trauma of the accident. Or maybe he was awake yet somehow dreaming at the same time. He still had not entirely ruled out a paranormal experience, which simply is a more legitimate way of saying that he was being haunted by someone or something. But if there was such a thing, it is doubtful it would be confined to any predictable pattern.

Also, if he was no longer simply blacking out without any memory of what happened, then his symptoms were improving. This could mean that it may never happen again. All in all, Noah decided, he had reason to be optimistic. Although the subject of the key still nagged him and whispered for his attention from time to time, it was something for another day, something for when his sanity was more firmly established.

Though the rain began to slow, the low, gray sky suggested that it was only an intermission. Noah took advantage of the lull and found his car. He turned the key. The car sputtered and coughed at first, then came to life. Noah let it idle, thinking he should burn off any water that may have found its way around the engine before he got back on the road. Just as evening darkness began to paint the world black, Noah made a U-turn and headed for home.

Noah suddenly felt a burning thirst. He realized he had not had even a sip of anything since leaving the house that morning. Strange, he thought, so much water around him, but nothing at all to drink. He remembered a tiny dive bar just outside of town called The Driftwood. He had stopped there before, but just to get six packs. He had never actually sat down to have a drink. No wonder. It was dark and smoky, and the few people Noah had seen there resembled grizzled hobos who might sooner cut a person with a rusty blade than offer even a nod of greeting. But the beer was cheap, and Noah wanted to get lost in a corner with his thoughts.

Noah parked around the back. There were only two other cars in the lot: an old rusty pickup truck and a Ford Taurus with a flat tire. Inside, he found a bearded man in a flannel shirt shooting pool by himself and another—much older—man in a raincoat sitting at end of the bar, furthest from the door, sipping a drink. Neither of them bothered to look up. Noah took a seat at the bar as far away from them as he could. He found his soaked wallet and pulled out a twenty-dollar bill. He smoothed it out on his thigh.

"What do you want?" A bored voice inquired.

Noah glanced up. The woman leaned against the back of the bar, smacking her lips as she chewed on a wad of gum. She was probably in her mid-thirties and would likely have been a knockout in high school. Although she was now overweight, Noah could discern an athletic build beneath the flabby surface. She wore a tight, faded black T-shirt that flattered a generous bosom, no doubt one of the few things she still felt good about when she looked in the mirror. She had shoulder-length brown hair and innocent cow eyes that always hoped yet were resigned to defeat in the end. Noah wondered how many times she had left the bar with drunk would-be saviors only to discover that they were just like the abusive father that had abandoned her when he got behind on the rent. Noah felt sorry for her. She seemed like the type of person who would always find the people willing to take advantage of her.

"You have Coors Light on tap?"

"It's your lucky day," she said while she reached under the bar for a glass. "That's about *all* we got. That and a couple bottles of Jack. Can't get no deliveries on account of the weather. We're just using up what we have. After that, who knows?"

"In that case, I'll take a shot of Jack and another beer, too, in case it runs out. That way I won't have to bother you for a while."

The woman shrugged. "Don't matter to me."

She leaned over the bar and placed three glasses in front of him. Noah caught the scent of perspiration and stale cigarettes.

"I'll be in the back; just holler if you need anything else."

Noah nodded, and the woman disappeared behind a drawn curtain at the far end of the bar.

Noah threw back the shot of whiskey. His throat convulsed, but he managed to swallow the fire without gagging. He stared at the empty glass for a moment. He had not had a naked shot of hard liquor since college. And now he knew why. It tasted like acid. But it was quick and to the point. He could feel his senses being laminated by the alcohol almost immediately. He quickly gulped down one beer. He watched a small television on the wall above him while he sipped the second one. It was a newscast, but there was no sound. Noah reached over the bar and found the remote. He turned it up.

The reporter said that although the storm had almost passed, it left widespread power outages across the eastern seaboard; Boston, New York, Philadelphia, and Washington DC, along with other major cities, were all experiencing power grid shutdowns. Looting and random acts of violence were on the rise. People were encouraged to stay indoors and off the roads. A state of emergency was still in effect. And it may get worse: a hurricane was brewing near Bermuda. The reporter cut to another talking head that posed a question: Was the storm caused by global warming or was it a natural cycle? Apparently, no one knew for certain. Either way, Noah thought, it's pretty fucking bad.

Noah searched through his coat for his cell phone. Just as he suspected, there was a text from work. The office was closed tomorrow because there was no power. Only truck drivers were to report. Normally, an unscheduled day off work would be reason to celebrate. But there was something ominous about it all that robbed him of any joy. Maybe he should be driving west instead of getting drunk in a bar. Noah imagined this is what the good citizens of Pompeii felt like just before they were wiped off the face of the earth.

Just then, the reporter said the western half of the country was being strangled by drought, and little snowfall was expected this year. Well, scrap the idea of getting out of Dodge, Noah thought. Might as well pretend that everything is fine and let the world fall all around you. If things ever came to that, Noah knew, he was a dead man anyway. Only people with skills and supernatural grit survived history-making disasters. Noah was nothing but cannon fodder. On that note, he chugged the rest of his second beer. He rapped loudly on the bar and called out for more.

"This time, two shots, one beer."

The woman came from behind the curtain. She stopped in front of him and folded her arms defiantly. Then she looked Noah up and down and furrowed her brow.

"You're not gonna be a problem, are you? I don't want no trouble. I wanna get home in one piece, same as you." Then she pointed to the empty glasses. "It hasn't been ten minutes! If you keep that pace up, you'll get mean or pass out. Either way, that's bad for me."

Noah suddenly felt like the scene was unfolding from a distance, as if he had been pulled to the back of his skull, and he was watching through pinhole eyes from the shadows of his mind. There was someone else inside his head, jostling for position, trying to crowd Noah out—someone who played evil games in the dark. Noah broke into a cold sweat.

He held up his finger. "Just a minute. Where's your bathroom?"

The bartender pointed to a door behind him. Noah nodded then excused himself. He just needed to walk around for a moment, get his bearings. He opened the flimsy door marked "Gents" and stumbled inside. A light flickered. Noah leaned on the sink with both hands and breathed deeply, methodically. He tried to focus, but his will felt mortally wounded, knocked out by booze and sad news. The cunning creature knew his defenses were down. Noah braced himself, then looked into the mirror.

⚷

The annoyed bartender waited for the retching. The man looked awfully unsteady after all. Put three drinks in anyone worn that thin and there was going to be a problem—her problem. She cursed under her breath while she searched for the mop and bucket. Her boss was too cheap to hire someone to clean the place, so it was her job to do everything from stocking the shelves to slinging drinks to mopping the floors at the end of her shift. And if someone puked in the bathroom, it was her nose-pinching job to clean it up.

She filled the bucket with hot water and soap then waited. This guy would be out on his ass the moment it happened, she decided. And if he gave her any shit, he'd get a bat across the bridge of his nose. It certainly wouldn't be the first time she put some drunk cowboy on the ground.

A toilet flushed, followed by the sound of running water. A figure emerged through the door. The man strode back to the bar, not even a hitch in his step. He sat down, yawned, and glanced around as if he were seeing the place for the first time.

"You all right?" she asked. "I thought you were gonna get sick or something."

"Nah, just a little tired. . . . Now, I got my second wind." The man looked up to meet her curious gaze. He examined her for a moment, then smiled with a hint of mischief. He reached his hand across the bar. "I'm Noah, what's your name?"

"Bernadette," she said softly, suddenly disarmed by Noah's interest, and she briefly took his hand.

"I have to say, Bernadette, maybe you and I didn't get off so well, but I can assure you that I won't give you cause for any concern." Noah reached into his wallet and put a fifty-dollar bill on the bar. "That's for your trouble . . . *so far.*"

Bernadette's eyes widened. "I'm grateful." She slipped the money into her back pocket.

Noah laughed quietly. "We'll see," he said playfully. "We will see."

Chapter 18

The Darkest Heart

EVEN IN OUR house, which is filled with warm light and fondness, there are cold, slithering things. For there can be no light without darkness, no goodness without the lack of it. The measure of us all was taken against the ones with black hearts, and they had their part to play. So, there was a place for them among us, though they always shrank from our presence, hiding just out of our view. And they were now, as they had been in the flesh, wringing gnarled hands and scheming. Unfortunately, we could deny them no more than we could deny ourselves. Though we loved them, we always feared for the havoc they might spread.

The rest of us, even though faulted to varying degrees, still strove eternally to be of service to our house. But the Dark Hearts, as we knew them, were not concerned with the needs of others, only themselves. No matter if they were called upon or not, they crept forward among us so that they might seize a host. Their opportunity to strike arose whenever and wherever there was doubt and fear, where they could find both camouflage and sustenance, just as a snake was drawn to the high grass where it could work an ambush.

There was one in particular that evaded the light most desperately. He appeared as a wisp of gray smoke or a fleeting, insubstantial mist that was always scurrying from our sight. Sometimes, his presence was felt more than seen, as when we were stricken by inexplicable sadness and a sense of foreboding. He had long ago discarded the title of our house and erased it from his memory. In its place, he bestowed on himself many false names that he used in a futile attempt to avoid accountability, names synonymous with the terrible deeds that we would never give voice to.

⚷

I was born in Maryland in 1862 to a simple farmer and his wife. By all accounts, my childhood was normal, and I grew up in the usual way except that I was extraordinarily precocious and self-absorbed. I attended church with my stoic parents and siblings and prayed before meals and sleep—I had been groomed for unconditional obedience and grueling physical labor. I was ill-suited for both, however, as I possessed an incisive mind perched precariously atop a gangly and uncoordinated frame. Thus, my work around the farm could best be described as long periods of bleary-eyed daydreaming interrupted by either the sting of my father's hand or an accident, which, again, gave cause to feel the sting of my father's hand. I excelled in the little education I received, which was cut short when, at age twelve, I was forced to leave school for good to work on the farm.

Most people I met seemed only slightly more capable of higher thought than the livestock. This convinced me that others should be manipulated to serve my needs. As a boy, this was an idea that I struggled to reconcile with the selflessness that the Bible prattled on about. If I was created in God's image, then did he not share my selfishness and my illicit desires?

Then I had an epiphany. On one rainy Sunday when I was thirteen years old, the preacher told a story about a man who became powerful by unabashedly using and deceiving others for his personal gain. Such a man, the preacher said, while he lived high on earth, could never reach heaven because his success was not the result of his own labors. *Not the result of his own labors?* Well, only the day before, after I had quite rightfully been accused of failing to latch the stall and allowing a horse to escape, I had successfully convinced my father, using deception that depended in large part on a convincing expression of sincerity, that my dim-witted brother was responsible because he was last in the barn. This was no small task, since my father always claimed he could see straight through a lie like a clean window. And so, I decided—just as cows and chickens and horses served my family—that if I worked diligently to advance myself by blind use of the human herd, there could be no complaint from God that I had not at least labored strenuously for the status I acquired in life. Anything else would simply be a waste of the talent God had seen fit to grant unto me.

When I was seventeen, I slipped away in the night with ten dollars stolen from my father, the clothes on my back, and two loaves of bread. I set out for new pastures in the burgeoning city of Baltimore. When I finally arrived, lean and foot sore, I purchased a newspaper. I immediately found the death notices. The name of my benefactor was soon revealed.

Ida Brinkhorn met all the requirements: middle-aged, childless, and the grieving widow of one of Baltimore's more noteworthy and wealthy citizens. Apparently, her husband, Matthew Brinkhorn, who was orphaned soon after birth, had made his way to Baltimore as a stowaway on a ship from New York. Mr. Brinkhorn had accumulated a fortune importing tea from abroad "through devotion to God and hard work," but had died suddenly at age fifty when his heart failed while out for an evening stroll. Though survived by his wife of thirty years, his only son, Matthew Jr., had been killed at the battle of Gettysburg.

I soon arrived at the Brinkhorn residence. It was a stately brick home with tall windows and red velvet curtains set far back from the dusty, rutted road. As I dared not be seen loitering about, I managed to climb into a densely leaved oak tree that sat at the edge of the side lawn. I found a perch by which I could recline in safety and half slept until nightfall.

Under cover of the darkness, I crept close and peeked into lamp-lit rooms. There was a library stacked with hundreds of books. I crawled around to the other side of the house, concealed from view by a row of hedges, and peered into a reclining room. There were plush leather chairs and a high table at one end of the room with crystal decanters. And there, above a fireplace, was a large portrait of who could only be Matthew Brinkhorn. Imagine my delight when I found a familiar face staring back. Although he was bald, his face was thin like mine, but not quite gaunt. And he had intelligent gray eyes, very much like a wolf, I thought—very similar to my own. Although I could glean little of his stature from only his portrait, certainly it was safe to assume that we were both of at least an average height, though I imagined I was more slightly built. Still, there was no sign of Ida Brinkhorn. I could not determine if my plan would work unless I could see her from afar first.

Finally, just past midnight, I caught a glimpse of a hunched female figure moving slowly from room to room. Her long dark hair, still tangled from restless sleep, fell about her face. She would pause in doorways, clutching a nightgown at her breast, and stare into the darkness for long moments as if searching for someone. Her suffering was palpable. I could barely contain my excitement. Ida Brinkhorn was low hanging fruit, ripe for the taking.

In fact, it proved even less difficult than I had anticipated.

The next afternoon, I rang the bell and introduced myself as William Hadson of New York. I explained that I had fled from an orphanage where the boys often talked late into the night about Matthew Brinkhorn, one of their own who had found great success in Baltimore. I said that I, too, wanted to be a man of action, so I risked the perils of the journey in the sincere hope that I might find work in the business of Mr. Brinkhorn.

I thought I might have to further embellish my tale so as to sufficiently pluck Ida Brinkhorn's heart strings, but I was immediately greeted with a firm embrace and a tearful rendition of her husband's recent death. And as he would turn no orphan away, Ida Brinkhorn explained that she could do no less. She said that I would immediately be put to work, but not before I was bathed and fed and otherwise made strong once again.

I was given a room above the stalls and charged primarily with assisting the groundskeeper, Mr. Tungstan, a surly and, at most times, intoxicated man who was always grumbling expletives under his breath. I took my meals in the kitchen and was often visited by Mrs. Brinkhorn. She provided me with clothes that once belonged to both her son and husband, to whom she occasionally remarked that I bore a striking resemblance in both appearance and intellect. And as I expressed a great interest in books, I was granted access to the vast library in her home.

Mrs. Brinkhorn was quick to recognize my intelligence, so she gradually allowed me to shoulder many of the responsibilities of managing her home. And I often caught her sideways, longing glances, her eyes always upon me. You see, I had ingratiated myself to her by proving indispensable. I had earned her trust by refusing any salary, replying always that her company was reward enough. Soon, she professed a romantic love for me and introduced me to the pleasures of the flesh. Although I was inwardly indifferent, I tearfully pledged myself to her nonetheless.

Of course, there were other household staff who were either suspicious of my intentions or jealous of my scandalous relationship with the widow, but as I had her confidence, any potential troublemakers soon found themselves put to the street. After many pleas, I was successful in convincing Mrs. Brinkhorn to cease communications with all her prior acquaintances and advisors for fear that they would do anything to acquire her wealth. I assured her that I, who loved her and expected no remuneration, was the only one she could trust.

One evening after lovemaking, I began to lament my circumstances in the event that I lost her favor or she suddenly passed. I told her that if she cast me aside or died, my own death would soon follow for the world held no joy without her. She assured me she could not live without me any more than I, her, but in the event of her death, she had already made provisions in her will that I should inherit her estate. Though I smiled in the dark, I scolded her softly for believing that something as thoroughly trivial and boring as money could be any substitute for our passion. She wept and said only that she was too old to wed me or bear me a child, so it was the best she could do to prove her love for me.

Chapter 19

NOT ONLY DID I devote a great deal of thought to the means by which I was going to murder the widow (so as to avoid detection), but I also contemplated the moral implications of such a crime. A crime, I say, because the premeditated intentional killing of another, if not to defend one's self or another, was an act that the populace believed was so heinous that it merited a swift hanging, sometimes even before the offender stood trial. But I must admit that I had a difficult time comprehending the reason for such a harsh punishment in every circumstance.

Certainly, if people went around killing each other all day, society would become unhinged. No person would leave the safety of their home, no work would be accomplished, and no crops would be harvested. We would very quickly be reduced to a pack of feral, starving animals incapable of rational speech or thought. But as we all had to die sometime, could there not be a case where killing another benefits the victim, the killer, and perhaps even society as a whole? I do not mean to suggest that dashing a child's brains on the sidewalk would result in any conceivable advantage to the killer—or anyone else for that matter. But say, for instance, where someone is suffering from a terminal illness. That person will inevitably die, but not before they endure great misery, not before precious resources are futilely expended in that individual's care. Would it not be preferable to spare the patient the suffering and spare the expense of their care so that the heirs might inherit the money instead and put it to any number of better uses?

But the widow Brinkman, while old, was certainly not ill. Though she was afflicted with the nagging ailments that marked her age, it could not be said that she was suffering. In fact, she seemed very spry when she undressed and took me to her breast. Still, she would, in the relatively near future, be bedridden and would require constant care. And she could pay to have the best doctors at her beck and call, the best medications, the very best of everything. Of course, that would leave less for me, which begs the question: Why should I wait until then? She has, by all accounts, had a good life. Now was the time for her to leave it, before the pain and the clammy fear of imminent death robbed her of her joy and replaced it with embarrassing, desperate prayers that would not and could not be answered.

I knew, though, that few people would concur in this decision and that if I were discovered, I would soon have a noose for a necktie. But why would no one else understand? Why would I be condemned rather than praised? Are not my reasons for this course of action logical? These were the most important questions, yet the answers eluded me as if I were trying to catch fog with a butterfly net. I understood, however, that the answer had something to do with empathy and sympathy with others. But that requires feelings, naked and undeniable compulsions that are powerful enough to stay the hand from doing harm no matter the benefit to the assailant. These emotions I simply did not possess, save the compulsion to serve myself.

As to the method of Mrs. Brinkhorn's demise, I ruled out poisons, as there were few substances to which I had access that did not leave some obvious sign of their use. However, I did consider arsenic, since it was already employed by the widow in various creams to improve her complexion. I could simply deposit it in her food over a period of time until she had consumed a sufficient amount to kill her. But since that manner of ingestion caused the victim to be violently ill and bedridden before death occurred, she would expend a great amount of money in her care, thus I would be cutting off my nose to spite my chin. Also, it would invite scrutiny, especially because I read recently that a physician had developed a means to test for toxin levels in the blood after death. If there were any question regarding the manner of my mistress's death, I would immediately by implicated in her demise if for no other reason than she had named a recently arrived, heretofore unknown man bearing a false name as her sole beneficiary.

I even gave thought to hiring someone else to kill her, perhaps designing a plan to make her death appear as a robbery gone wrong. That meant, however, a conspiracy. And conspirators, if caught, tended to reveal the identity of other conspirators to save their own necks.

An accident, however, if properly designed, could sufficiently prevent suspicion of my complicity. People die every day from one manner of mishap or the other. The newspaper was replete with tragic headlines of human error. I remembered reading about people crushed beneath the wheels of runaway carriages or overcome by fires that spread from unattended stoves. The very means of daily living were deadly and would serve as the perfect disguise for my deed.

I arranged to visit the docks overnight one day each week under the guise of conducting a thorough inventory and accounting of goods at the warehouse, which could only be efficiently accomplished after hours. Although the widow protested my absence at first for fear of being alone in the home at night, I assured her that she would be fine and that perhaps she might even benefit from a time of personal reflection without any distraction I might pose. Though I am sure that she pined away for me at first, she grew to at least tolerate the inconvenience.

For several months, on every Tuesday, I walked to the dock at eight in the evening and settled down to a desk in a dreary corner room on the second floor of the warehouse and began to examine the daily records. I arranged myself so that I sat with my back to the only window, my figure cast in a hunched silhouette by the glow of several candles and a fire that burned in a small coal stove that sat along the interior wall.

I made certain to find the old night watchman, Butch, each evening I arrived, just to let him know I was there, and I spoke with him briefly just before I departed each morning right before dawn, when the docks would begin to swarm with laborers. Butch, who was probably nearing sixty, had once been a dockhand, but due to his age and infirmity, he had been relegated to the lonely post of night watchman. He appeared permanently stooped, as if all the cargo he had ever hoisted still weighed, unseen, upon his shoulders. And seeing as how tea and coffee held little interest for any thieves, Butch's biggest threat was boredom. Thus, he was grateful for the conversation, which was mostly borne by me because he could enunciate only a few words for lack of a vocabulary and most of his teeth. I always greeted him with feigned warmness, and I often brought him luxuries such as scented tobacco or a bottle of fine whisky, which always drew the loose skin of his sunworn face into a quivering grin.

Like most people, Butch was a slave to his habits. While sitting in my perch, I learned that he only made one round of the warehouse and the dock at night. Between ten and ten fifteen, Butch always appeared beneath my office window and paused. I knew he could see me because at first, I sometimes turned and raised my hand for a moment to acknowledge his watchful eye, and he waved an oil lantern back and forth in confirmation. However, I grew to ignore his presence, leaving my back to him as though I were thoroughly engaged in work, as I did not want the lack of our cursory exchange to be cause for alarm or investigation.

I took to bolting downstairs after Butch passed so I could follow him. He always walked around the sprawling warehouse from my office in a clockwise rotation, checking doors and chasing away the shadows with the lantern that dangled from his outstretched arm. He stopped at the tip of the dock to smoke his pipe while he gazed absentmindedly across the sloshing, moon-glazed waters, then he continued on his way until he returned to his starting point, which was nothing more than a rickety stool sheltered by the frame of a recessed storeroom door. Sometimes, he leaned the stool on two legs against the door, folded his arms, and fell asleep. Sometimes, he just sat in the dark and smoked his pipe, the smoldering orange ember occasionally casting his face in an eerie glow.

I began to substitute a likeness for myself that would closely resemble a man hunched over his desk. While Butch was on his round one night, I placed a pillow I had brought from home across the back of my chair, then draped my coat on top of that. I then stood outside, under the window to observe. Backlit only sparsely by candlelight, it certainly conveyed the desired impression. Still, it had to be put to the test. So, for the next several weeks, just before Butch was out and about, I pre-pared the ruse and lay quietly on the floor. No alarm was sounded. In fact, Butch stopped me and voiced his concern for my wellbeing when I departed one morning.

"Beg your pardon sir, but you might hurt your eyes, them bein' buried all night in your papers, can't be good for ya."

I tried to hide a satisfied smile.

"Never fear, my good man; my work is nearing completion." I rested a comforting hand on his shoulder.

Butch shrank back and stared at the ground like a spurned mutt.

"Sad to hear," he managed. "It was nice, havin' company, I mean."

"Well, I still have some things to do, so I'll be back and forth for a bit. But I cannot thank you enough for keeping such a close watch on things and making certain I have not been disturbed. When my time is ended here, perhaps we can find you another position, something in the warehouse, where you can see your old mates. Would you like that Butch?"

"Oh, sir," he gushed, "I would be grateful; the missus, too! We don't see much of each other, me being up all night and her sleepin'—ain't natural that is."

"You just keep up the good work, Butch; I will take care of every-thing else." I turned to leave. I struggled to contain my excitement. Butch would be my greatest advocate.

Chapter 20

THAT FINAL NIGHT, I greeted Butch as usual, then settled down at my desk. As soon as he began his patrol, I arranged the prop of myself and quietly descended to the first floor. I slowly opened the door. I could see Butch's lantern shrinking in the distance then finally disappear as he turned the corner.

It would not be possible to accomplish the deed in sufficient time before Butch completed his rounds, but I could sneak back in unseen once Butch had taken up his pipe and stool.

I fastened my black coat and donned a black woolen cap, then slipped away into the night. I crept from shadow to shadow, often pausing to scan for the movement of any possible witness. But for the lonely howl of a dog in the distance, the world was under the spell of a cool fall night that seemed to bestow deep slumber upon any living creature.

I entered the house quietly using my key, though making no real effort to conceal my presence. The widow was the only person in the house in any event, at least until the kitchen staff began arriving after dawn. I walked to the spiral staircase and gleefully ascended. The pale glow of a single candle appeared at the far end of the hall—a hand was trying desperately to push back the sea of blackness.

"Is . . . someone there?" a feeble voice asked. "I say, again, . . . is someone there?" The light grew closer. Hidden by the darkness, I simply watched. She shuffled unsteadily, one hand holding her gown closed. The other, which held the candle, was trembling so terrifically I thought the widow might inadvertently extinguish the flame. My excitement and anticipation grew in direct proportion to her increasing agony.

"I'm sorry to startle you, my dear," I said cheerfully as I suddenly stepped into the light directly in front of her, "but I finished early tonight." She gasped and stumbled backward, but I caught her just before she tumbled to floor.

"Dear Lord!" she screamed. "I was so frightened; I heard a sound. . . . I didn't know what to do." I held her close for a moment, feeling her breath begin to slow.

"It's only me, darling. I was trying not to startle you. Obviously, I failed." She began to cry on my shoulder. "Hush now, everything is fine," I said, trying to soothe her. Then I held her at arm's length. "But I'm glad that you are awake now; I have something interesting to show you, something I found regarding the accounts. I think there is a problem that requires your immediate attention."

"What . . . right now?" She asked incredulously through her tears. "It's the middle of the night—surely it can wait until morning?"

"It won't take but a moment, my love," I said as I took the candle from her and led her by the hand to the stairs. Though she still searched my face with a confused expression, she moved weakly forward. I paused on the top stair, waiting for her to catch up. As soon as she began to descend, I moved behind her and took a step back. I loaded my weight on my back foot, then with all my might, I shoved her forward. For a brief moment, she was weightless, floating silently in the dark, defying all physical laws like some image from a dream. I could not see her face just then, but I could imagine how the horror, disbelief, and then finally the realization of betrayal must have manifested in her violently twisting expressions and bulging eyes. Never had she been more beautiful and desirable, I decided.

The widow's return to earth, however, was far less graceful. It was a cacophony of thuds, gasps, and muffled cracks as she tumbled out of sight. It lasted far longer than I would have anticipated, and I thought that perhaps she had made it the length of the stairway, all the way to the marble floor below.

I followed slowly, counting the steps as I went. I found her on her back on step forty-two of fifty. Her body was deathly still. Her right arm was hanging at an odd angle, and one of her legs was folded underneath her body, making it appear as though it had been severed just below the knee. I kneeled down and held the candle close to her face. I searched for some sign of emotion, of lingering thoughts, of evidence of the divine. But her eyes had rolled back, revealing only the bloodshot whites. Perhaps this signified some sort of self-examination, I thought.

I was startled when she began gasping for breath, puckering frantically like a fish out of water. I thought I might have to take further action to end her misery, such as covering her face with a pillow. I knew that the longer I remained, the more interaction I would have with the corpse, which meant that there would be a greater chance for me to make a mistake or for others to call into question what would otherwise be the scene of a simple, yet gruesome, accident. However, she just twitched several times before growing still once more. As the blood drained from her face, it seemed that she had been painted a waxy pale white.

She was gone, and no angel or hissing demon was there to whisk her away. Death itself, I found, was actually quite boring: nothing more involved than the simple act of snuffing out a candle. The playful moments before death, however, while someone walked the knifepoint of the hereafter, were quite intriguing. Next time, I decided, I would be patient. I would nurture the suspense on my own terms, free from prying eyes.

I did not linger, but I crept unseen back to the docks, tiptoed past Butch, who was dozing off, and quietly ascended the stairs to my office. I threw the pillow into the stove and arranged myself in the chair at the desk and eagerly awaited first light. When dawn's chariot finally began to arc across the sky, I knew there would soon be a terrible shriek from the maid that marked the macabre discovery of my mistress. The news would be spreading, and it would not be long before I was sought after.

I gathered my things and made my way casually down the stairs at the routine time. As always, Butch was waiting for me.

"How do you fare this fine mornin' sir?" Butch inquired with unusual cheerfulness as he pressed fresh tobacco into his pipe.

"Fine, Butch, fine, but I must confess that I am exhausted. Looking forward to a good sleep!"

Butch nodded. "Amen to that, sir." He struck a match on the bottom of his shoe and sucked the flame down into his pipe until it glowed pink. Sweet cherry-perfumed smoke hung like a curtain in the humid air.

"That must be the Virginia tobacco I gave you. What do you make of it, Butch?"

"Truly, sir, it shouldn't been wasted on an old fool like me, but it's the finest smoke I ever had."

"Well, you deserve it, being a loyal watchman," I said. "You are always alert and vigilant.... By the way, I meant to ask, did anything untoward occur last night? I thought I heard footsteps down below my window."

Butch thought for a moment. "Not at all, sir; it was quiet as a church at midnight. Ya probably heard me is all. Sometimes I stop there and look up on ya, make sure there's no one botherin' ya, or ya don't want for nothin'."

At that moment, a small figure emerged from the low light and sprinted toward us. I only knew him as Thomas, one of the stable boys that kept his mistress's carriage horses. He was no more than ten or eleven. He doubled over to catch his breath before he spoke.

"I been sent to bring you back.... There was an accident.... The constable wants you to come right away!"

"What is it boy? Speak up now. Is someone hurt?"

The boy grabbed me by the hand. "They didn't say what, sir. They got me from the barn,... said that somethin' bad happened and ya was needed right away!"

Butch pleaded to accompany me, but I reminded him of his duty to remain and keep watch until properly relieved. I then followed the boy as quickly as I could, but he was forced to stop every so often and wait until I caught up. I arrived breathless and soaked with sweat. I stumbled into the kitchen where I found most of the staff huddled together at the table, openly weeping.

I donned a mask of an appropriate mix of fear and concern. I searched the wide-eyed faces. "Well, what is it? What has happened?"

One of the maids pointed toward the doorway. "In there," she said, her face quivering.

I rushed through the dining room and into the hallway, where I was immediately greeted by a portly middle-aged man dressed in a blue uniform with polished brass buttons. His gray hair was slicked back, and he wore a bushy mustache twisted to fine points with wax. He had intelligent brown eyes that narrowed to gun slits while he sized me up.

"I am Chief Constable Hubert Mannion. And you are?" he demanded.

"William Hadson, of course. I am Widow Brinkhorn's assistant. Surely you must have been told. And now that I have responded to a question you already know the answer to, would you be so kind as to enlighten me? What has happened? Nobody will say. Where is Mrs. Brinkhorn?"

The constable continued. "And where were you last evening? I am told you keep quarters in the house, but you were not here when the maid arrived this morning just after daybreak."

I feigned anger. "You know very well that I was at the docks, where I spent the night reconciling the accounts. The staff or Mrs. Brinkhorn told you, that is why the boy was sent for me! I must insist that you tell me the cause for this alarm!"

Hubert Manion folded his arms across his chest and exhaled slowly. "Perhaps," he said, "it is best that I simply show you." He stepped out of the way and nodded toward the stairs. I could feel his piercing gaze on me scrutinizing my every action and reaction, searching for the slightest flicker of satisfaction at the sight he knew I was to behold.

I walked slowly toward the staircase. I could see wrinkled patches of white cloth through the spindles as I approached. As I turned and squared myself with the bottom step, the shattered corpse of the widow, clad in her favorite nightgown, came into view. Her unblinking doll eyes stared strangely at the ceiling, as if she were intently searching for a defect. I gasped and covered my mouth with my handkerchief, which seemed a plausible response to such a sight, though I felt virtually nothing. It was simply a sack of flesh and bones to be tossed in a hole. She was just as dead as she would have been had nature taken its course in the years to come. Could I be blamed any more than the far crueler lord of time that saw fit to strip us of all dignity before we expired?

"My God! Poor Mrs. Brinkhorn. How could this be! How could this be?" I began to sob loudly. I felt the constable's hand on my shoulder. His other hand swept up along the staircase as he explained.

"We found a candle near the top there. It appears as though she got up during the night and used it to guide her. As she began to descend, she fell, dropping the candle and tumbling down to where you see her now." The constable reached into his pocket for his own handkerchief and dabbed droplets of sweat that had condensed on his forehead. "The doctor was here already." He pointed to the corpse. "She has several fractures. But it was the broken neck that killed her."

"Why did she get up?"

The constable shrugged his shoulders. "I was certainly hoping you might shed some light on that."

"I told you, sir, I was not here last night. Though, I know that she often complained about her inability to sleep; even the slightest noise disturbed her. And this house emits many strange creaks and groans that seem all the more sinister in the dark."

The constable sucked his teeth as his eyes followed down the stairs, as if reenacting the incident in his mind. I sat down on a nearby chair and buried my face in my hands. The constable was certainly no fool, and I would give him no cause to note any unusual reaction. If I expressed any passionate emotion, he may suspect a more intimate connection between the widow and myself, which of course could explain a motive for murder. On the other hand, if I appeared too distant and detached, he would obviously conclude that I had some role in the widow's death, especially when he discovered that I was bequeathed the widow's entire estate.

I released a long, loud breath. It seemed a natural expression of dismay at word of the death of one's employer, one which denoted sadness for the loss of someone well respected mixed with an aspect of self-pity in light of an uncertain financial future.

"You needn't worry," the constable mentioned, "at least about your prospects for income."

I dropped my hands and turned my head slowly toward the inspector with a confused expression. "Meaning?"

"Meaning that all this will soon be yours, . . . once my inquiry is complete, of course."

"What exactly are you referring to, Mr. Manion, this house?"

The constable began to pace back and forth slowly in the hallway while he spoke. "I took the liberty of reading Mrs. Brinkhorn's last will and testament, which I found among her documents. It seems that everything was to be left to you: the house, the business, and all the chattel." He then approached and stood directly over me, eclipsing the still-rising sun that filled the window just across from me and enveloping me in shadow. "And what do you make of that, Mr. Hadson?" he asked menacingly.

My eyes widened with an expression of disbelief. "But, . . . but why? Is there any mention?"

"Only that it is for lack of her own heirs and in recognition of your loyal service."

I shook my head and began to sob. "I am truly at a loss for words!" After several moments I composed myself and stood. "What do you need of me?"

"As you can imagine, I must rule out any involvement on your part in the widow's death, since you have much to gain by it."

I narrowed my eyes with anger. "I can assure you that I was not aware that I was a beneficiary until just this moment, thus I can assure you I had no cause to harm Mrs. Brinkhorn!"

"Perhaps, but I must inquire nonetheless. You said you were at the docks last night—is that correct?"

I nodded.

"All night?"

"Of course."

"And you never left until you were summoned this morning?"

"That is correct."

"And is there any way that I can confirm your assertions, or must I rely strictly upon your word?"

I stared at the ceiling, pretending to think. "There is a watchman on the docks at night," I finally mentioned. "His name is Butch. You can speak with him if you wish, though I do not know precisely where he resides."

"And I shall then, this very morning. You will remain here in the house until I return." The constable retrieved his hat from a hook near the front door. "I have men posted outside; please, do not make any attempt to leave. Do you understand?"

I nodded. "I'll be here."

"And the widow's remains will be retrieved while I'm gone. I also ask that you not interfere."

"Of course."

I went to the window in the library and watched the constable make his way down the stairs to the street. He spoke briefly with two young men in uniform, then climbed aboard a black carriage and disappeared from my sight. The other policemen took up their posts on either side of the walkway leading from the front door. I could only assume others were positioned in the rear of the house to ensure that I remained.

Everything now depended on Butch, whom I was certain would exonerate me. After all, he would tell the truth, and the truth was that he saw me (or at least believed that he saw me) at regular intervals huddled over my desk throughout the night. He would tell them there would not have been enough time for me to leave, kill the widow, and return before he would have noticed my absence. The gifts and goodwill I bestowed on him would make him all the more anxious to defend me.

Though I carefully avoided the hallway where the widow was being moved to a litter, I strolled confidently throughout the rest of the house, making a mental inventory of everything that now belonged to me. I would, of course, not reside here, as I would be too well known and otherwise loathed. I would sell everything, including the business, for a tidy sum. I would change my name once again and disappear. I would soon be a quiet stranger on a carriage bound for someplace where I might explore my new interests free from scrutiny.

It was not long before I caught sight of the constable slowly walking up to the front steps. His shoulders were hunched, and his hands were thrust into his trouser pockets. He silently dismissed his men with an agitated flick of his hand. They exchanged a curious glance, and one of them shrugged. They began to walk to the street. I smiled. It seemed the good inspector had not received the news I am certain he was hoping for.

I sat in the library and forced salty tears down my cheeks. I quickly tousled my hair as I heard the front door open. I still had to remain in character.

"Mr. Hadson?" he called out.

"In here, in the library," I responded with a gravelly, emotionally worn voice. Heavy footsteps came in my direction. Soon the inspector was standing before me, although this time, at a respectful distance.

"The watchman is giving a signed statement. He accounts for your presence throughout the night."

I remained silent, staring blankly out a nearby window. Finally, I turned toward the inspector. "What else do you require of me?" I asked softly.

"Nothing as of this moment. Though my investigation is not officially completed, I intend to close this matter in the near future. A simple stumble in the dark it seems." His eyes studied me once more. "Still, if a need should arise, I expect I will find you here?"

"You will," I said as I turned back toward the window. "Where else would I go?" I asked my own somber reflection.

The inspector's footfalls echoed down the hall. The front door opened then gently closed. After several moments, I let free a long pent-up sigh of relief. I could contain my joy no longer, so I snatched a pillow from the couch and howled into it, lest any ears be pressed to my doors. At that moment, I was certain that God had never given life to a more perfect creature than myself.

Chapter 21

NOAH WOKE UP, but he did not open his eyes. He sensed that somebody was lying next to him, so he pretended to be asleep until he could piece things together.

His heart fluttered, and his head pounded with a ferocious headache. He last remembered being in the bathroom at the bar, staring at a face in the mirror that, though familiar, bore a cruel, devilish grin that made Noah recoil. Then, everything went black. But it was not a smooth and gentle sleep like before, rather he felt as if he had been drugged and tossed into a dark hole, like a press-ganged sailor who woke up bruised and battered below decks and already far out to sea.

Noah dared a glance. He did not recognize the place. A naked woman lay next to him on a bare mattress, the sheets tangled around her feet. It was the bartender. The ripe smell of sticky, unwashed bodies permeated the air. Though it was quite dark, a beam of dusty sunlight found its way in through a hole in the shades. Clothes were strewn about, and several beer and liquor bottles sat upon a dresser. An ashtray on the windowsill was overflowing. *Her place, maybe?* Noah noticed that he was naked as well, and with all the care his trembling hands could manage, he slowly pulled the sheet from underneath her feet until it covered him to the waist. He closed his eyes again.

His mind began to fit some shattered images together once more. There was the drunken laughter and reckless, mindless sex. He cringed. As if exchanging bodily fluids with a complete stranger was not disconcerting enough, there was something else between them, something far more devious. Noah squeezed his eyes and concentrated. He was relatively certain that he had tied her up somehow and that he had had his hands around her neck. He had made her beg, and he lied and promised her everything so she would let him do whatever he wanted. But what else had he done?

Was she breathing? Her back was to him, so he could not tell right off. He sat up and loomed over her. There was only stillness. His heart leaped to the back of his throat. Finally, her chest rose and fell, then again, and again. He watched for a minute or so just to be certain. He could only think of leaving.

Noah reached over the side of the bed and found his jeans along with his wallet and keys on the floor next to him. He rolled out of bed and pulled his pants on. He found his shirt balled up on a chair near the door, then he slipped outside without any thought of the rest of his things.

He found himself in the parking lot of a shabby motel. He remembered seeing it from the road before. It was on Route 50, thankfully not too far from home. He padded gingerly on bare feet to his car that was parked cockeyed in a space in front of the manager's office. He checked his rearview mirror just in time to see the door to the room open. He pulled away as she poked her head outside.

Noah floored it. He drove recklessly, drifting into the opposing lane on the turns, refusing to slow down. But some downed tree limbs appeared in the road ahead, forcing him to jam on the brakes and stop.

He was going insane now, he was sure of that. He had heard that blows to the head can cause this sort of thing. A once buttoned-down family man had turned into a raging alcoholic after he had slipped on ice and hit his head; an admired football player had committed suicide by cop, his brain fundamentally altered by concussions. What sort of snickering demons haunted them when they closed their eyes? What finally drove them to disregard all notions of self-preservation and seek out a violent death? Noah was beginning to understand. When you can no longer make sense of things you see, there is only one thing left to do, and there is only one thing you can do: jump into the endless, silent abyss.

When Noah finally looked up, he found the windows fogged. He wiped the windshield with his hand. It was raining again. He opened his window and took in several long breaths. If he could make it until tomorrow, he decided, he would drive to the nearest hospital and check himself in. The doctors could pump him full of drugs and lock him away in a room until they found a cure.

Noah put the car in gear. He proceeded slowly and found a way through the roadblock. He turned on the radio, but once more, the news was all bad. Thousands of dead fish were washing ashore in California, and no one had a clue as to why. A suicide bomber blew himself up in a busy market in Istanbul. Hundreds were dead; body parts were everywhere.

An idea popped into Noah's head. As ridiculous as it seemed, Noah believed his fate and that of the world were somehow inextricably intertwined. It seemed as though his internal anarchy was being carried out across the globe in a wave, manifesting itself as disease, war, and disorder, as if he were the proverbial stone that had been sent skipping across the quiet pond. Still, Noah was not yet too far gone to realize that it was always the unwavering conviction of mad men that they could shrink the world and put it on a mantle.

Chapter 22

THE NEXT THING Noah remembered was standing in his house and staring at the closet in the hallway. He knew that deep inside, behind the rack of old musty coats, behind a pair of long, unused skis, was a 12-gauge shotgun propped against the wall. It was a gift from his uncle, an avid hunter, for Noah's sixteenth birthday. He could not recall the last time he had used it, because long-ago memories, like mirages, eluded his grasp at that moment. Even more importantly, he did not know whether it was loaded or whether he had any ammunition for it. He could have just dug through the closet and inspected it to be certain, but somehow, he knew that once he touched it, he would be more likely to use it, as if by that time, the deed would almost be done, so he might as well finish it. After a moment, Noah turned away and shuffled off.

Noah sat on his bed and rubbed his temples. He mumbled some half-baked affirmations that he remembered hearing from a self-help guru he had seen on TV while he was in the hospital. He repeated it over and over again, waiting for the power of positive thinking to wash him out into a calm and peaceful sea.

"I am healthy. I am happy. I am whole."

But the more he said it, the more obvious it was that he possessed none of these qualities, which cast him into abject despair.

Then, a picture of the key drifted into his mind. *That key!* He suddenly became enraged. It was not him at all, he decided; there was absolutely nothing wrong with him. It was that dull silver . . . *thing*. All of Noah's insanity had started just after his grandmother gave it to him. It was a talisman, he knew, a conductor of ghosts and ill will that filled him with dread.

Noah stood up. He ripped the drawer from his nightstand and dumped the contents onto his bed. He sifted through the junk until he found it. He used a tissue to pick it up, as if it were coated with lethal poison, then hurried through the house, out the front door, and to the edge of his yard. He took a running start then flung the key sidelong like a flat stone. It sailed high over the road and into a fallow, muddy field on the other side. Noah suddenly felt like a deflated balloon, and he collapsed to his knees, heaving for breath. Then the pain set in, like vice grips on his limbs. But he welcomed the agony if it meant that the evil token was now gone, its magic radiating out harmlessly into the mud until it was finally dissolved by time and the elements entirely.

After a hot shower, Noah crawled into bed. He already felt better, lighter, as if he barely made an impression in the mattress. Lifted up and weightless as he was, his awareness was crackling with electricity. Something or someone was beckoning him, waiting for him. If only he could see further. Noah concentrated on the ceiling: the frozen paint strokes and the plaster surface beneath. Gradually, the layers of all coverings, even the roof of his house, seemed to peel away until there was a glowing, pale blue sky, which then only thinly veiled the great black expanse beyond. Noah shot toward it like a rocket. A face with two burning blue eyes appeared.

"For the one who sees me, . . . welcome," the voice said. "There is so much you must learn."

Chapter 23

CHERYL WYATT STOOD outside the First National Bank building in Darryville, Washington, on a gray fall day smoking a cigarette and contemplating her fate: death by boredom. And she was only 25, which meant that she had a long time to suffer before the end.

She flipped up the hood on her jacket, trying to block out a damp gust of wind that was buffeting traffic lights and twisting rusty street signs. She started to shiver. It was going to be a long, dark winter, she thought. She could feel it looming, gathering strength somewhere over the horizon. She could feel it in her bones.

The mailman, Thomas Barwill, strode by and nodded. Cheryl smiled reflexively. Several cars passed by; she recognized the faces. She shook her head. Cheryl knew almost everything about Darryville and its 550 occupants.

It seemed all conversations in town eventually devolved to the subject of the town's "proud" history, perhaps as a way fill the silent void that had long ago descended on this place. Cheryl had heard it said so many times she could recite it in her sleep.

Darryville was laid out along the Sauk River, surrounded by the North Cascade Mountains. The tallest of these, Whitehorse, towers more than 6,000 feet above and can be seen from Seattle, some seventy-five miles away, on a clear day. Though the mountain's height is only relatively modest, it strikes most people as menacing due to its jagged peak and extremely steep slope, which poses a constant threat of avalanche in the winter.

Darryville, briefly known as "End of the Road," began as a gold rush boomtown, but it soon drew the attention of timber barons for the virtually limitless supply of lush fir, cedar, and hemlock trees that stretched as far as the eye could see. After the Northern Pacific Railroad laid tracks all the way to Darryville in 1901, sawmills sprung up all over the valley almost overnight, and Darryville instantly became a bustling, wealthy logging town. The First National Bank building where Cheryl worked was built in 1903 to protect and increase the fortunes of the timber industry and is today listed on the National Register of Historic Places.

Things began to go sideways, however, in the late seventies. Some say it was because all the good trees were gone or because the timber industry collapsed under the weight of too many regulations. Others said it was just cheaper to get wood from other countries. Whatever the reason, the big mills closed, and people packed up and left. The final blow was when the railroad tracks were ripped up in 1991. Any hope that people had that big lumber might make a comeback was crushed. Darryville became a ghost town.

Cheryl painfully realized that her cigarette had burned down to her fingers. As she bent over to rub it out on the sidewalk, she glanced up at the imposing three-story bank building, which now served mostly as a sore reminder of better times. It was built with crimson bricks and beveled sandstone blocks that framed tall, yawning windows. It offered a perfect view of the half-mile downtown, since it was easily the tallest building for miles around. It was also one of the oldest continually operated banks in the state of Washington. Like the town though, the bank's glory had faded long ago. The upper floors, once filled with crisply dressed executives, clerks, and secretaries, were now relegated to the storage of old documents and dusty furniture. What precious little business the bank still conducted in the building was confined to the first floor, where only a skeleton crew remained.

Still, even if ragged around the edges, the bank had weathered time far better than most of the businesses in town. With the exception of a pharmacy, barber, hairdresser, drycleaner, and Mike's—the local bar—Main Street was a collection of dark and shuttered storefronts, most of which had faded For Sale signs taped to the inside of windows. The rest of the merchants had either moved out to the strip malls on the highway or had gone out of business altogether as the population dwindled.

Cheryl checked her watch. Break time was almost over. She hurried along the walkway to the bank's gilded front doors. She hung her jacket in a small closet, smoothed her skirt, and then made her way to the counter. Her high heeled shoes clattered loudly across the marble floor. Her manager, Ms. Alice Wayhill, frumpy and twice divorced, glanced up from her desk for a moment, her eyes squinting with disapproval. Cheryl winced, then walked awkwardly on her toes the rest of the way. It certainly wasn't necessary for Cheryl to wear dress shoes, considering that no customer actually saw her feet, but they made her feel pretty. Besides, wearing flat shoes or sneakers with business wear seemed cheap and tawdry, like slapping a crooked bumper sticker on a new Mercedes.

Cheryl nervously cleared her throat and took up her assigned station. She was a bank teller, and she made twelve dollars an hour. That wasn't much, at least in rest of the country, but in Darryville, that was a good job. It paid the bills and left you with some spending money at the end of the week.

But she had dreamed of so much more.

What had happened?

Cheryl made it a point to ask herself this question quite often. It kept her uncomfortable, unhappy, and dissatisfied. That was a good thing, because it meant that she had not given up and that there was still a chance to find joy.

She had been accepted to the University of Washington on a partial academic scholarship. She was going to major in archaeology. She loved history, and she wanted to be the first to find it, smell it, and hold in her hands before it was sealed in a museum. That summer after high school, Cheryl was bursting at the seams: young, confident, and drunk with promise.

But just two weeks before first-year orientation, her mother had been diagnosed with pancreatic cancer and given just months to live. Cheryl deferred her acceptance to college and bore down to the bleak business of comforting her mother as best she could until the end. Her father, on the other hand, already disabled by a heart condition, could not rise to the occasion. He seemed completely lost and required almost as much care as her mother. After her mother's death, Cheryl's father refused to leave the house at all. And he increasingly relied on Cheryl, who was forced to take over the household finances, shopping, cooking, and cleaning.

Cheryl kept putting off college. Though some part of her thought that her father was being selfish and that he deserved to be alone, mostly, she was afraid that he would simply waste away and die if she left. One day, she received a letter from the school. There would be no more deferments. She would have to reapply.

Most of the kids in her high school class stayed put. They found shitty jobs or got married to people who had shitty jobs or both. They were perfectly happy to discourage Cheryl. After all, who was she to think she could do any better? She worked at the bank and spent her free time looking for Indigenous relics along the river and reading as much as she could about the latest and greatest archeological finds. She dreamed about a day when she would look back over her shoulder at Darryville, Washington, for the last time, though it would likely be after her father went into a nursing home or passed away. She cursed herself for hoping that would be sooner rather than later.

Chapter 24

IT WAS ONE hour before the bank's doors closed for the day. Cheryl gazed out of the nearest window, counting the seconds. The sky still looked angry: two high clouds resembled furrowed brows. It was quickly growing darker as the sun began to settle. She decided to check her receipts once more, mostly to look busy, and pulled her stool in closer. She heard the heavy front doors open and slow, hesitant footsteps coming closer.

Cheryl glanced up and forced a warm smile, the kind that had landed her picture in a billboard advertising campaign for the bank last year. She was a bit startled though, as it had been a long time since a stranger had stood at the counter.

He was wearing jeans and a mid-length wool coat with the collar turned up. His attire alone was a dead giveaway that he had to be from some far-off civilization, maybe Seattle, where a person could find an example of modern male fashion, though maybe a few years out of date. He had short black hair and perhaps a two-day beard. She guessed he was about thirty, give or take. Cheryl decided he was handsome, if only for his eyes. They were the kind that were deeply stirring and rendered you speechless for a moment while you gazed into them, trying to figure out exactly what color they were. Her first impression was that they were blue. But as he got closer, they seemed to change colors: blue, gray, even green, depending on the light.

"How may I help you?"

The man returned a polite, pleasant smile. He reached slowly into his coat pocket and placed a small, plain key on the counter in front of Cheryl.

"I would like to open one of your safety deposit boxes."

Cheryl took the key and examined it closely. There had been only a handful of times when customers made this request, at least while she was working, but she remembered that the keys were always engraved with the number of the matching deposit box. Of course, she always knew the customer. Cheryl gave the man a puzzled look.

"It goes to box 5239," he said, anticipating her next question, "that's the date the box was first rented, May 2, 1939."

"Is this your account? . . . Did you rent it?"

The man laughed. "I hope I don't look that old!"

Chery knew that was a stupid question even before she finished asking it. But there was something about him that made her feel dumb and confused.

"I'm sorry. . . . This is just a bit unusual."

"Well," he began, "my grandfather rented it. When he died, it passed to my grandmother. She gave the key to me."

Cheryl glanced at the key once more. She coughed to fill the silence while she thought of what she was supposed to do. She finally remembered the procedure.

"The way this usually works is that when someone dies, there is an estate, and the executor of that estate gets a court order to open the box."

The man stared at her curiously.

"I mean," she continued, "and I'm not saying you would do this, but without the customer here to verify this, or without a court order, how do we know the key wasn't stolen? People usually keep valuable things in a security box. We, and especially *me*, could get into a lot of trouble if we handed the box over to someone who was not supposed to have it. . . . I'm sorry."

The man nodded. "I understand now." He paused for a moment. "I thought this might be a problem," he said, as if thinking out loud. Then he held the key up while he spoke. "My name is Noah Batson. Edward Batson was my grandfather. I think he left instructions with the contract he signed, which should clear everything up. Is it possible for you to get that somehow? I know it may not be easy, but I came a long way to get this."

Cheryl bit her lip. "Unless he left instructions that it must go directly to you, which he could not have done because you weren't born yet, then I know that my manager won't let you open it, at least without a court order." Then she leaned close and whispered. "My manager is strictly by the book; again, I'm sorry."

The man was undeterred. "No, no, of course. I get it. But I'm sure my grandfather gave some . . . unusual instructions that will make it unnecessary for me to go to court. If you would at least look into it, I would really appreciate it. Like I said, I came a long way."

Cheryl glanced at her watch. "We close very soon, and I'm not sure where to look for records that old or even whether we still have them here. Can you come back tomorrow? We open at nine. That should give me enough time to talk to my manager and track down the file if there is one."

The man exhaled with apparent relief. "Thank you. I'll be back tomorrow then. . . . Sorry, one more thing. Do you have any idea where I could stay for the night? Anything would be fine. I'm not picky."

Cheryl squinted into the distance. "Well, there's a motel on 120, about 10 miles out of town. It really isn't much, a lot of truckers use it, but that's the closest one I know of."

"Once more, thanks," he said gratefully. "I'll see you tomorrow."

When he reached the front doors, Noah Batson turned his head and nodded toward Cheryl, once more indicating his appreciation, then disappeared behind the curtain of afternoon gloom.

As soon as Noah Batson was gone, Cheryl raced off to speak with her manager, who frowned suspiciously while Cheryl excitedly recounted her conversation with him. When she was finished, Ms. Wayhill punched some keys on her computer and stared intently at the screen for several silent seconds. She finally swiveled her chair around to face Cheryl.

"Any records that old must be upstairs," she explained. "It seems they have not been scanned into the computer yet." Ms. Wayhill held up a stubby finger to pause the moment, then bent forward and searched through one of her desk drawers. "Ah, here they are," she said as she handed Cheryl a set of keys. "I'm not sure which one is which, so you may have to try them all. But the files will be in room 205. They're organized by year; you should see it on the file cabinets. I just don't have the time right now."

Cheryl snatched the keys. "I told him to come back tomorrow. I hope I can find it by then."

"This may all be pointless," Ms. Wayhill warned. "Even if he has the right key, without proper authority, he will not be permitted to access the safety deposit box. Still, we should have the file in case this man wants to dispute it. So, once you find it, bring it to me right away. Make sure you talk to me *before* you talk to this Mr. Batson. Do you understand?"

Cheryl nodded. "I'll come in a little early tomorrow to get a head start."

Ms. Wayhill picked up the phone, then waved Cheryl away.

Chapter 25

CHERYL WAS UP well before dawn, impatiently scanning the mottled darkness outside her bedroom window for the first sign of daylight. She had already showered and picked out her best (and sexiest) clothes, barely able to contain her excitement. Certainly, it was only a small mystery, but it was *her* mystery. Rather than it being something she only heard about, she was a character woven into it, pushing it toward a conclusion. To top it off, it was dropped into her lap by a strangely handsome, and, by Washington small-town standards, exotic man from places unknown. It was a feeling she had not known since she was just a hair's breadth from becoming a shiny freshman. She was determined to savor every minute of it because it would likely be a very long time before any intrigue was thrust upon her again. Or maybe, just maybe, she thought, this was the sign she had been waiting for. Perhaps she would pack her bags and go find adventure for herself.

Even though she would head out before her father was awake, Cheryl made coffee and French toast for him, which she put in the oven to warm until he was ready. By the time she got dressed, the lazy sun was just beginning to climb to its seat in the sky. Cheryl checked her watch. She would be more than an hour early, but the guard would let her in. She poured herself some coffee but forgot it on the counter. She grabbed the car keys and set off.

Cheryl set her things below the counter at her station and made her way to a long hallway that led to the rear doors. There was an elevator, but she ignored it. Cheryl's heels clattered on the tiled floor, but there was no one around to complain about it yet. She climbed the stairs to the second floor. The sickly gray light that found its way in through the windows was immediately swallowed up by mahogany-paneled walls that kept the hallway shrouded in half darkness. It gave the place the ambiance of a medieval castle, she decided. Cheryl finally found a light switch, and fluorescent bulbs flickered and began to glow noisily. The office doors still bore the names of dead or retired bank officers and staff. The door to room 205 swung open with a creak. Dust bunnies scurried for cover.

All four walls were lined with sturdy black file cabinets that were no doubt fire rated to withstand the horrific conflagrations that had brought many cities to ruin at the time of their manufacture around the turn of the century. In stark contrast, a flimsy particle board desk and folding metal chair sat squarely in the middle of the room.

Upon closer inspection, Cheryl found that each cabinet had six drawers that were marked with dates, beginning in 1880. She located the cabinet with the drawer marked "1930–1940." She pulled on it, but it did not budge. She found a keyhole on the upper right-hand side of the cabinet and tried three keys before one slid into place. It turned smoothly and was followed by several muffled clicks, indicating that the drawers had been freed for use.

Cheryl's fingers skipped across the dividers until she found the right year: 1939. A moment later, she pulled the file marked "Batson, Edward" that was, anachronistically, printed perfectly on a computer-generated label. They must have reorganized everything to prepare the files for scanning, she thought.

Cheryl placed the file on the desk and pulled the chair in with a loud screech. She took several tissues from her pocket and wiped off a thin coating of grime from the desk. Then, slowly and very carefully, as if they might turn to dust at any moment, she lifted the yellowed documents from the folder and placed them on the table. She cringed when she found that the bottoms of the pages were folded over to make them fit into the folder. Cheryl gently unfolded the pages, doing her best to smooth them out so she could read everything.

The top page appeared to be a pre-printed form titled "Contract for Secure Storage Box." Below that, it read, "Between First National Bank of Washington and _____." On that line, a name had been neatly written in blue ink: Edward G. Batson. Cheryl continued reading.

Although it contained a great deal of formal language or legalese that made it somewhat difficult to understand, she could grasp the basic terms of the agreement: the bank promised to safely keep the belongings of the depositor in exchange for a monthly rent, which, oddly, was not filled in. Instead, a handwritten line that ended in an arrow pointed to the bottom of the page. There, printed in the same hand, were several lines that read, "After negotiation, Depositor, as specified herein, shall make a one-time, non-refundable, lump sum payment of $15,000.00, which shall entitle the Depositor, his heirs or assigns, to the use of Safety Deposit Box 5239 in perpetuity unless terminated earlier by the Depositor."

Cheryl raised her eyebrows. That did seem strange, but that was a lot of money back then, enough to make the bean counters drool, so the bank probably gave Mr. Batson whatever he wanted. She went to the second page to see what it said about access to the box. Once more, an arrow drew her attention to the bottom of the page. "The parties hereby agree that an unmarked key for the aforesaid Secure Storage Box shall be provided to the Depositor (although the Bank shall retain a key bearing the Secure Storage Box Number) and that access to the Storage Box shall be granted to any person who possesses and presents the key, without further scrutiny or inquiry by the Bank. Such person shall be deemed to be an assign of the Depositor and such person shall stand in place of the Depositor for all purposes, including the enforcement of the terms of this Agreement in a Court of Law."

"Wow!" Cheryl blurted out.

So, the mystery deepened. What could possibly be in that box? The strange terms of the agreement suggested it was something so important and perhaps valuable that it had to be secured forever, yet, on the other hand, they also implied that it was something so ordinary and insignificant that it did not matter who took possession of it, so long as that person had the key!

Just to be sure, Cheryl checked the signatures. Edward Batson signed it, and so did Matthew Hornsby, a name she recognized from one of the portraits on the wall in the lobby. He was the bank president at the time. It was an important person indeed who had access to the bank president. Even today, he was rarely seen; his business carried on in strategic board meetings in a modern office building in Seattle.

Cheryl reasoned that there had to be a log of people who had gotten into the box, and she quickly returned to the folder. She found the form, essentially the same one the bank still used, which was the only other piece of paper inside, but there were no entries. Nobody had been in it since Edward Batson on the day he rented it in 1939! Once more, she thought, Wow!

Cheryl checked her watch. Although there was still plenty of time before Noah Batson arrived, once Ms. Wayhill heard the news, she would need to call the higher-ups, and that may take a while. Cheryl put the contract and the log back in the file and then raced downstairs.

Ms. Wayhill put on her reading glasses and followed along with Cheryl while she pointed to the handwritten portions of the contract and explained what she had found. Ms. Wayhill grunted then roughly snatched the papers from Cheryl to read them for herself. After a few moments, she glanced up, obviously annoyed.

"What time is he coming, this Mr. Batson?" she asked sharply.

"I don't know, but I'm sure he'll be here soon; this is the only reason he's in town."

Ms. Wayhill picked up her phone and dialed. Cheryl waited. Ms. Wayhill shot her a perturbed look. "Go on now. Just get back to your station; I'll let you know."

Cheryl walked back behind the counter and sat on her stool. She began to log in the checks left in the overnight deposit slot, but she was so distracted that she found herself simply unable to complete any tasks involving numbers, which seemed like so many illegible symbols at that moment. Instead, she occupied herself by cleaning her computer screen and disinfecting the keyboard.

Finally, she heard Ms. Wayhill's office door open and shut. They must have reached a decision. Cheryl busied herself once more with the deposits, simply for show. Ms. Wayhill was soon standing behind her.

"Cheryl," she said. "I have been instructed to allow Mr. Batson inside the box. I don't agree with this decision, but the vice president believes we must honor the contract, however extraordinary it might be. But, we want him to take the contents and go so that we can consider our obligation now terminated." Then she produced a silver key, like the one the stranger had, only this key had the number of the box engraved on it. She handed it to Cheryl. "Now, do you remember how to do this?"

Cheryl nodded. "I stay with him until the box is unlocked. Then I leave before he opens it. I come back when he's done."

"That's right. But be sure that you get a copy of his driver's license and that he signs the log. If he takes everything out of the box, just have him write that on the log. If he doesn't take everything, let me know, and I'll speak to him. Do you understand?"

Cheryl nodded once more.

"Good. Keep me posted."

Chapter 26

NOAH SAT FOG-EYED in his car, which was parked along the street on the opposite side of the bank. He had been up all night staring at the television in his tiny motel room with cardboard walls and shag carpet. Finally, he decided to shower, drive to the bank, and simply wait in the dark for it to open. As the sun began to crown the horizon, Noah could feel his pulse quicken and throb in his ears. His sanity was held together now by nothing more than Scotch Tape. He had quit his job without explanation and spent a great deal of the money he had left to get there. Either he would soon have vindicating answers, or he would have a gun in his mouth. Noah glanced around at the silent, neglected neighborhood that slowly began to take shape in the cold dawn light. He shook his head. How strange, he thought, that his fate should meet a fork in the road so far from home, in a forgotten town in the Washington wilderness.

At first, Noah thought his grandfather was directly addressing him in the "vision," but after he thought about it some more, Noah felt certain that even though his grandfather seemed to be looking at him, he was actually staring through him. It was as if he were filming himself for posterity. The words would only appear to be directed to the person who saw the film, yet it was meant for anybody who happened to watch it. In Noah's case, it was meant for the person his grandfather never met, the person who "saw" him, the person who had the key. Noah made sure to dictate the words into his cell phone while he could still remember what Edward Batson had said, and he looped it over and over again while he waited.

"If you see me now, then it's fair to assume that you have seen many others who you do not recognize," his grandfather said. "That seems to be the order of things." Then he smiled warmly. "But you should not be overcome; the same things happened to me. I know you have suffered, but you are not stalked by ghosts, and you are not a lunatic. Quite the contrary—you have been blessed beyond imagination! I will not reveal much more to you, at least at this moment, and I have taken great pains to erase certain experiences from my mind so as not to give anything else away. However, as to the key, it belongs to the First National Bank of Washington, to a branch in Darryville, Washington. It opens a safety security box, number 5239. That number also coincides with the date I opened the account, May 2nd, 1939." His grandfather appeared to shrug his shoulders. "That was not necessary; I just thought it was a nice touch. In any event, in that box you will find the information that you are no doubt seeking."

Noah paused the playback at that moment. He was reminded once more of how foolish he had been to throw the key away and how lucky he had been to find it. He had been on his hands and knees in the muddy field for several hours frantically searching for it before he got the idea to buy a metal detector. Even with that, it was several more hours before he found it, and not before he hit on some coins, two screws, a nail, and several crushed tin cans. Without that key, he would not have had even the chance to know the truth. Noah thought he would likely have already done himself in.

Noah took the recording off pause.

"Perhaps I should also explain why I have not simply let you know everything and saved you all the effort. Why did I need to put something in a deposit box? First, if what I tell you about the box in Darryville proves accurate, and I know it will, it will convince you that this is real and that it is not some hallucination. Second, by requiring you to make the journey, you must work just a bit harder to get to the truth, which demonstrates your commitment and should impress upon you the gravity of your gift." Then his voice took on a serious tone. "Finally, I have done this to protect the world from you as best I can! What I mean by this is that there is a chance, though it may be slight, that you could be a truly evil and corrupted person. There is no way I can know. If you are, then it is quite possible that you may be in prison or otherwise notorious. Either circumstance could prevent you from getting the box and thus acquiring power that you could use to cause untold harm to others. This is certainly not foolproof, but it at least offers the world some measure of protection from you should you be so inclined."

At this point, Noah remembered that Edward Batson took several long breaths, then leaned closer to the "lens." "One last thing. Use it for the best," he pleaded, "to help others, not just to better your own circumstances. I have given our house a motto to guide you: *Non Sibi Sed Orbi*; . . . Not for Self, but for the World."

Just as the recording ended, Noah glimpsed a lithe figure hurrying along the walkway toward the bank. It was the teller that had waited on him yesterday. She was young and very pretty, with shiny, eager eyes, the kind that silently hinted at a sharp intellect. Noah decided that her presence in this town must have belied more far-reaching ambitions. While in another time he might have at least tried to make the small talk that leads to more, today was the day when he would find out if he lives or dies, and the best he could do was not to appear like a wild-eyed inmate who had escaped from a padded cell. The box existed or it did not. If it was there, even if there was nothing at all in it, then at least he could be certain he was not crazy. If the box was not real, then Noah would find a quiet place and he would blow his brains out in the car.

Noah reached under his seat and found the pistol. He let his fingers gently glide along its cold length, just to assure himself it was still there. He checked his look in the mirror. Not too bad, he thought, though it would have been better if he had shaved.

Noah looked down at the clock in his car. It was time.

Chapter 27

EVERY TIME NOAH took a step forward, it seemed as though the world moved one step further away. His mind was trying to trick him to turn back, perhaps to save itself from extinction. But Noah leaned into the wind and forged ahead. He would find his path today, he decided, no matter if it led him off a cliff. After what seemed like an eternity, Noah finally reached the bank doors and stepped inside.

He immediately found the attractive teller, who had not yet seen him, as she was talking on the phone and checking something on her computer. Noah did his best to drain the emotion from his face and force a nonchalant expression, as if he were just running some errands. A crazy man in a bank was sure to come away with nothing except perhaps a police escort. Noah straightened up and thrust out his chin, moving with the casual confidence of one who had nothing to hide. The teller looked up as he approached.

As soon as she saw Noah, her eyes grew wide and were almost sparkling with excitement. It was clear she had much to tell, which meant that maybe the "ghost" was right: the box could actually be there! Noah hurried the last few steps. She eagerly leaned out over the counter to greet him.

"Hello, Mr. Batson," she blurted out loudly. Then she caught herself and looked around sheepishly. She lowered her voice. "I found the paperwork. It is very, very interesting!" Noah's jaw dropped, but she did not seem to notice. "Your grandfather paid one lump sum to rent the box in 1939, May 2nd, 1939, just as you said! No one has been back for it since then. And it also says anyone who presents the key should be granted access to the box." She paused to catch her breath. "This is very unusual; nobody here has ever heard of something like that!

I mean, what if the key had been stolen from him? Anyone could then walk in here and look in the box. I . . . I'm not saying you are a thief or anything; I mean, I'm sure you're his grandson—it's just so strange! I just need to copy your driver's license, then we can get started."

Noah fumbled for his wallet and retrieved the license. He handed it to the teller, doing his best to hide the fact that his hands were shaking.

"I'll be right back." She disappeared into a room at the end of the counter.

Noah leaned on the counter while he let it sink in. For lack of a better description, Noah was filled with a bursting awe. It was a realization so powerful that for the tiniest fraction of a second, Noah felt as if he could see through the veil to the very heart of the universe. Everything made sense, and he felt like he'd been suddenly snatched back from the brink. He imagined there were so few people who may have ever known the feeling that it never merited a proper name or definition. The first to sail over the edge of the world may have understood it, and some great explorers and scientists since then, but no doubt it could be experienced only when the utterly impossible had actually come to pass.

The teller returned to the counter and handed Noah his license back. She was staring at him, as if waiting for him to say something. Somehow, Noah was able to compose himself. "I wasn't quite sure this would work. You're right though, very weird." Noah read her name tag. "So, . . . Cheryl, can we take a look—how does this work?" She gave a puzzled look, and Noah nodded toward her blouse. "There," Noah said, and she glanced down. She looked up again, and her cheeks were brushed red.

"Sorry," she laughed, "I forget I'm wearing it sometimes." Noah waited, though his anticipation must have been evident because she slipped back into a professional voice. "Of course," she said, "you want to see the box. We have to go downstairs to the vault. I use your key to unlock the box, then I leave you to it."

"Great," Noah said.

He followed Cheryl as she walked around the counter toward a glass door in the far wall. She peered over her shoulder to be certain he was behind her. They made their way down a set of marble steps to a door that opened into a small wood-paneled room warmly lit by wall sconces. There was a desk with two chairs set against one of the walls.

"The vault is next door," she said. "I'll get the box and bring it back. It'll just be a moment."

Noah nodded and pulled out one of the chairs but did not sit down. He heard the door shut behind him. He closed his eyes and began to sway, as if he were drunk. He leaned against the wall to steady himself. Exhaustion crept into every fiber of his being. He almost did not care what he found in the box. The mere fact that it existed was sweet relief and proof that he had not lost his mind. If he had wanted, he could have turned around and left without a word. He could have returned to his old life and his blissful ignorance. Maybe the faces would be gone, maybe his dreams would no longer be a torture chamber. It took all his will to keep from lying down on the tiled floor and falling into a deep sleep, the kind that could only be surpassed by death itself.

The door swung open slowly. Noah straightened up and thrust his arms onto his hips.

"Here it is," Cheryl said cheerfully as she held the box out for his inspection. "It was a little dusty, so I wiped it down."

The metal container, which was painted dull black, was a bit larger than a shoebox and had a metal tag bearing the number "5239." There was a single keyhole. Cheryl set it on the desk. It made a distant, tinny sound. Noah's heart sank a little. It was obvious the box was light, which almost certainly meant it held no treasure, at least the kind he could cash in to cover his losses.

Cheryl turned to him. "If I could have your key, just to be sure it works, then I'll be out of your hair."

Noah fished the key from his pocket and set it gently into her hand. He let his fingertips brush her palm ever so lightly as he pulled his hand back. Her skin was soft and slightly moist. He glanced up to see if she had noticed, but she was already turning toward the table. He chided himself. That must have been creepy for her, he thought, and he wondered why he did it. Perhaps it was because he wanted to assure himself that this was still grounded in reality and not just one of his episodes. Maybe he wanted to be sure that he wasn't just a sick man

only dreaming he was cured. Or maybe, he just needed to touch someone, to share a human connection that he had so long been without.

Cheryl turned the key. There was a gritty click.

"It works!" she exclaimed.

Cheryl backed away slowly but kept her eyes on the box. Noah
laughed to himself. He thought she was even more desperate than he
was to know what was inside. Then he understood what a commotion
he must have caused. A strange man, and a strange key! He would be
the topic of conversations in this town for years to come.

"Who knows," he heard himself say. "Maybe there's nothing at all."

Cheryl tore her eyes from the box and shot him a sidelong, astonished look.

"Or maybe there is!" she said, her voice trembling with excitement,
Then she caught herself and lowered her gaze. She headed for the door.
"When you're done, use the intercom button on the wall. It goes to me."

Noah nodded. He did not hear the door hiss shut behind her.

Chapter 28

NOAH COULD FEEL the hairs standing up on the back of his neck as he reached for the box. He let his hands rest on it for a moment. It was tombstone cold, and a quivering chill went up his spine. He shook it off then pulled his chair into the desk. He flipped the lid open and slowly folded it back. He reached in. Nothing. He felt around for a moment, and his fingers touched *something*. It was square-shaped. A book, perhaps? He gently pulled it out into the light.

It appeared to be journal, or perhaps a diary, roughly the size of a motel bible. It had a plain black leather cover worn soft around the corners. The edges of the pages were gilded with silver, but it had rubbed off in places. Noah reached back into the box but found only emptiness. He turned it over and shook it up and down. Nothing. He set the box down on the table then slid it away from him. He squared the book in front of him and opened the cover.

The first page bore his grandfather's name, "Edward Batson," printed neatly by a steady hand, followed by a date: 1918. He carefully turned the page by the upper right-hand corner so as to not damage the paper. The words began immediately at the top and filled the entire page. The ink was fading, thus it was difficult to read at first glance. Noah leaned closer. He could make out the words *terror* and *given up for lost* in the first sentence. He felt dizzy but kept reading. At the bottom of the page, several words were underlined: *So, the hell began.* Suddenly, Noah felt heavy with realization once more, as if his limbs were filled with cement and he were sitting on quicksand. He had read enough already to understand that he and his grandfather were bound by something more than blood. His grandfather, like himself, had been to edge of the unknown and suffered dearly for it. Yet he had obviously managed to persevere. It seemed to Noah that people who had been stretched to the limits of sanity no doubt bore an invisible scar that could not be hidden from their own kind. Perhaps it was because they never really came all the way back. And just as two cancer or disaster survivors who have never met might recognize each other across a crowded room, Noah was certain that he and Edward Batson had been tormented by the same demons.

Noah quickly, though gently, thumbed through the journal. He found page after cluttered page, as if the journal consisted of one long undivided stream of consciousness at times. It would take hours, or perhaps even days to read, decipher, and digest its contents, a task that certainly could not be accomplished in his present surroundings.

Noah gathered up the journal. It fit in the pocket inside of his coat. He stood up and found the call button.

"Are you finished, Mr. Batson?" Cheryl asked.

"Yes, I'm done. Should I just come up?"

"Will you be taking the contents with you? If you are, just leave the box on the table and come up."

"Yeah, I won't need the box anymore."

Cheryl was waiting at the top of the stairs when Noah opened the door. She searched his face for clues as she passed him a form on a clipboard. Noah signed it before she even had a chance to explain what it was.

Cheryl looked around for a moment. "I know it's none of my business," she whispered, "and I could be fired for even asking this, but did you find what you were looking for?"

Noah smiled. "No, it's okay. If I were you, I'd probably be even less subtle. But that's a hard question to answer." Noah patted his coat. "Let's just say I don't know exactly what it is yet, but I already know that it saved my life."

Cheryl's jaw went slack, and her eyes widened to shiny brown marbles for a moment before narrowing once again. She opened her mouth to speak but must have thought better of it. They stared at each other for an awkward moment. Finally, Noah stepped closer to her. Cheryl did not move away. "I can't explain it any better than that, at least for now. But I promise that once I sort things out, if you still want to know, I'll come back."

Just then, Noah noticed a squat figure looming behind Cheryl. Her arms were folded impatiently. Cheryl cocked her head to the side, following Noah's gaze. She no doubt realized that her scowling manager was hovering about.

Cheryl pointed to the clipboard. "You signed that already, but this means you have taken the contents of the box and that we have permission to close the account."

"Of course," Noah responded. He handed the clipboard back along with the key. Cheryl smoothly removed a slip of paper from the pocket of her blazer and wrote something while she pretended to examine the form.

Cheryl extended her hand. "Thank you, Mr. Batson," she said loudly for the benefit of her boss, "if you need anything else, please stop by anytime." Noah raised his arm, and Cheryl slipped the paper into his outstretched hand.

Noah nodded understandingly. "It's been a pleasure, thank you."

Once outside, safely away from the bank, Noah opened the note. It was her phone number followed by an exclamation point. He put the paper in his wallet then tilted his face to the sky. Although the sun was not hidden by clouds any longer, it still glowed tentatively in the distance, as if ready to bolt at the first sign of winter.

He felt his pocket, just to be sure the journal was still there. He looked longingly back over his shoulder toward the bank where Cheryl spent her days. Love, life, and the future were all just an impossible dream for him, he realized. At least for now. Noah swallowed a lump in his throat and crossed the street to his car. He set the book gently down on the seat next to him.

Noah was soon back at the motel, but he was in such a daze that he did not clearly remember driving there. He decided that he simply could not wait until he got home to analyze the journal. He gave the clerk all the cash he could spare, which bought him three more days. When the clerk was out of sight, Noah pocketed the cheap pair of reading glasses she left on the counter. He shut the door to his room and locked it. He unplugged the phone and the digital clock on the nightstand, then pulled the curtains shut. He plugged his laptop into the wall, just in case he needed it. There would be no day or night, no clicking notches of time until he was done.

Noah found a big bottle of Southern Comfort and took a long pull. He stripped down to his boxers and plopped down at the tiny desk. He turned on the table lamp and pulled it close. He placed the journal in front of him and rested his hand on it for a moment before he dove in.

Chapter 29

September 2, 1918

Before I begin to recount the strange and terrible events that have shaped my life as of late, perhaps some context is necessary for the person who reads this.

I am nineteen years of age. I grew up in the St. Christopher Orphanage in San Francisco, where I learned to read and write. I was left there as a toddler with nothing but my name, if even that is accurate. I believe myself to be intelligent and otherwise able-bodied, thus I traveled north to Seattle last year to learn a trade and find work, as the city is rapidly expanding and there are a great deal of high-wage jobs available in new-home construction. I very quickly secured employment and a room in a boarding house that overlooked the busy shipyards.

Soon after my arrival, however, whispers of a plague came to these shores. In fact, the Spanish flu followed so close on my heels that I secretly harbored the irrational belief that I was the unwitting harbinger of doom. Perhaps that is why, at least in the beginning, I thought I was getting no more than I deserved . . .

Not quite two months past, on an unusually warm and humid day, I, along with several other sturdy men, was installing a tin plate roof on a large home in the Georgetown neighborhood; I remember pausing to wipe my brow and noticing that most people on the street below wore flu masks as they skittishly hurried about their business. That was when I first truly felt the dark, heavy pall that the terrible disease cast over the city. The next thing I knew, I awoke under the shade of a nearby tree and found several of the men standing over me, dousing me with water and fanning me with rags. They said I had lost consciousness, presumably as a result of heat exhaustion, and had tumbled from the roof. Lucky for me, I fell onto the narrow scaffold just a few feet below. My fellow workers lowered me by pulley to the ground, where they resuscitated me. When I could stand, I was brought to the physician who prescribed salt pills, hydration, and a week of bed rest.

This, unfortunately, marked the start of my trials.

Every night following my injury, I began to have odd dreams. I would see the faces of strangers, sometimes one at a time and sometimes they came in rapid succession with such speed that I could barely discern man from woman, young from old. On occasion, the faces appeared all at once, all talking, like a collage of floating, living heads. However, just when I began to question my sanity, the dreams ceased as inexplicably as they had begun.

But something far more sinister took their place.

I began to sleepwalk. I would often wake from slumber blocks away in the middle of the night with no memory of how I had arrived there. And if that was not alarming enough, eight days ago, I woke in bed, covered in blood belonging to some other person or beast!

Of course, I searched for news of a corresponding crime I may have committed, though I could find no reports that might explain it. Still, I was convinced that I was insane or possessed by some malicious entity that could harm others.

To prevent myself from roaming at night, I thought it best to install a deadbolt on the outside of my door. Of course, I needed someone to lock me in at night and let me out at first light. I was able to convince the house matron to perform this duty only upon the promise of extra coin, of which I had little to spare at the time. Nevertheless, I thought it was necessary to protect society against me.

While I was able to successfully cage my physical body, my mind traveled in its stead. Each night that I was confined to my room, my spirit, or my consciousness perhaps, seemed to wander off to live out other people's lives. By this, I mean that I believe I have been experiencing fleeting yet intense moments from lives across time, as if I could see past events unfolding from behind other people's eyes. How many people? I cannot say for certain, but mostly, they seem to be the same four people that I experience each night, For this reason, I believe they must be the strongest ones, since they have been drawing me in time and again. I have bestowed on them titles

in accordance with what I believe to be their elemental natures:
The Healer
The Warrior
The Leader
The Darkest Heart

Though Noah was sitting down, he felt dizzy and just about fell out of his chair. Each name smashed him in the face like a boxer's jab. Noah, of course, knew them all as well. However, Noah's experience was the mirror image of his grandfather's. Rather than passively watching their lives play out each time, they invaded Noah and acted out their lives through him! That explained the lost hours and why he felt like a blind, helpless passenger every time he came to. Even though Noah's experience was different than his grandfather's, there could be no doubt: as sure as Noah knew his own name, he was certain he had somehow fused himself to the same apparitions.

But there was more. Noah's grandfather even included detailed descriptions of their faces, making a point to note that they all shared some things in common:

Rich blue or gray eyes.

Dark curly hair.

And Noah could now be counted among them. But why should there be any common thread?

Noah's question lingered in space only as long as it took him to turn the page. Where most every blank space in the journal had been filled with writing, the entire next page was blank except for one underlined word followed by a question mark.

"Ancestors?"

Chapter 30

ACCEPTING WHAT HE knew about his "ancestors" to be histori-
cally accurate, Edward Batson wrote that there would be no point
in looking for the trail of either the Healer or the Warrior, because they
had lived and died in Europe. So, he decided to set out for the East
Coast, to Pennsylvania and Maryland, where he could find some evidence of the either the Leader or the Darkest Heart. Ironically, because
the latter lived more recently, he would prove easier to find. Yet, he
was the one ancestor Noah's grandfather said that he truly dreaded to
uncover. On November 3, 1918, Edward Batson seemed to confidently
declare in his journal that he was "bound for the unknown and whatever may come." He had saved enough money to purchase a train ticket
that would get him all the way to Baltimore, a trip he thought might
take about two weeks. He had enough to spare for meals and lodging
for several days after he arrived. He did not say anything about what
he would do once the money was gone.

November 20, 1918
Baltimore, Maryland

*Today, I visited the George Peabody Library, which proved to be one of
the most magnificent buildings I have yet laid eyes upon. So much so, in
fact, that for a brief time, I forgot my true purpose. Imagine, if you will,
five tiers of ornate cast-iron balconies illuminated by a massive skylight in
the domed ceiling more than sixty feet above! It was truly awe-inspiring.*

*More significant than the house, however, was the knowledge I found
within it.*

With the help of the librarian's assistant, I studied old newspaper editions, which were replete with references to Matthew and Ida Brinkhorn, including both of their obituaries. There followed an article about a mysterious and unnamed beneficiary who had inherited the Brinkhorn fortune and then disappeared without a trace. . . .

This, of course, filled with me with equal measures of relief and horror. On the one hand, I now have at least some proof, though it be indirect and inconclusive, that the Darkest Heart is not just a figment of a troubled mind; thus, I am closer to explaining my illness. On the other hand, perhaps my kin was a murderer, which could mean that evil and madness were my family heirlooms after all.

I must know more. I must know everything.

Chapter 31

December 1, 1918

I alighted from the train in Easton, Pennsylvania, an old industrial city at the confluence of the Lehigh and Delaware Rivers.

It proved to be a watershed day.

Though I was exhausted, I immediately set out in search of the Leader. I made my way to the city center and inquired of various persons about a tobacco merchant named William Coddington. None, however, claimed to have heard of this name. Finally, a friendly street sweeper directed me to a man by the name of Red, who could be found occupying his stoop only one block away. It was told to me that Red, being of a ripe old age, was a repository of local history.

Between puffs on his corn cob pipe, Red confirmed that the Coddingtons once owned a tobacco and dry goods store along the Delaware River, but it had been shuttered long ago, when Red was just a boy. He said that he had not heard any word on the fate of the family since.

After I told Red that I wanted to see the place myself, he took my pen and drew a map for me. He depicted Easton as an upside-down triangle wedged between the two rivers at their crossroads. He included several street names for reference. An X marked the old Coddington store at the northwest tip of the triangle, a block or so from the Delaware River, beneath a railroad bridge that spanned the water to New Jersey.

It was not long before I found the old bones of a once bustling riverfront. Dilapidated docks poked out into the muddy water like gnarled fingers. A now silent jumble of warehouses seemed to have been hastily erected to meet the demands of once constant river traffic. I wondered about the cause of the waterfront's demise and decided that the trains, which were at that moment thundering along the bridge overhead, must have had a great deal to do with it.

I followed a carriage-rutted street that led directly from the heart of town toward the river. I soon found many derelict clapboard buildings that I worried might be full of scoundrels. When I consulted the map once more, the X appeared to be drawn at the corner of the last intersection, where the road abruptly ended at the skeleton of an old pier.

I found a boarded-up storefront attached to a narrow two-story brick warehouse that stretched the length of the block. The porch roof had partially collapsed, thus I had to duck underneath to gain access to the door. I spied the inside through a gap in the boards that were nailed across the front window. There was a counter in the back, and the walls were lined with empty shelves. Several barrels were tossed about the floor.

I heaved a shoulder against the door, and it gave way easily. Although the place had clearly not served as a business for some time, there was evidence that squatters had been there recently. There was a pile of blankets serving as a makeshift mattress in the corner, and empty whiskey bottles were lined up neatly on the floor nearby.

I walked behind the counter. I rested my hands on it. Suddenly, a chill galloped through me.

I could feel it with concrete certainty.

I had been there many times.

Then I shuddered once more. When I opened my eyes, I found the store was pristine and alive with activity. A woman in a linen gown with a swaddled child was examining the shelves behind me. She rocked her child while she apparently considered something she wanted to buy. An older man with a knee-length coat, breeches, and a greasy tricorne hat stood behind her, tapping his cane impatiently on the floor.

It was John Tollthorn; I remembered that he was always quite difficult.

I could see others through the windows who were standing on the porch outside, no doubt discussing the weather or the news of the day. The vision was so real that I could even recall where each and every item was located throughout the store.

Then, it was like a bolt from the blue: there was a trap door below the counter! I dropped to my knees and wiped away the dust, and sure enough, it was there.

Though I found nothing inside, the mere facts that it existed at all and that I knew right where to find it brought my theory into even sharper focus. I am not insane; I am now certain of that. Quite simply, I own the memories of other people from long ago. Many questions, however, remained unanswered. I still could not say for certain that they were my ancestors, because I was an orphan and had no knowledge of my family history. And I still cannot say how or why any of it happened in the first place.

Edward Batson wrote little more about his East Coast sojourn until he boarded the train once more, this time bound for Seattle.

"All quiet. Settling in for the long ride back," he curtly noted on December 2, 1919. "Though I know more now than before I arrived, there will still be much to do once I get home."

Noah took a deep breath and read on.

Chapter 32

January 23, 1919

For the past three weeks, the same dreams, the same memories, have returned. But there is more. There are new ones, too, coming ever more quickly. These lives are unfolding before me in the most rapid pace. Along with them comes a new spectrum of emotions experienced at the same blurring speed. I struggle to remember any details, any reference that can be verified, because it is all moving so fast. Each morning leaves me more exhausted than the last, with no end in sight.

Since the flu had subsided, I took to vigorous, late-night walks before bed, which made for better rest and thus seemed to offer some respite from my suffering. During one of these strolls, I was drawn to a crowd gathered in a park near a banner which read: Van Maven the Mysterious; astounding magic and mind control.

The magician said that he could use the mere power of suggestion to make a person do almost anything he wanted. He said that he could make the biggest, strongest man meow like a cat or bark like a dog. Of course, most people present, including myself, laughed at this.

Nonetheless, a large, surly looking fellow took up the magician's challenge and stepped forward. I remember he shook his cinderblock-sized fist at the magician and told him that if it did not work, he would punch him in the nose.

Unfazed, Van Maven directed the man to a chair on the platform. He stood in front of the man and produced a round silver locket hanging from a chain, which he held high for inspection by the crowd for a moment before he brought it close to his subject and swung it slowly back and forth at eye level.

Van Maven instructed the crowd to be silent and for the man to follow the locket with his eyes and give his attention to nothing else. After a short while, the magician leaned close to the man and told him to close his eyes and fall asleep. The man seemed to do just that.

Then, the magician dramatically wheeled about to face the crowd. He commanded the man to bark like a dog. To my astonishment, the man gave several hoarse whelps. Then Van Maven told the man to get down on all fours and howl for a meal. The man immediately slumped forward onto his hands and knees on the platform and began to bay loudly. The crowd stared in shocked silence.

Having achieved the desired result, Van Maven directed the man to return to his chair. The man quietly got to his feet, found the chair, and sat down. He stared blankly into the distance.

The magician then told the crowd that he also had the power to force a person to experience even lost childhood memories. Van Maven turned to his subject once more and said: "You are four years old. Your mother has sent you to bed without supper because you were so naughty. What did you say to her?'"

The man immediately began to sob, then buried his head in his hands. He soon began to cry out for his mother in a child's high-pitched voice. Van Maven bowed, and the crowd erupted with cheers and whistles. The man in the chair kept sobbing, however. Fascinated by his transformation, I could not tear my eyes from him.

I watched closely for any clue of a hoax. I soon found myself shouting out to Van Maven to show mercy and release the once proud fool from his psychic hold, but the magician seemed lost in the adoration of the crowd. I then noticed something very strange.

The man began to speak. I pushed closer to the stage for a better view. He seemed to be arguing with himself. Now, Seattle was a port city, so I had heard many languages spoken, but his words did not sound even similar to anything I had heard before. I was alarmed, and I began to wave my arms to get Van Maven's attention. Finally, the magician caught my eye, and I pointed several times to his subject. Van Maven instantly turned and dashed across the platform. He kneeled next to the man and whispered something in his ear. The man opened his eyes, which darted about as if he had no idea of where he was. Van Maven looked to me and nodded, then guided the man from the stage. I approached the magician once the crowd dispersed and he was preparing to depart. I told him I was the one who pointed to the man. Van Maven stared at me for a moment.

He thanked me and said that he had forgotten to release the man from the spell. I then inquired about the strange way the man was speaking. Van Maven explained that on occasion, when he takes a person's mind back in time, it keeps regressing until the trance is broken. When I asked him what he meant, he only shrugged and said perhaps the mind begins to channel times that came before or people that came before.

I stayed in the park until it was nearly dawn, thinking about what the magician had said.

I then set about discovering everything I could about hypnosis. In addition to reading the works of Franz Mesmer, which I admit were very technical and difficult to understand, I attended several lectures on the subject at Seattle University. While there existed different opinions as to the cause and effects of hypnosis, one thing seemed certain: hypnotism allowed a subject to access long-repressed memories. I soon discovered a method by which a person could hypnotize themselves without the aid of another by using a simple metronome.

The technique was most important. It requires one to first be motivated for hypnosis. Second, a person must achieve complete relaxation. Third, a subject must be able to concentrate on the task outside of all distraction. And finally, a person must have a specific goal to achieve through the hypnosis.

There could be no doubt that I was sufficiently motivated, but the ability to relax and focus were qualities I did not possess, especially in my desperate state. This is why the metronome was so beneficial. By focusing on the sound and precise movement of the arm, it enables one to concentrate wholly on the experience and to thus achieve peace of mind. As to my goals, well that was quite simple: uncover the nature and source of my suffering.

My first attempts failed miserably. I simply could not find any solace. However, I gradually discovered, using powerful images, that I could guide myself into and out of a trance with ease.

When I was about twelve, I was quite small for my age and was relentlessly taunted by most of the other boys in the orphanage. One day, I ran away into the forest like my favorite character, Huck Finn, with a stolen jar of preserves and a loaf of bread. I followed a narrow deer path for several hours and emerged in a small clearing where I found the ruins of an old log cabin. I claimed it as my own private island and lived there quite blissfully for several days until I was discovered by a search party. It was the only thing I truly missed when I put the orphanage to my back.

I began to picture that place once more, and I remembered how happy and awestruck I had felt when I had stumbled upon it. I decided this memory could help me.

To guide myself into a trance, I close my eyes, and I imagine I am walking into the forest along that winding, tangled path that seems to grow gloomier by the moment. While I am frightened, all I have to do is make my way toward the clearing, the light in the dark, and then, I am safe once more.

I thought of this as a metaphor for my journey into my subconscious through the hypnosis. When I employed this imagery while the metronome swayed, I found that I could consistently slip free and return once more.

It is very difficult to explain what I found, as it would be for any person to describe finding a place never seen by human eyes. It is almost impossible to put into words what happens when a person visits the forest deep in their own mind. For posterity, however, I will do my best.

There was darkness of course, or maybe it was just the absence of anything else. Soon though, it seemed like thousands of voices rose up in unison, followed by layer upon layer of fast-moving images, things seen from the perspective of the beholder. Like my dreams, it was as if so many lives were unfolding all around me, all at once, and with terrific speed. The word confusion cannot begin to convey such a scene. Perhaps madness is a better word. In any event, I was overwhelmed, reduced to a single emotion: fear. Yet, I realized that I was under no spell but my own and that I could make a dash for the sun-bathed clearing anytime I wanted. When I awoke, I checked my watch and found that fifteen minutes had passed. I decided to try once more and to go right back in, this time with some backbone, for was it not my own house that I needed to get in order?

Now, knowing what to expect, I was better prepared for it. And when it came, the million sights and sounds, I concentrated with all my might and demanded order from the chaos. I had no particular idea about exactly *how things should be organized, but at that moment, I happened to think of the orphanage and how every night, the screeching, squirming boys were put to their rooms so that everything was finally quiet. That is precisely how things took shape in my mind.*

Doors. To the left, to the right, up and down, stacked neatly on top of one another. Doors. As far as the eye could see in every direction. And each resembled the doors from the orphanage, with chipped and faded paint and dented knobs.

After this point, several pages had been torn away. The next entry offered some explanation.

After a great deal of thought, I have removed and burned the pages that came before this. This was a difficult decision, but I believe it was for the best.

Over these past several months, by thinning the barrier between my conscious and unconscious mind, I have acquired knowledge that could cause a great deal of harm if it fell into the hands of scoundrels. Now, I do not think that just any person could do what I have done simply by reading the information and instructions I provided, but I cannot take the chance that such power could be acquired by a person not already predisposed. I suspect that only someone who is born with this gift can realize its full potential. But, if such a person reads this, I have some advice: The strongest ones are always calling to you, finding you. This includes the Darkest Heart. If you let down your guard, even for a moment, he will seize your mind and fill it with bloodlust. He has no <u>skills</u> that you can make use of.

⛊⟶

Noah understood why his grandfather had emphasized the word *skills*. He thought back to the man on the motorcycle and the incident at the rest stop. Noah had done things that he simply did not know how to do, however difficult it was for him to accept. He had used skills that he had never learned. Now, at least, he could begin to explain why.

But Noah's grandfather did not stop there.

Chapter 33

January 2, 1939.

In all this time, I still have not seen my parents. Or perhaps I just can't recognize them. Either way, without this reference point, I still cannot determine if all my benefactors are indeed my ancestors. This is the most important question yet to be answered. I will leave for the East Coast once more—New York City—tomorrow, as I believe my fate lies in that direction. There are more resources and more information available there that may yet provide an answer. If I can prove my theory, my life's work will be accomplished.

I have made more money than I will ever need, even after giving most of it away as anonymous charitable donations. I still do not feel comfortable employing my unique knowledge for financial gain, although I suppose it is no different than anyone who uses any of their God-given talents to improve their position in life.

I also have another concern. I am forty years old, and I still have not taken a wife nor have I produced any children. This must be remedied for two reasons: first, I should not be the last to enjoy my gift—which in turn should be used to benefit others—and second, my offspring could be the very means to prove my theory.

January 7, 1939

The train stopped in Pennsylvania for repairs, in Easton, coincidentally. It was very cold. I was milling about with other passengers in the station when I saw a beautiful young woman. Although she was about half of my age, I pressed on. I met her gaze, and she returned my smile. That was the only sign I needed. I decided then and there that I would look no further: she would be my wife. I strolled over and struck up a conversation with her.

Her name was Miranda. She was waiting for her father, a trolley driver, who would soon finish work. I made my intentions known immediately. I asked if I could call on her in the near future, and she agreed. I waited until her father arrived, then took him aside and introduced myself. I explained that I intended to court his daughter, with his permission of course, and that I had sufficient money to support her and any children we may have. Though he seemed quite bewildered, he gave his assent.

⊶—⚷

In the days that followed, Edward Batson explained that he purchased a large home near the top of a hill just outside of the city, and he plied Miranda and her family with expensive gifts. He proposed to her two months later. She accepted without hesitation.

April 15, 1939

It is time to implement my plan. If all falls into place, the riddle may finally be solved, though perhaps not within my lifetime. As I write this, I am traveling to a place where I will conceal this journal and my notes until one like me finds it. Miranda does not know where I am because I told her nothing except that I would be out of town to conclude some business.

I will deposit my journal in a safety deposit box in Darryville, Washington. My train stopped there on my first trip to the East Coast. I remember that there were several stalwart, longstanding banks in the town that would serve my purposes. I will insist on renting the box in perpetuity. I will also insist that I be provided with a key for the box that bears no indication from where it came. Finally, I must secure terms from the bank that permits access to any person who holds the key. All these steps are necessary because I do not know the identity of the next person with my talents who may come along, nor do I know how long it might take. It could be my own child, or it could be several generations before my line produces another.

On my wedding night, before the marriage is consummated and my seed is possibly sowed, I will directly address my heir. I have prepared some remarks that I will repeat in front of my own reflection, something to help them to make sense of all the turmoil and to encourage them to find the truth. I will give the safety deposit box key to my wife, and I will instruct her that she must hold the key dearly, because in the likely event she outlives me, she must give it to the one that sees me. If, before her death, no such person comes forth, she will pass the key on to our children with the same instructions.

I understand, however, that there are many obstacles. I could die on this trip, before I am even married. The banks could fail or be destroyed. The box could be stolen. Perhaps Miranda and I will not be able to have children. Even the key could be lost over time (although that would not prevent my heir from knowing where to find my journal). But these risks are unavoidable in light of what I am trying to accomplish.

When my heir reads this journal, they will find some guidance and thus be spared a great deal of suffering that I endured. And most importantly, they will know what I could never be certain of: this is an inheritance passed in the blood.

⚷

The final undated entry in the journal seemed to speak directly to Noah.

⚷

Whoever might be reading this, so long as you came by this knowledge as I intended, using the clues and the selected memories I left behind, you are truly blessed. I have given you, I believe, just enough of my experiences so that you may be led to discovering, in your own way, all the power that you possess. And such power is worth more than all the money and riches of the world. I can only pray that you are virtuous enough to make use of this mostly for the greater good. For if you were selfish, you could bring untold misery to those around you.

The motto of our house should be your conscience: Not for Self, but for the World.

Chapter 34

NOAH SHUT THE journal, pushed his chair back from the desk, and stood slowly. He stretched out his arms toward the ceiling and then bent over to touch his toes. He had been sitting so long that his joints felt like rusty hinges. His mind, on the other hand, was a boiling pot of questions with no real answers.

Assuming that everything his grandfather wrote in the journal was true, how could Edward Batson possibly access and experience the memories of people that died long ago? How could he make use of their skills? He believed it was "in the blood," but that is just another way of saying that the ability was inherited from his ancestors. The word *ancestors* conjured up images of moldy crypts and blurry old photographs. Ancestors could give you their looks or hair color, but memories? The idea made no real-world sense: memories were ethereal and abstract— otherwise incapable of being weighed, measured, or photographed. Noah simply could not wrap his numb, exhausted mind around it or much else for that matter. It was all so beyond him, he realized; it was meant for gods or at least the steel-trap minds of the scientists at NASA who graduated from Ivy League schools at the age of sixteen.

Noah decided he needed some fresh air to clear his head. He opened the door to his room just a crack. Cold air whistled in, and his body erupted in goosebumps. He put his face to the opening and took long, deep breaths. After a minute or so, he shut the door and locked it. Only then did Noah notice a ripe smell.

He looked around for a source. Pizza boxes were strewn about. The handle of Southern Comfort was long gone. The empty bottle was lying on the floor by the desk. The garbage pail was filled to the top with things that Noah could not recall discarding. *Take your pick, I guess.*

Then Noah lifted his arm and sniffed at his armpit. "Gross," he said aloud. It was definitely him. He had been at it for what . . . two days, maybe three? And he had not bathed or brushed his teeth even once. After a taste of the outdoors, his half-lit, disarranged room suddenly seemed like a prison cell with the walls closing in.

After Noah straightened things up a bit, he started the shower. He tested the water and then parked himself under the weak stream.

When Noah was in high school, one of his science teachers, Mrs. Blumfield, said that the universe was without any limit; it went on forever and could have no end. Normally, Noah's lessons went in one ear and right out of the other. But he remembered that moment. He could appreciate that there had been something profound in his teacher's words, but he had just been too dull to work it out at the time. And he must have looked stupid and confused, because his teacher focused on Noah while she explained.

"When you stare at the night sky, you see planets and stars, tiny points of light. But the naked eye can only see so far, so you might use a telescope. Things become clearer, and you can see a bit further. And when you do, you see more stars in the distance. And with a giant telescope you can see further, well beyond our galaxy. And what do you find? More stars than you could see before. And when probes are shot into space and they send back pictures, what do they show? More space, more blackness, more things even further away."

Noah said that maybe there is a brick wall somewhere out there, where everything ends. His teacher smiled.

"And how thick is that wall? What is behind it?" Noah could only shrug. "You see," she said. "Do you follow? There must always be *some-thing* there, whatever that something is, which means the universe can have no end." Noah felt just as small now as he had in science class that day. But Mrs. Blumfield had a knack for making things clear. Perhaps she could even help him now.

As soon as he dried off and brushed his teeth, Noah returned to the desk and fired up his laptop. He prayed Mrs. Blumfield was still there.

Chapter 35

NOAH GOT DRESSED then stepped outside his cheerless motel room into the daylight. He tried to guess the time before looking at his watch. The sun looked as if it was just beginning on the downslope to the west. He thought it was about two in the afternoon. His watch almost agreed. It was one twenty-seven p.m. The sky was clear, but it was quite cold, so Noah ducked back into the room for a moment to grab his heavy, insulated sweatshirt.

Noah's room faced a lonely highway and dark, misty forest that stretched beyond his sight. He found a plastic chair laying on its side in front of the room next to his. He dragged it to his door, turned it over, and sat down. He pulled his hood up and leaned back on two legs until the back of the chair rested against the wall. He yawned, then folded his arms across his chest. His eyes fluttered, then closed just before his phone chimed.

Noah planted the chair firmly on the ground and rifled through his pockets until he found it. He did not know the number, but the area code was right.

"Hello?"

A woman's voice answered. "Mr. Batson? This is Rita Blumfield calling. . . . I got your email."

"Thank you for calling, Mrs. Blumfield."

She chuckled. "It's Rita. I have not been your teacher for a long time."

"Of course, . . . Rita. I don't know if you remember me, but I was—"

She cut Noah off. "Of course, I do. You were curious; you asked questions. Teachers don't forget things like that; or, at least, I don't."

"I appreciate that you took some time out to call me in the middle of a school day, but I could not think of a better person to ask. I did a little research on the internet, but I couldn't find much. Maybe I just did not know where to look."

"Your question is certainly interesting: Can a person inherit the memories of an ancestor? Well, there is no recorded instance of this that I am aware of. In theory, however, it might be possible. I'll explain what I mean. . . ."

Noah's pulse quickened. *Here we go!*

"Take instinct. How does an eagle raised in captivity know that it can dive below the surface of a lake to catch fish without drowning if it had never witnessed that behavior before? What is instinct if not a form of genetic or inherited memory? There are many examples, but this is one that comes to mind. Also, did you take Ms. Day's biology class?"

Memories flooded back. "Yes, but I was not crazy about dissecting cats—that part I wanted to forget."

Rita laughed once again. "Of course, but that was not the only thing you dissected, right? Do you remember planaria, more commonly referred to as flatworms?"

"Sure, we cut them into pieces, and each one grew back to form a new worm. One worm became two, four, or even eight worms."

"That's right. In fact, one planarian can be cut into as many as two hundred and forty-nine pieces, each one of those bits being capable of growing into an adult individual! That's why they are described as 'immortal under the knife.' Well, in the 50s, two professors at the University of Michigan conducted a fascinating experiment. They subjected planaria to electric shock every time they turned on a light, to the point that the worms convulsed every time the light was turned on, even after they weren't being shocked anymore. The natural offspring of those worms, which were never subjected to the stimulus, also shuddered every time the light was turned on. These professors theorized that memories of the experiment were being genetically passed on to a new generation of planaria."

"But worms are pretty simple things, right? I mean humans, . . . I would think we are far more complicated. Seems like apples and oranges."

"Not necessarily. As it turns out, *we share many of the same genes with this lowly creature!* Also, because I had time during my morning break today, I found some recent articles about the Michigan experiment. Scientists at Princeton and Duke have built on those findings. Using food rewards, they painstakingly taught planaria the way through a complicated maze. The offspring of those worms immediately found their way through the maze to the food without any prompting! The only way this could happen is if the offspring *remembered* the experience of their parents!"

"But I would think someone would have already found a gene for that if it existed. There are genes for hair color, skin color, even alcoholism I thought I read somewhere. Shouldn't we know about that?"

"Well, first of all, we still have not identified one percent of our genes, and no one is sure what we may find there. But, while we have mapped out ninety-nine percent of our genes, we still do not know what most of them do. Let's just say there is a lot of room for discovery.

"And think about this, Noah. Evolution is always trying to make us better suited to our environment, right? To that end, it might make a lot of sense if we were able to access the memories of our ancestors. We would be better at avoiding danger, better at finding food and shelter, and better at surviving because we would have the benefit of their experience to guide us, even after they were dead and gone. Maybe it's only a matter of time until someone comes along who has that ability. . . . I hope this helps to clear things up a little."

After many thanks and a heartfelt goodbye, Noah pocketed his phone. He leaned the chair back once again and stared blankly into the distance.

Okay, he got the concept now. But that did not make him feel any better. The idea that he could know every moment of every life in his family that came before trembled him to his core. He could barely unspool the thread of his own simple existence, let alone endure the personal triumphs and tragedies of the hundreds of generations of people in his line. The nightmares and the strange incidents suddenly seemed puny and only slightly inconvenient compared to that possibility. If he delved into his mind and stumbled upon the dark corner where they all waited for him, what happened if he could not escape as his grandfather had done? What if he was trapped there with the multitudes of incessant voices forever clamoring for him? Then his suffering would be virtually as limitless as the universe itself. It was better left for someone stronger who may come along, he reasoned.

Noah started to shiver and noticed that the sun had disappeared behind the distant peaks. He walked back inside the room, put the journal on the desk, and collapsed into bed. He stared blankly at the ceiling for a while, trying to imagine the sky beyond and all the space and nothingness that lay beyond that. Finally, he propped himself up on his elbows and eyed the journal amid the clutter of scraps of paper. He could not help but feel a sense of destiny slowly creeping up on him. It would be difficult to turn back now, he thought. The key and the safety deposit box were gone for good, and the journal was now his. He could attempt to recreate the signposts for another, assuming there would be such a person, but Noah had no inkling of how to control or refine his abilities, thus the attempt would have as much a chance of success as a toddler writing a symphony. And without this lifeline, the next one might drown in the depths of insanity, as Noah had almost done.

After a trip to the liquor store, and after half of the bottle he had bought was gone, Noah plunged into much-needed sleep with the fragile conviction that he must take on this burden or others would surely suffer dearly for it.

Chapter 36

THE NEXT DAY, following his grandfather's example, Noah worked on some visualization techniques. When he was a child, his parents had often taken him to a public pool near his home where he had learned to swim and had spent many carefree days. The pool was unusually large due to the fact it was a WPA project from the Depression era. This meant that the government had hired people who were out of work to build things as a way to stimulate the economy. Because the government wanted these people to stay busy as long and as often as possible, the end result was something often far larger and more elaborate than could otherwise be justified. In this example, the pool filled almost half of the length and width of a football field. It had four diving boards and gradually decreased from a depth of twelve feet to two feet, with the latter depth serving as a baby pool. The pool had a large concession stand and a two-story gatehouse made from smooth local river stones. The windows and doors were arched to a fine point, giving the building a Middle-Eastern look. It always seemed strangely out of place in a dingy slate mining town with only few thousand residents. Nevertheless, it attracted people from miles around.

When Noah was a gangly youngster and it seemed that there was little respite from muggy summer days, the pool was an oasis. His mother would drop him off after lunch with a warning that he should wait at least an hour before he swam, lest he get a cramp and drown. Noah would hurry through the creepy, dark tunnel of sweating stones in the gatehouse as fast as he could, for fear of what may be gaining on him, and emerge at the shimmering expanse of water, confident and cocky. The latest hits were always playing over the loudspeakers amid a shrill chorus of giddy screams and lifeguard whistles. The scent of grilled burgers, chlorine, and freshly cut grass wafted into his nostrils. After he found his friends, he cast his towel off in a heap and then hurled himself into the cool water to join them.

Perhaps it was just that fond memories of childhood always seem to be filmed through a soft filter, but Noah could not recall any other time or place where he had felt more whole and perfect than when he was on the event horizon of his teenage years, swimming and playing and trying to drum up the courage to do a double front flip off the diving board. If there was any memory that could shed light in a dark place and show him the way, it was this. Noah cast himself back to this time over and over again in his mind until he could instantly conjure up a detailed scene, down to the way the pretty girls had begun to fill out their bathing suits.

Next, as his grandfather had instructed, Noah bought a metronome. This proved more difficult than he expected, but he finally found one in a pawn shop in Appleton, twenty miles away. After some internet research, Noah decided it would be best to attach a small picture of an eye to the arm of the metronome, since this apparently made it easier to follow, which in turn should make it easier for him to slip into a trance.

Once Noah had properly modified the metronome, he cleaned the hotel room thoroughly, shut the blinds, and shut and locked the door to prevent any distraction. He started the metronome at what seemed like a leisurely pace, then placed a chair directly in front of it and sat down. He closed his eyes to reset for a moment, then began to track the gentle motion of the metronome, focusing all his will upon the swaying arm.

And then, there was . . . nothing.

Noah stood up and paced back and forth, trying to clear his mind. He sat down once more and started again. Still nothing. He clenched his fists and pounded on his thighs, but his outburst only seemed to draw him further away from the scene.

Noah instantly knew what he was missing. Relaxation. It had been so long since he had experienced any real peace of mind. Noah could not think of the last time he was able to just sit and simply be. In his quiet moments, all he could think of was how to avoid himself, to turn on the television, or to get on to the next task.

Noah stopped the metronome. He climbed into bed and buried his face in the pillows. He began to sob. It was more than self-pity though, he realized. On some level, he was actually mourning the loss of his simple existence, no matter how much he had disdained it. If you hated yourself, you hated everyone else, and nothing could truly wound you because you expected no less from the world. Noah understood that he could never be that man again, not with all that had happened. Mother Nature had seen to that.

After a few hours, when Noah did not feel like a raw, exposed nerve any longer, he made his way to the bathroom and splashed his face with cold water. He worked up his courage and stared at himself in the mirror unflinchingly. He took in the depths of his own eyes and felt no emotion at all. He was finally an empty vessel. There could be no better time, he thought.

Noah wound the metronome and started it once more. He settled in easily. After a few moments, he noticed that each click began to echo, sounding slower than the last. As the arm moved back and forth, the paper eye stared back. It seemed to glisten with color and life, as if it sensed Noah's receptiveness. Noah pictured his twelve-year-old self making his way into the black tunnel of the gatehouse. Noah could feel his breaths deepen. Suddenly, everything swirled together.

Then, there was . . . *everything*.

Chapter 37

I T WAS SOMEWHERE in his mind presumably, or in the twisting strands of his DNA, or both, where no laws, physical or otherwise, applied. It was a "place" where thousands of his ancestors from different ages in history existed all at once, like actors packed on a stage the size of an ocean. It is not to say that Noah saw any people, at least not at first, but he could *feel* each one, all at the same time. He could hear and see and do things as each one of them, as if he were living behind each pair of eyes.

The voices, the fears, and the lovers, found and lost, of these multitudes flowed through Noah like electricity. The word *chaos* cannot even begin to describe the condition. If Noah had not had the benefit of his grandfather's guidance on this point, he would not have had the strength or courage to force it all to take a recognizable shape.

Once more, Noah reached back into the memories of his childhood. He could not have been more than six or seven years old when his mother had brought him to his father's office for the first time. Noah was instantly drawn to a large Rolodex that sat on the desk. Noah's father had explained that the important things about each person he knew could be shrunk to fit on cards and placed in a device that was so pleasing to spin. Noah was fascinated. Even after the Rolodex was made irrelevant by a computer, Noah's father kept it for Noah to play with whenever he visited him at work.

With this picture in his mind, Noah willed everything and everyone to be silent and for all to take their places.

All at once, he was in a plain room with white walls and a bare light bulb swinging overhead. There was a desk and a chair like his father's. A Rolodex was the only thing sitting on the desk. Noah examined it.

The confusion and chaos had taken a familiar form, one that Noah could easily control and manipulate. He sat down and began to spin the dial. After several turns, he was still not through even the As. Noah took his hands away and sat back. Strangely, he somehow knew the name on each card as well as he knew his own, and he could see, even feel, their greatest achievements and most catastrophic failures with as much clarity as he could recall his own experiences. Even their monotonous, quiet moments belonged to him. And Noah had a face to put with each name. They were reflections, not just in mirrors or in pools of still water, but sometimes in the eyes of loved ones and enemies.

Noah immediately felt the weight of his gift.

He leaned back in his father's chair and "closed" his eyes. He visualized the pool at the end of the tunnel. He made for it, walking out into the sun and company of his friends. Noah had the blue water in his sights. He launched into the air, then made himself into a perfect cannonball. Just before splashdown, he found himself staring at the ceiling of his shoebox motel room.

Noah crawled into bed and instantly nodded off into something resembling a heavy, anesthetic-induced sleep. When he eventually woke, he glanced at his watch. It was a little after nine a.m. He had been out for almost ten hours! He swung his feet onto the floor and rubbed the sleep from his eyes.

Noah stood up, then veered into the bathroom and started the shower. When he was done, he dressed and began to gather and pack his things. He checked his wallet to be sure he still had the paper with Cheryl's phone number. He could not escape a fluttering feeling in his stomach that she still had a part to play in all this. But that future was foggy and obscured. All he knew for certain was that he would be a different man if ever he came back this way again.

Noah examined the room once more to be sure he had left nothing behind, then he shut the door behind him. He pushed the keys through a rusty mail slot in the motel office door and made his way to his car. There would be no need to stop. The radio and pure adrenaline would sustain him for as long as it took.

Chapter 38

NOAH WAS SITTING on the edge of his bed, staring mechanically into the distance. He was so immersed in his thoughts that he could only for a split second register that the wind had snatched up the few remaining leaves that still clung to the red oak tree outside his window and had carried them off in a perfect spiral.

How did his grandfather do it? How did he know how to make practical use of the skills of his ancestors? To do that, Noah considered, he would need to have their memories at his fingertips, ready for instantaneous use. Otherwise, it seemed so ponderous, having to use hypnosis every time he wanted to find somebody and tap into their knowledge. Beyond that, how was his grandfather able to control them to the point where he could pick and choose the particular skills or talents he wanted? Clearly Edward Batson had done it, so Noah was determined that he could, too. And this was all that mattered, he decided.

He suddenly had an idea.

Noah started the metronome and settled himself into the chair he had placed directly in front of it. He leaned back, letting the sound soothe him and take him. His breaths slowed. His eyes quickly grew heavy. Shadows closed in on him and shut out all light.

As before, he was dropped into a roaring, packed stadium of churning, mixed-up people, memories, and emotions. He concentrated until everything was once more shrink-wrapped into the Rolodex. It was open already to Abreas, the great healer, one of the elementals that had somehow pierced the veil of this world without being summoned. It was just as his grandfather had predicted. The memories of all the strong ones were virtually jumping off the pages for Noah, ready to offer their services, with one exception: the Darkest Heart, the monster that led him to a flea-bitten motel with a woman who was certainly in far more danger than she ever realized. Somehow, it had escaped Noah's attempt to tab, organize, and control it. So, if it was not here, then where was it hiding?

Noah began to feel frustration welling up inside him, then hot flashes of anger. He focused all his will to find him, as if he were squeezing his mind in a vice, but there was no sign of the evil creature. Noah resolved to destroy him somehow, to obliterate his memories and banish him forever. Just then, when the searing hate threatened to undue his trance prematurely, Noah noticed something. In dark corners where the light was turned aside, something moved. It was like a ripple in the very fabric of the shadows rather than something concealed by it. It was pulsing and vibrating, as if excited.

He had found the Darkest Heart. Or perhaps, the Darkest Heart had found Noah, for he noticed that the abomination had unfurled gossamer tendrils that were stretching and slithering toward him, searching for purchase. Noah had already had a taste of that and refused to allow the thing to take hold again. Its mere presence infected Noah with the most loathsome emotions. But the Darkest Heart would not dare to face Noah directly, because its shame made it a parasite that could only whisper, deceive, and ambush to gain the advantage. Sensing that it had been discovered, the shapeless malice instantly contracted and seemingly disappeared. However, fear and doubt could never be banished entirely, Noah realized, so he would always have to monitor it— like a malignant cancer in remission—otherwise, by the time he knew it was growing inside him, it would be too late to do anything about it.

As for the task at hand, Noah had the idea to start small and work his way up. That is to say, that it stood to reason that the greatest, most powerful of his ancestors would be difficult to control, so Noah decided he would focus on one of his more obscure, more simple predecessors first, presuming that their memories would be easier to manipulate. The question, though, was *who*.

Noah scanned his database as the Rolodex spun blindingly fast, dog-eared cards whipping by. Then it stopped. Strange, Noah thought, as he studied the card. Noah stared at the bewildered, mud-smeared face. It all came flooding back to him.

Alice Raines led a curious life. She was born in 1787 in western Pennsylvania and was the youngest of three children of a frontier family. She had dirty blonde hair and small green eyes with a lean face that most people would not find very pretty. When she was eight years old, she was abducted by the Lenape tribe in retaliation for some indignation she could never understand. Her memories of people and conversations were often simple, blurry, and jumbled, as if she lived in a perpetual state of confusion. This might have been the result of the hardships of a brutal life, though it seemed more likely that she had some form of mental disability.

Several months after her capture, Alice had learned only a few words of the Lenape tongue. While she helped clean game and plant crops, she had otherwise failed to assimilate to her new life, mostly because she lacked the capacity, Noah thought. As a result, she was subject to ridicule by the tribe and often felt the stinging end of a switch for her perceived incompetence and dullness, that is, until her hosts discovered that she was quite adept at finding and gathering medicinal plants.

Though no one had ever cared to notice before, it was always true that Alice came alive when she was alone in the forest, where she was not mocked, scolded, or tested. She did not have to think of or know the right thing to say. Her sight was sharp as an eagle's, and she instinctively knew where things would be, even before they came into view. And she was young and strong and could skip from rock to rock with the soft touch of a feather.

It was not long before Alice became renowned for her knowledge of the local plants and her agility and skill in finding them in the thick forest. This finally earned her the respect of her enslavers. They even bestowed on her a name denoting great regard, which roughly translates to Leaps-Like-Deer.

However, several years after she was kidnapped, she once more traded cultures. One cold night, Alice was startled from sleep by the sound of gunfire and war cries, so she sprinted into the forest and hid among the trees. White men were searching the wigwams, killing any man, woman, or child who had not already fled. Soon, rough hands grabbed her from behind, and she was hauled off.

Although she was returned to her family, Alice could find no home. Strangely, she felt a Lenape heart beating in her chest. She refused to speak, she refused any food, and, at the first opportunity, she attempted escape. But this had apparently been expected, because her father was waiting for her with an axe handle, which he applied liberally to her temple. There was a dull thud, then blackness. When Alice woke, her hands and ankles were chained.

It was said that her mind had been made feeble by her treatment at the hands of the Lenape, and people came from miles around to catch a glimpse of her. In fact, her father often trotted her out like livestock so the wide-eyed spectators could get a better view. He told them Alice had been struck both deaf and dumb by her torture and that they should return the favor if ever they found themselves in the company of one of the Lenape.

Alice was freed only after it was certain that her Lenape hosts had been hunted down and eradicated and that there was nothing left for Alice to run off to. However, she quickly returned to her wild ways, dancing lightly in the forest and sniffing out the healing herbs whenever she had the chance. Alice's father usually recoiled at the sight and smell of the "weeds" and threw them into the stove or ground them into the mud with the heel of his boot. But word of her abilities was whispered about town, and pacified Native people and white men alike sought her out. Of course, Alice's father saw the profit in such trade, and he very quickly amassed a tidy sum, little of which was ever spent for Alice's benefit.

Regardless, Alice began to notice a finely dressed young man who came to the farm often to purchase herbs. He was pale and quite skinny, though he had gentle eyes and an honest smile. She heard her father say that he was a new doctor in a town several miles away and that he found great use for the herbs in his practice. Alice liked to spy on him from hidden places whenever he was around. She felt things stirring inside her at the mere sight of him, and for the first time, she could imagine not being alone.

In time, Alice allowed the man to see her, and he curtly bowed his head and smiled. Soon, they were exchanging greetings, and the man always waited patiently until Alice could find the words. As often as he could, the man would stop just to see her and make sure she was getting enough to eat. Alice would often comment, however, that he was the one who should be eating, sapling-thin as he was.

One day, Alice emerged from the woods to find the man and her father discussing something. Though she was not quite close enough to hear, she guessed it concerned her, for her father had his arms folded across his chest and was shaking his head back and forth while the man appeared to plead with him. After the man left, Alice asked her father about it. But he refused to discuss it in the least and shooed her off to finish her work in the garden.

In the deep of that night, there was a knock on Alice's window. The man said she should go with him to be his wife. He said that her father would never approve, that he thinks her a dullard and not fit to be any man's wife. Alice knew the truth though: her father was afraid for her to leave because he would be a poor farmer once more.

Alice and the man hurried off to his carriage. They were married the very next day. No sooner had they left the magistrate's office when her father appeared with the sheriff, intent on taking her home. But, seeing as how Alice was an adult, the sheriff said, there was nothing he could do.

It was not long before Alice conceived a child. At that magical moment, somewhere in the murky depths of her chromosomes, the memories of her life jumped ship to a new generation.

⊶

But to take with him only what he wanted, that was still the question. So, before Noah put Alice back in the Rolodex, he thought about the sun and the pool and the girls who sometimes gave him a second look, and he was instantly returned to his bed, bathed in waning afternoon light.

Noah sat up. He looked around for a moment, just to be sure of where he was, then walked into the bathroom and examined himself in the mirror. It was certainly him, but he could feel that Alice, or at least the memory of Alice, was sharing the space inside him. Everything she said or did was roiling about in his mind, always on the tip of his tongue.

Noah would put it to the test.

He pulled on a pair of sneakers and dashed out the front door. There was a dense strip of forest just down the road. He dove right in.

Noah had played with his friends in the woods a great deal when he was a child, but he did not *know* the forest. Noah and his buddies had splashed in streams, thrown rocks, and knocked over rotted trees, but Noah had never thought seriously as to how anything in the forest could feed him or heal him. Beyond recognizing the obvious difference between an oak tree and a pine tree, Noah knew nothing of the breadth and wealth of the forest's resources.

This time, it was different.

He had only to kneel down to find yellow dock, a stalky plant with coffee-like berries growing at the edge of the forest. Before that moment, Noah had thought of it as nothing more than a noxious weed. But now, he examined it with pure fascination. Not only was it food, but its roots could be crushed and made into a soothing ointment.

Just several steps away, there was no mistaking a clump of buckbrush arching its branches over the ground. The tea made from its root was a powerful diuretic. A few feet away from that was a black gum tree standing straight at attention. Noah ran his hand down the trunk, remembering that the alligator-like bark could be used to relieve chest pain and angina.

Virtually everywhere Noah looked, he found either food or precious medicine that grew wild just a stone's throw from his house, resources that he had never before known existed.

Noah could feel the deeper, darker forest calling, and he sprang forward into the cool stillness. His muscles coiled and flexed, infused with Alice's fleet-footed memories. Automatic legs carried him smoothly over stones and fallen branches as if they had tiny minds of their own that were always scanning and marking the uneven terrain ahead.

Noah stopped suddenly in a damp, low-slung patch of ground draped with a thick mat of leaves, brush, and ferns. Bright green moss clung to the few rocks that poked through the cover. A faint ginger smell caught his attention. The elusive and coveted snake root was nearby. Noah squatted down and searched through the detritus. Two heart-shaped leaves marked the spot. He followed the stems with his hands down to the long, pale roots, which appeared to slither like tiny snakes across the rich black earth below, hence the name. The herb had long been prized for its many healing properties, which include its ability to instantly relieve headaches as well as indigestion. A strong, hot infusion of the roots could also rid the lungs of excess mucous. If enough was available, it was also used as a spice for cooking. And this was just to name a few of its positive properties.

Virtually everywhere Noah turned, he instantly recognized something useful. There was common mint, heart's ease, cattail, and sumac, each of which provided at least one medicinal benefit. If he had wanted, Noah could have gathered quite a vast natural and valuable pharmacy.

In an instant, using Alice's borrowed memories, Noah had been transformed from a dumb beast into a medicine man. But what happened now? Would the knowledge just evaporate in an hour, or would his mind perhaps be wiped clean overnight while he slept? Only time would tell, he concluded. Noah made his way home as darkness closed its curtain, and he collapsed on his couch without even bothering to change clothes.

8—ᛜ

When Noah finally stirred from his nap, he smiled because he could feel that Alice was still with him. He remembered the forest and the plants; the knowledge of it all seemed to be permanently etched into his conscious mind now. He felt a wave of excitement. There would be no need for a trance to find her anymore, or perhaps anyone else for that matter.

A theory was now emerging: If Noah brought anyone back from the Rolodex, that person's memories now belonged to him, stored away in the same place with all of his own memories, and were just as familiar. So, what if he somehow retrieved the whole Rolodex next time? Would his head explode? Would he go crazy and claw out his eyes? He did not know, but he suspected it could be done. He believed his grandfather alluded to it when he wrote that he had found a way to dissolve the barrier to his subconscious mind—another test for Noah to pass.

He took a deep, calming breath. "Let's get to it," he said aloud.

Noah started the metronome. He went straight to the Rolodex. He was trying to wrap his mind around its untold human layers. He started probing it, anticipating the collective weight and strength of so many slices of so many lives. Noah could feel the incredible density of the thing, as if he were holding a collapsed star in his hands. It was just too much, he decided as he began to take fright. If he brought them all back with him, he was suddenly sure it would turn him inside out. He would literally explode so violently and with so much force that he would leave nothing behind but pink mist painted on the walls of his bedroom. He imagined stunned police detectives standing around and scratching their heads while they tried to explain what had happened to him.

Noah dropped the Rolodex and sprinted madly for the light.

Chapter 39

THOUGH IT TOOK every ounce of courage he had, Noah went back in the next day. Much to his relief, he found the unassuming organizer sitting intact on the desk, exuding no clue of the chaos it contained. But Noah would not try packing it out again, at least not until he had a plan. He was only there for his grandfather. He found the card, though there was virtually nothing on it, at least nothing Noah did not already know. His grandfather mentioned that he had somehow hidden his memories from Noah, mostly all of them it seemed.

Noah could understand why Edward Batson might not want him to know *everything*; that would be too easy. Noah had to figure some things out for himself, and he got that. But on this critical point? Could his grandfather not at least have offered a clue about how to swallow a universe-size memory box?

As soon as Noah came to, he climbed into bed and rested with his hands behind his head. It was nearly midnight, but he was not tired. He grabbed the journal from his nightstand and started to flip through it as he had done many times before. After a moment, he threw it aside. He knew there was nothing there to help him either.

Perhaps if he were stronger, braver, and smarter, it would come to him. Maybe if he had not wasted so much time being foolish, he would have had an answer by now. His father had said it best: Noah was always trying to fill an emptiness inside him with nonsense. . . . Noah's heart just about stopped, and he sat up. *Wait, . . . emptiness? If there was a void inside him, obviously something was missing.* The tumblers fell sharply into place. Noah instantly grasped that a piece of him had always been missing—that he had felt incomplete for as long as he could remember. The law school debacle was just a symptom of the problem, not the cause of it! He did not actually want to be a lawyer, he was only using it to try and fill the hollow inside his chest, and when that failed, he tried to consume just about everything and anyone else he could find to make himself feel whole, including Violet.

Just as Noah could sense the solidness of the immense Rolodex, he could, at that moment, measure the utter vastness of the cavern inside him with equal certainty. He decided it was the perfect fit.

Noah jumped out of bed and started the metronome. He materialized at the desk. He put his hands on the Rolodex.

Noah gave a silent prayer, then let them all loose.

They burst forth from the pages in a furious torrent, like a pent-up river exploding through a dam. Noah could feel himself filling up with it. He quickly visualized the pinpoint of light and water at the end of the dark tunnel. He shot for it.

Noah opened his eyes. His head felt like an anvil filled with a swarm of bees. Voices and emotions were swirling around inside, searching for space, a place to settle. Noah concentrated with all his might on the image of the Rolodex, and it began to take shape once more, this time in his throbbing, conscious mind. Micron by micron, it seemed, the Rolodex was being tediously 3D printed in his brain. From time to time over the next couple of weeks, Noah would check in on the progress when he had a quiet moment and watch his creation flesh itself out a little more each time, with a sense of pride and accomplishment that he had never known before. Finally, one day, Noah took a peek, and everything was still. They had all taken their places. They were finally home.

Chapter 40

THE NEXT DAY, Noah packed his car with as much as it could hold and set off. He would immerse himself in his "memories" and rely only on them for sustenance. Noah reasoned this was the best way he could think of to learn about himself and refine his abilities. Stated more simply, he would sink or swim. To avoid winding up in a missing person's report, however, he concocted a story for his family and neighbors that he had taken a sales job that kept him busy and out of touch for long periods of time.

First, Noah thought as he pulled away, he would need significant funds to finance such an epic road trip, and there could be no better way than to steal already-stolen money. He soon found himself at a casino in Atlantic City, where he exchanged the few thousand dollars he had left for chips and took a seat at the blackjack table. What the electronic eyes of the casino could not have seen was the card counter in Noah's head.

Many years ago, there lived a man, now long forgotten, who possessed such a skill, and Noah knew him well. When the cards were dealt, Noah closed and rubbed his eyes for a brief moment while he spun the Rolodex.

Philip Sokamp could often be found at a small table in the darkest corner of a foul-smelling pub in medieval Paris, always ready to take a day's pay from anyone drunk enough or foolish enough to wager on a game of cards. Since he had been accused many times of cheating, he took to playing in nothing but his breeches to avoid any suspicion. And he rarely lost, except by design, which served to either hustle his prey or avoid having his throat cut by a particularly sore loser.

Phillip's secret was simply that he had the innate ability to remember every card shown so that he could almost instantly determine an opponent's hand and calculate his chances of success. Had he managed to steer clear of the wine and the prostitutes that waited for him in the alley outside, he might have saved enough money to purchase a cottage in the country, far away from the filthy, plague-infested streets of Paris. Yet if he had, perhaps he never would have passed his seed to his bastard child of one of the prostitutes, which allowed him to keep his secret alive for Noah.

But there was also another.

Edith Bricker was the daughter of a Baptist minister in Springfield, Missouri. She was thin and graceful, with long black hair and intense, green eyes that conveyed a voracious intellect. She was born with a rare eidetic, or "photographic," memory, which she could only secretly cultivate on the pretext of casual visits to her local library. Women of the late nineteenth century were, tragically, deemed fit only for domestic work. Yet her husband was tolerant of her "hobby" so long as she was gone no longer than an hour or two. Noah could feel her suppressed rage, which she sometimes gave voice to by screaming into a closet to avoid being overheard. By the time she had conceived her fourth child at age thirty-two, she had accepted her fate. Still, she could never quite forgive the world that would have been better off had she been allowed a proper place in it.

When Noah turned his attention back to the game, Phillip Sokamp and Edith Bricker were perched on either shoulder, and they lent him their combined skills. By the end of that night, and for the following week, Noah owned the tables, much to the chagrin of the security staff who, by the end, were constantly looming over him. When they finally escorted him to the door and dumped him roughly on the boardwalk, Noah had almost $100,000 in his pocket.

After he flipped his scowling hosts the bird, he jumped into his car and headed south.

Chapter 41

PERHAPS IT WAS because all the music Noah heard on the car stereo seemed so silly and vacuous, but he felt inexorably drawn to news and current event channels.

Of course, the news was bad. That is precisely why it sold, why people wanted to hear about it. In addition to the usual violence and political unrest, the news was punctuated with stories of an increasingly angry mother nature. There was more frequent and intense storm activity, which Noah had now lived long enough to bear witness to, mass animal extinctions, melting glaciers, and rising sea levels. Apparently, we were even due for a magnetic pole shift which, while not fatal in and of itself, would fuel climate change like gasoline poured on a fire.

Noah could not help but shake his head in disgust while a geologist explained during one broadcast that the Great Plains Aquifer, which lies beneath eight Midwestern states and covers more than 174,000 square miles, was being rapidly depleted by irrigation, which, in conjunction with drought in the Western states, would mean the collapse of food production in the US. This in turn would result in starvation and famine around the world. Although this was a worst-case scenario, the scientist explained, there was no cause for alarm because we still had time to avoid it, if we acted now.

Noah was slapped with yet another epiphany. He pulled the car to the litter-strewn shoulder of the highway and came to a screeching stop. He closed his eyes and frantically tore through the Rolodex in his head.

The man lived so distantly in the past that the images were fragmented and scattered, as if diluted over the millennia. Trying to reassemble them was like gathering once more a single drop of oil spread over the surface of pond. Eventually, Noah could piece together a picture in his mind of a young man with an unpronounceable name resting in the shade of a tree to escape the blistering sun at a time that could not have been long after the dawn of humans. The man began to think about his world. It had been many days since he made a kill, owing to the animals being particularly wary and skittish. The man could not deny that he, too, felt uneasy, as if there were an unseen menace rolling over the plains, drawing closer each day.

Although it was the hot time, the nights were unusually cold, so he always had to keep himself covered or find a place near the fire. And it was drier than he remembered. Even the strongest trees and plants had begun to wither, something he had never seen before in his short life. But what scared the man most was that the big animals had begun moving off to forbidden lands. Only small, burrowing things remained, and they could not for long feed even the man's small group. If they had no food, they would soon turn on each other.

The man glanced up to gray sky and lifted his nose to the breeze. There was always smoke in the air these days, spewing from the mountain crowned with fire in the distance. The man often saw flames turning the plains to ashes in his dreams.

The man had finally found enough courage to stand before the elders and tell them they must go where the herds go because the land was sick, which is why the animals had fled. They were angry with the man and threw small rocks at him, the traditional expression of their displeasure. The animals would come back, they said, as they always did, and they would survive until that day. They said the man was too young to understand the way of things. Besides, they reminded the man, no one had ever been beyond the eyes of the great mountain and was ever seen again.

But the man believed in signs, as did the thundering herds who left their trail in the grasses. That is why the man and a few strong others gathered their supplies and set off to follow. They walked for many long days before finally sighting some of the thirsty beasts gathered at a watering hole.

Just as the man settled down to sleep under a veiled moon, there was a great explosion, and night was turned into day. All he could do was watch helplessly as the horizon from whence he came was set on fire.

There was another, Reginald Potts, who was acutely aware of signs, perhaps because his birth coincided with a most auspicious event. In 1307, he was born in London to a baker and his wife. Reginald was the fourth of six children and the only one to live to adulthood. That same year, winter lasted for six months in northern Europe, and the Baltic Sea froze over for the first time in recorded history.

When he was a child, Reginald heard his parents talking about the endless snow that some said was slowly creeping further south each winter. But there was no cause to worry, they assured themselves, because in those days, when most people rarely strayed more than a few miles from their birthplace, the Baltic nations might as well have been worlds away. Even then, Reginald remembered wondering how people could deny something as plain as the nose on their faces.

When he was twenty, pox-scarred and all but blind in one eye, there was much talk in the bakery about mass starvation in Scotland, where early frost had claimed the crops before they could be harvested. Though none believed England could suffer such a fate, Reginald had not failed to notice that the mornings had grown chillier with each passing year and that it would not be long before the wheat began to yield less for his bread.

In Reginald's twenty-ninth year, in what would be the autumn of his life, the damp cold had finally settled in England. Just as he had predicted, grain had become scarce because the wheat had rotted and prices had exploded. Those that could afford the bread came less often. Those that could not tried to steal it, to the point that Reginald had to always keep a dagger close at hand. But there was almost none who were not by that time lean with sharp angles showing through baggy clothes.

Then, there were rumors of a ghost ship washed up in Sicily with dead and dying men at the oars, their bodies erupting with black boils. It was said that all who set foot on deck died soon after due to this same scourge, which then spread through the Mediterranean turning towns into festering piles of corpses. Still, some said, there should be no panic because God made the Channel to keep England safe.

Reginald was certain, however, that it would not be long before a ship of death docked in London, which he could see was ripe for destruction. No food meant famine, and famine always invited disease, which especially made use of crowded places like his city because it had less distance to travel. Reginald could sense that an invisible wave had crested and was about to crash down and obliterate even his isolated isle. However, flight meant he had a chance to survive. He had long ago planned that he would strike off to Wales when the time came. There, a skilled baker was sure to find employment, ideally in a secluded lord's manor or a monastery. He had squirrelled away a purse of coin that he hid under the floor that would see him through. And because he had been widowed, he needed only to provide for himself unless or until he found another wife (which, of course, he did, lest Noah would never have known him).

Noah saw that there were others, too, all survivors who had the forethought to understand the signs of a coming catastrophe. Or perhaps it was just that they lacked the mechanism of denial. Regardless of the skill that they possessed, Noah found that they had survived and evolved to find a place in a world that had forever changed.

Noah, too, thought he saw signs everywhere: in the clinging smog in the distance, in the wet, unseasonably warm air that made his car smell like the cup of coffee he had spilled between the seats a couple of months before, and in the decaying row homes of rusty industrial cities that stretched from Boston to Miami. But there was something else, something beyond these obvious portents that no one talked about.

Noah often studied the faces of passing drivers and pedestrians who hurried across intersections. He concluded that there was palpable exhaustion and frustration in their expressions, as if they were all at their wits' end. And it could not be hidden by makeup or sunglasses or whatever mask they put on for the world. At least it could not be hidden from Noah, who benefitted from spies who had watched the rise and fall of civilizations for thousands of years. Mother Nature had always been a violent killer, but the threat now to society, Noah believed, was from without *and* within. And it would come to a head soon, though in what form, he could not be sure.

Chapter 42

AFTER NOAH FILLED the tank at a 7-11, he bought a dried-out hot dog and a soda. As he sat on the hood of his car and ate, his thoughts drifted back to the questions of how and why all this had happened to him. How it had occurred seemed fairly straightforward, he decided. He had inherited the ability to remember everything that the thousands of ancestors who had contributed to his DNA remembered. Why should that be the case? Noah thought the answer to that question was obvious, too. As Mrs. Blumfield pointed out, in biological terms, anyone that could access the talents and skills of their ancestors would be much more likely to avoid danger, survive and reproduce, thus passing the desired memory trait on to a new generation.

So, that left the vexing question of why now. Why didn't Noah know about it right out of the gate, from the time he could walk and talk? It had been the same with his grandfather, who was already an adult when his ability manifested itself.

The light bulb suddenly went on. Edward Batson mentioned in his journal that people had been dying from the Spanish flu. Noah recalled some things about the Spanish flu he had learned in a history class in college. The word *flu* was a misnomer, because it implied that it was merely an inconvenient sickness that took people out of circulation for a week or two. But the truth was far darker. The Spanish flu killed six percent of the world's population between 1918 and 1920, almost one hundred million people. It was described as perhaps the worst medical catastrophe in the history of the world, killing even more people than the Black Plague of the Middle Ages. It is still argued today that it shifted the balance of power to the Allied nations in World War I because the mortality rate from the disease was much higher in Germany and Austria than in England or the United States.

Noah suspected that the world in his grandfather's day was stressed and stretched to its limit, nudged over the precipice toward a fundamental correction by the epidemic. However, because the Spanish flu fizzled out so rapidly, due mostly to the fact that it killed its hosts so quickly, society never unraveled to the point where Edward Batson's survival even remotely hinged upon his unique skill set.

Noah considered that the situation was probably just as dire now, one hundred years later. If the experts were right, and all the dominos fell, people will begin to face one crisis after another, like a set of tidal waves pounding the beach. Climate change would cause sea levels to rise, forcing people inland from the coasts. It would also cause massive crop failures, which in turn would make it difficult to feed everybody. The few viable food-producing regions that remained would be overburdened and would fail. So, even the people who managed to flee to the safety of higher ground would soon find themselves starving. And their weakened immune systems would make them easy pickings for a host of diseases that have long been smoldering in the poorest parts of the world. Those that were hardy enough and lucky enough to survive starvation and disease would soon find themselves in the midst of war and violence while governments competed to secure any remaining resources.

Even though Noah did not believe in worst-case scenarios, because just about everything, even catastrophe, never goes according to plan, he nonetheless felt certain that a very painful change was in the making and that it would happen far more quickly than most people expected. The world would surely spin on, and people would continue to rule it (perhaps less arrogantly), but there would certainly be some mayhem and tragedy that would leave no one untouched before it had run its course.

As Noah took the last bite of his hot dog, he agreed with himself that his ability was likely triggered by stress. He had internalized society's escalating worries and anxiety, which in turn had set off a call to arms deep inside the very fiber of his being. The strange people he saw on the night of his accident; maybe that was the final straw. As a result, his body let its perfect weapon off the chain to make sure that he survived. The same thing must have been true for his grandfather.

Noah felt a wave of urgency when he realized there was likely precious little time to perfect his gift. Any idea he had of a graceful cinematic journey of self-discovery was assassinated and replaced by a grim determination to fill his fingertips with as much practical information as he could in as little time as possible.

Chapter 43

DONNA WELLER SAT on her porch alone and wrapped in a blanket in the middle of a cold night. Sleep proved almost impossible lately.

Donna squinted into the darkness. She could still make out the soft black outline of the mountains in the distance. She found some relief from her agony in imagining herself there in the quiet stillness. Donna stood slowly and let the blanket drop to the floor at her feet. She was so close. All she had to do was take that first step, and she would be gone. But something froze her like a statue, something still tethered her to her prison.

Her children.

They were sleeping blissfully inside. She would not leave without them. Certainly, they would be confused at first, and they would miss their father, but they were still so young, so malleable. Donna would show them, she would lift the blindfolds from their eyes, and they would finally *see*.

She thought her husband, of all people, would understand. After all, they used to always be on the same page. She told him she knew it sounded crazy, but she was sure she was being poisoned by things in her own house. The phones, the computers (even the washer and dryer had computers!), the internet—the waves of energy and information they vomited out every second of every day was somehow making her sick. There was the constant humming in her ears. And she had headaches and nausea that lasted for days. Even when she was not in pain, there was haziness and confusion, like she always had a cold or a bad hangover.

And it was getting worse.

Donna could no longer stand the sight of her cell phone and tablet, even when they were turned off. Yesterday, she buried them in the bottom of the kitchen garbage just before her husband took it out to the garage. And every night now, she unplugged the computer and appliances before bed. Even that did not work, because the mere thought of them gave her a terrible migraine and made her feel like she would throw up. Besides, there were computers she could not turn off: computers in the thermostat, the water heater, and the boxes on the electrical lines outside with blinking lights. And cars were the worst. They were just big, thumping computers on wheels, and they were everywhere.

She begged him; they had to get away to a place where the invisible torturers could not harm them. She said there were a lot more like her. Before it had become unbearable to sit in front of a screen, Donna had found several obscure chat rooms where people like her were making plans for their escape.

Unfortunately, Donna's husband was not on the same page. When he realized she was serious, he hauled her off to the emergency room. Donna told the doctor about how she felt, but she was very careful not to mention anything about wanting to run away because shrinks did not like that kind of talk; she might get sent away for saying something like that. In the end, the doctor said that she had anxiety, that she'd probably had it for a while, so he gave her pills. Donna took a few, but they did not help. She flushed the rest down the toilet.

Donna thought a lot about what the doctor said though, about her having it for a while. It was true; she had not felt right for some time. Maybe it was a slow-burning fuse.

It started with small things, things that could be nothing at all. A year or so ago, she started to get tired all the time. She thought it was the kids. A nine-year-old and a seven-year-old took a lot out of her. But there had been sadness, too, and a feeling of being out of place a lot. It was like she was wearing the wrong glasses, and everything was out of focus. Then she became physically ill. Headaches morphed into migraines, and an upset stomach became full-blown nausea. After that, there had been the strange buzzing in her ears, like a tiny mosquito was stuck in her head all the time.

More and more, she felt inexorably drawn to the wilderness, where no human had yet left a mark. She did not just want to trade her house for one like it minus the electrical guts though. She wanted, no *needed*, to claim a patch of shaded forest and feel the uneven ground beneath her bare feet. Only then might her sanity be restored. She needed to start from scratch, as if everything that came before had never existed all.

When she continued to cry and complain, her husband became angry. He became violent, too. One night, after an argument, he pinned her against the wall by her shoulders. He said she could go off and live in the woods like an animal, but she was not taking the kids. He said if she ever mentioned it again, he would kick her out and take her to court for custody. Donna was scared, not just because he was strong, but he made all the money. Donna had not worked in years. Even back then, she worked in retail for minimum wage. She had no chance.

Donna did not say anything else to her husband about how bad she felt after that. Instead, she suffered quietly and came up with plans and kept it all to herself. It took a little time, but it turned out to be easy. She took money from a vacation account. She hid everything she bought in the attic behind a rack of her old clothes. He never looked there.

She did not know who her husband was anymore. She did not know who a lot of people were anymore. But she fooled them anyway. Her husband started to smile again and give her a peck on the cheek when he came home from work. His mother did not stop by to look in on her anymore. They could have it all. They could choke on it, too.

It was almost time.

Chapter 44

Macon, Georgia: The Blacksmith

WHILE NOAH GENERALLY knew that blacksmiths worked by heating pieces of metal until they became hot enough to shape into the desired form, he had no clue as to how that actually happened. So, at first, Noah could only stand helplessly in the blacksmith's studio he had rented for the day. While there were many tools he recognized, like hammers, chisels, and the iconic anvil, he had absolutely no idea what to do with them, despite what he had said when he had forked over the cash and signed the release forms.

That changed very quickly after he searched his mind and plucked an ash-smeared face from the Rolodex.

"By hammer and hand do all things stand."

The blacksmith's motto, in some derivation, was ancient even in the year 950, when Obecco Abel plied his trade in Burgos, Spain. He often thought proudly on the motto's implications and meanings when he hammered and shaped diverse things from nails to plowshares to the occasional and tediously constructed sword commissioned by wealthier patrons.

Noah could feel his forearms and hands begin to pulse with muscle memories honed by countless hammer blows that had rung out more than a thousand years ago. He surveyed the room once more, this time with a practiced eye. He instantly tallied up the inventory and was satisfied that he had everything he needed.

Although the forge was heated by propane instead of the charcoal used by Obecco, it mattered little because Noah could immediately tell by the metal's consistency and color when it was ready to be made into something useful.

Noah was soon pounding a glowing piece of truck spring, which began to take the shape of a flanged spear tip. He flattened and spread it to a fine point, then he quenched it in oil to make it tough and hard. Some filing made the edges razor sharp.

Next, Noah made a dozen iron nails with the help of a header, a tool designed to flatten one end of the nail for striking. Finally, out of a steel ingot, he created a three-pound hammer head, being sure to apply coal dust to keep the punch from getting stuck while he forced a hole through the center, in which he would later fasten the handle.

As Noah worked, he could not help but dwell on the motto as well, recognizing its truth on so many levels.

Clay County, Tennessee: The Hunter

Noah parked his car along an old, rutted logging road. He stepped out and scanned the distance. The sky was clear and bright, but the air was quite cold, especially for mid-October. A thin crust of snow clung to the ground. Noah squatted down for a better look.

There was no mistaking the hoof prints of whitetail deer that traveled down the road, then veered off into a dormant corn field that lay like a welcome mat to the forest beyond. Noah shaded his eyes against the sun, alert for any sign of movement, but there was nothing.

It seemed obvious to Noah that the ability to track and find wild game might prove particularly useful if ever food became scarce, and he had no shortage of ancestors who possessed varying degrees of hunting skill. But there was one in particular who could always be counted on to make the kill. More than 150 years ago, Jonathan Begrew stalked whitetail deer, bear, and rabbits not far from where Noah found himself at that moment. Johnathan learned from an early age how to handle the prized Sharps rifle that his father had looted from a dead Yankee after the battle at Chancellorsville. While his father may have made it home from the war without so much as a scratch on his body, he had taken some invisible wound that he had attempted to remedy with liquor and hate until the day he wandered off and drowned in a creek. But before his will broke and it fell to Jonathan to put food on the table, his father had taught him how to hunt.

"Any fool could throw out corn for the deer and wait for somethin' to come stumblin' across the sights. There ain't no skill in that. And what if it don't come? What then? The only sure way is to go out and find it, or you go home hungry," his father had said.

Noah examined the hoof prints at his feet through Jonathan's keen eyes. Snow made for good tracking, he knew, because Jonathan Begrew had known that so many years before. Noah traced the depression with his fingers. He could tell from the way the ice was smoothed around the edges that the prints were a day or two old, having thawed a bit in daylight, then freezing again overnight. Most were faint heart shapes left by agile does that appeared to almost skip across the snow.

Then something caught Noah's attention. A heavy, flat-footed track with fractured crystal-like edges that screamed to a skilled hunter like Jonathan Begrew that a big buck had just passed this way. Noah followed the meandering trail. The tracks were about twenty inches apart, which meant the buck was only walking. Occasionally, the tracks doubled back and then vanished. This was a defensive maneuver often used by bucks to confuse predators that hunt by scent. But after only the slightest pause, Noah recovered the trail and pushed on. Because walking whitetails often stop on odd numbered steps, Noah mimicked their canter, so that even if the crunchy snow gave him away, a deer might not yet suspect the presence of a hunter. When he reached the forest, he stopped for a moment to take a long breath and gather Jonathan's thoughts on the pursuit.

Though his back was to the wind and whitetails have an acute sense of smell, Noah decided it was worth the risk to stay on the buck's heels. Attempting to circle around in the thick cover would take a great deal more effort and time. Noah knew, from Jonathan's experience, that the biggest mistake a tracker could make was to move too slowly, arriving only after the opportunity for a shot was long gone. In fact, Jonathan had made a number of kills downwind because he had struck so swiftly.

Noah noticed small twigs that were resting lightly on top of the snow, likely broken by the deer's rack as he had passed through. Noah suddenly ran into a wall of musky stench, and he knew it was near. He walked hunched over to lower his profile, this time moving slowly on his toes to avoid any sound. Noah parted some brush and found the buck feeding on acorns, its favorite meal, completely unaware of Noah's presence. Noah formed an imaginary rifle with his hands and pointed it at the buck, aiming for the heart. He could almost feel its drumming beat.

"Bang!" Noah said aloud.

In that instant, the deer swung twitching ears around toward the sound of Noah's voice and shot off, thundering through the trees.

As Noah gleefully retraced his steps, he looked up to find three huddled figures walking determinedly past his car down the road. They presented a strange sight. There was a woman and two young children, a boy and a girl. The children, who looked to be no more than eight or nine years old, were bundled up in heavy coats and carried cartoon-themed backpacks. The woman was wearing a heavy frame pack and pulling a long trailer piled high with gear that was covered with a blue tarp. It seemed to Noah an odd time of year to go camping, especially with kids.

As Noah got closer, the woman seemed to finally notice him. She abruptly turned away, as if to hide her face, then bent down and said something to the children. A few seconds later, they started off once again, this time at a much quicker pace. Noah raised his hand to wave, but they put their eyes to the ground, obviously trying to ignore him.

Noah watched as the group hurried down the road and then started across the field toward the bronzed sea of trees. Occasionally, the woman glanced back over her shoulder, as if to see whether Noah was following them. Eventually, the woman shooed the children into the forest, which swallowed them from view. The woman took one last look about before following them into the trees.

Noah was abruptly gripped by what he could only describe as a powerful sense of déjà vu. He was cast back to the night of his accident, when he had almost mowed down the strange people frozen in his headlights. The woman had the same frightened look, the same fidgety, nervous moves, like a desperate refugee trying but failing to slip by unnoticed. Though she had said nothing, Noah could not help but think that had he blocked her way and demanded answers, she would have pleaded tearfully with him to let her go. She might have told him that there was no point in stopping her because she was *already gone*— she was *not here anymore*.

The hue and cry rose from deep inside Noah. "Be aware of portents and signs!" his spies firmly reminded him.

Noah glanced up and searched the wide sky once more. There was no thunder of war, no smoke on the horizon, no mass exodus. Though Noah, too, could feel invisible walls closing in, except for a gentle wind, everything was silent and perfectly calm. *What is coming?* He pled with the Rolodex. But there was no answer.

Near Wilmington, Delaware: The Survivor

Noah parted the curtains and stared out the window that could not be opened. He was at yet another ubiquitous motel nestled in the midst of highways and chain restaurants. He sorely missed his home and the red oak tree outside his window.

Noah kicked off his shoes and lay down on the bed. He was satisfied that he had now honed his skill to the point that whenever he snatched somebody from the Rolodex, they never went back. Their lives and their memories, including all their acumen and expertise, were always front and center, fresh in his mind. Noah was able to use whatever piece of them he wanted instantaneously, without any mental gymnastics. He had all the tools he would need to carry on, but that was still no guarantee he would make it through some catastrophe.

Noah had long been fascinated by stories of people who against all odds clawed their way out of the most desperate situations. For example, Noah remembered reading a story about a man in his seventies who had gotten lost in the wilderness of Alaska after his car had crashed in a ditch along a remote road. Despite suffering from diabetes, a lack of warm clothing, and subzero temperatures, the man stumbled into a ranger station six days later. By that time, he was severely dehydrated, and frostbite had claimed his nose, four fingers, and six toes. He had managed to stave off hypothermia with almost constant movement and by stuffing dried leaves inside his shirt and pants for extra insulation. He was even able to scare off a pack of wolves by throwing stones and screaming at the top of his lungs.

On the flip side, many people, even those younger, fitter, and better prepared for that kind of emergency, would have laid down and died long before finding help. Almost everyone who has ever heard a story like that has wondered whether they had what it took to walk out the other side of a disaster. That is precisely what made tales of survival so interesting. But the question was this: What was *it*? Was *it* will, determination, even stupidity?

Noah searched for one that could teach him. The Rolodex stopped on a dime.

⊶

She popped up to the surface of the water just in time to witness the broken schooner being swallowed by the waves, along with her infant child and every last thing that she owned, save the clothes on her back.

It had all happened in the blink of an eye, so fast that she wondered whether she had only dreamed that she was Rebecca Rowan, a widowed wife and now childless mother. For how is it possible to heap so much misfortune upon one person, if not in a nightmare? She tried to convince herself that she was back in Nantucket, lying in bed half asleep, her baby tucked into the crook of her arm. It would not be long before her husband arrived home from the docks, dropped his muddy boots by the door, and stealthily made his way under the quilt, molding his body to her own.

Rebecca blinked several times, but nothing changed. She was bobbing in the waves in the middle of the cold, deep ocean, and everything was still gone, as if it had never existed at all. She reached back into her mind for answers. Scenes came flooding back.

Though the day had been overcast with bruised skies, the wind and the water were strangely calm, especially considering that an early September storm had threaded its way between Nantucket and Hyannis only the day before. As Rebecca and her son had no other choice but to leave on the next ship for the mainland, it seemed particularly fortuitous that the sea offered a gentle hand to bear them.

Her husband had died six months before, thinned to the bone and finally suffocated by consumption. They had met three years before that, when his whaler had docked in Batavia, her home in the East Indies, to trade for supplies. He was lean and strong and had been made so dark by the sun that his skin appeared only a shade lighter than her own. When he sent for her the next year, she never could have imagined the strange world where she would soon find herself. Except at the height of the summer, Nantucket was chilly and windswept and was often battered by rough, foamy seas. It seemed so barren and colorless compared to her homeland, as if it were teetering on the edge of a flat world.

At first, she proved quite a curiosity to the stern New Englanders inhabiting the island, who often found occasion to stop by and welcome her, if only to catch a glimpse of the pretty dark-skinned woman from faraway lands. Though none would truly call her *friend*, they seemed content at least to tolerate her presence, mostly on account of her husband, who was by then a captain of his own ship.

Soon after the birth of their son, Jacob, Rebecca's husband grew too ill to sail, so he instead purchased a share in a whale processing station on the island. After he died, creditors took most everything and "with great regret" cast her and her son into the street. She had been left with enough money only for the passage to Hyannis, where she hoped to find work and earn her way back to the East Indies. Though her prospects there as a single mother might be no better, at least her family would share what little they had.

But as Rebecca was standing on the bow of the ship with her sleeping child in her arms, uneasily scanning the horizon for any sign of their destination, a cry went up. There was a rogue wave! Icy fingers clutched her heart.

Rebecca's husband once told her that he had seen a sturdy ship swamped and sunk without a trace by one such monster.

"Like a bolt from the blue," he had said. "It roared out of the fog on smooth seas, perhaps forty feet tall. It passed before me so quickly that it had already taken one of the fleet in its path before I could give warning."

By the time Rebecca turned to follow the gaze of the stunned deckhands, the sickly green wall of water, as tall as the main mast itself, was upon them. She felt a powerful gust of damp air just before it struck. She drew her son to her tightly. The wave seemed to growl angrily as it fell. She closed her eyes. There was the sound of splintering wood, then she was tumbling and knocked about under the water. She was as powerless as a leaf sucked up in a hurricane, and her son was soon torn from her arms and claimed by the sea. Just before she thought her lungs might burst, she popped to the surface where she now found herself, a speck in the sea and by her estimate, at least fifteen miles from Hyannis.

Rebecca soon noticed fragments of the ship and other items appear on the surface around her. There was a broken spar and some rigging floating next to her, but they were not sufficient to keep her afloat. Then a steamer trunk drifted by. Rebecca grabbed it and climbed on top, but it soon filled with water and disappeared beneath her.

Rebecca struggled mightily to keep her head above the surface. She felt something dragging her down. Perhaps it was the hand of death itself. She panicked for a moment but quickly realized that her long dress and undergarments were pulling her under as if she had lead weights strapped to her back. If she was going to die and follow her son down into the deep dark, all she had to was stop struggling and just let herself go. It would only hurt for a moment. As she descended and the light above her was extinguished by the depths, she would let the spent air go and take one long, deep breath.

On the other hand, if she had any chance to survive, she would have to get moving. It would take every shred of fight she had to get to shore. However, the longer she pondered the question, she knew, the more of her strength and precious warmth would be leached into the hungry sea.

Rebecca chose the way of suffering and pain. But why?

⸎

In one word, hope. Although she may not have been able to articulate the feeling at precisely that moment, Noah had the luxury of being able to replay those few seconds in his mind over and over again until he filtered out one feeling, one compulsion that was only disguised by fear and sorrow. She unknowingly clung to the belief that she still had a part to play, and that gave her the strength to shed her heavy clothes and begin the long, tortuous swim. Hope quelled the panic. It calmed her breathing and gave her a steady stroke.

8—ᴛ

Soon though, Rebecca was faced with a different dilemma. She saw something floating just ahead, directly in her path. And it was moving. At first, she thought it was just some debris from the boat being jostled by the waves, but as she closed on it, she made out a single hand waving, though rather weakly, trying to get her attention. A terror-stricken face emerged. It was a man struggling to stay afloat. No name came to mind, but she recognized him as one of crew.

Rebecca's first thought, incredible as it may seem, was to ask if the man had seen her son. The sight of another survivor triggered a bizarre belief that her son might yet live. Rebecca created any number of fantastic scenarios in her mind by which he could have survived, including a wild vision of her son being gently borne above the water by a pod of dolphins. But the man's mind had already been made feeble by the disaster, and he could only give words to but one thought.

"Help me," he said over and over again in a desperate whisper.

Rebecca regarded him for a moment. His sad state brought her crashing back to reality. He had a long, deep cut across his forehead that was pouring out blood, and his left arm dangled limply at his side. She could see that it was badly broken and hung at an unnatural angle. His legs, however, seemed fine, because he was kicking ferociously to keep his head above the water. He could not long maintain that effort, however. Rebecca could think of nothing more than taking him into her arms and calming him. Perhaps with their combined strength, they could find a way for both of them to get home.

In a flash, with what seemed like supernatural strength, the man lunged for Rebecca with his good hand, but she instinctively pulled away to avoid his grasp. In his state of mind, she thought, he would drown her if he got hold of her. He would claw his way to the top of her like a raft and doom them both. She thought about using some clothing as a rope so she could haul him behind her, but seeing that she may not have even the strength to get herself to land, any dead weight would only lessen her chances. She would leave him behind, she decided, and let him die. There was no empathy, sympathy, or any other emotion in her at that point, there was only the lack of it: a hard indifference to the fate of anything or anyone that could not aid her.

As Rebecca swam away, the man's senses seemed to suddenly return to him.

"Please," he implored, "I have a wife; . . . she'll be worried!" He began to weep and shake his head. "Not like this. Dear God. Please, . . . help me!"

But Rebecca would not look back. The part of her that would have paused for just such a heart-wrenching plea a few moments ago had died, and she would not retreat even one inch now until she could feel the ground beneath her feet. She dug in with slow, methodical strokes that she timed to match her breaths. Once the man's cries faded into the distance, Rebecca knew for certain now that she would make it. The only thing that was left to chance was when and where.

Every so often, she stopped to get her bearings by the sun. Though it was difficult to tell because of the low clouds, the sun's glow had begun to wane as it made for the west in the hazy distance. Rebecca picked up her pace lest she lose the light and veer off course. She blocked out thoughts of her helpless son and dolphins and drowned deck hands. She swam until she was numb and darkness fell.

The next thing Rebecca remembered was waking up under clean sheets in an unfamiliar room. She tried to speak, but she could only manage hoarse breaths. Her throat, and virtually every other part of her for that matter, had been left raw and swollen by the sea water. When her eyes adjusted, she found a frail old woman beside her gently lifting her head so that Rebecca could sip some water.

Seeing the confusion in Rebecca's eyes, the woman pulled a chair beside her and explained that her husband had been fishing out on his skiff the day before when he had found Rebecca about half a mile from shore. The woman laughed when she explained that her "fool" husband could not believe his eyes because he thought she was a mermaid, at least until he finally hauled her battered body into the boat.

It seemed Rebecca was right to have hope after all. The elderly couple welcomed her into their home, and she, in turn, cared for them for several years until they passed on, one three months after the other. Though Rebecca would never return to the East Indies, she found love once more and bore inquisitive children who struck out into the world, who, in turn, bore children of their own.

Now Noah had his answer; now the pale monster had been dragged into the light. For all the dreams and passions of the dead that swirled around inside his head, Noah realized he had none for himself. Zero. He was just a shabby container for better things, a cracked vase filled with beautiful flowers.

So, where would Noah find hope or purpose when the time came? What would keep him from the abyss? He stared blankly at the ceiling. Nothing came to mind. He had the feeling though that something grand was there, but he just could not tease it apart from everything else going on inside his mind.

Not to mention there was still the matter of the strongest ones. Not only did they appear when not summoned, but they hijacked his body completely. There were few things more terrifying than knowing he might have to answer for actions over which he had almost no control. Noah had the feeling that until he mastered them, he would still be incomplete. And if he was only mostly himself, he could never grasp the big picture.

Noah got up and paced back and forth in front of his bed. It was not long before he had devised a simple plan to bring the elemental ancestors to heel.

Chapter 44

NOAH TOOK OFF his jacket and then stripped to his waist. Some in the tightly packed crowd chuckled.

"Like I told ya," Little P reminded him in a thick Philly accent, a freshly lit cigarette dangling from his lips, "it don't matter this is your first time; this ain't for show." Little P tilted his head toward the crowd. "They're not only bettin' on this fight, but they expect some blood and guts. It whets the appetite for the main event, so don't disappoint, get it? And remember, there ain't no ambulances comin' if ya go down. Someone *might* dump ya at the hospital if they feel charitable. Or they might just dump ya in the river. Got that?" Noah nodded. Then the man grabbed Noah by the shoulders for a moment and flashed a crooked smile. "And if ya do good, maybe ya come back." Noah nodded once more. He took his place under the lights in the center of the bare, concrete floor to wait for his opponent.

Underground fighting, Noah had learned, was big business. And in Philadelphia, there was no shortage of tournaments to gamble on. Every spectator had favorites and money in the game. It had only taken a few days for Noah to find one such gathering that convened regularly in the bowels of a leaky warehouse in the Elmwood section of Philadelphia, a tough, drug-infested neighborhood where even police feared to tread except in dire emergency, and even then, only in numbers. It had taken several weeks to convince the "promoter," a fat man with dyed black hair and a lazy eye, ironically known only as Little P, to let him fight in an exhibition match or "try out," which was designed to vet newcomers and whip spectators into a betting frenzy for the main fight card.

A figure suddenly stepped into the light across from Noah and was immediately met with adoration from the crowd. They whistled and drunkenly shouted "Pit Bull" over and over. And his sobriquet, Noah noted, while a bit cliché, was quite appropriate. Though Pit Bull was several inches shorter, he weighed at least as much, if not more than, Noah, due mostly to his wide, muscular build that gave Noah the impression of a cinderblock. His hair was shaved close to his head, which emphasized his mangled, cauliflower ears. He stared at Noah menacingly and rubbed his hands together in a calculated display designed to intimidate him.

"Fresh meat!" he yelled out to the fans, though he always kept his eyes on Noah. "Won't be but a minute or two!"

Traditionally, the fighters stood for inspection by the crowd and waited briefly for any last bets to be cast. This was expected even in a "try out," so Noah faced the group. During the lull, fear was quickly scaling Noah's spine, and he began to seriously debate his decision to test his theory in a place that was, at least figuratively, so far from civilization. But it could be no other way. If he should fail to control the great warrior, Allard Davey, and badly hurt or even kill the man facing him, police would never know. However, if this were to happen in a legitimate bout, Noah would certainly land in prison. While this was a double-edged sword (because Noah would be risking his own life and unceremonious disposal), at least from a moral perspective, both men knew and accepted the risks.

As Little P addressed the crowd, Noah turned his eyes inward and found the hulking soldier staring back at him. Like before, as the Warrior's memories were unleashed, Noah could feel himself being thrown about and battered inside of his own mind, as if being trampled by a stampeding herd of buffalo. But this time, instead of being cast aside, Noah stood his ground.

"You will stop!" he screamed inside his head.

There followed an immediate stillness, as if he had at least gotten the Warrior's attention. Noah reasoned that Allard Davey existed to serve, conditioned from birth to take orders from his aristocrats. If Noah could convincingly play, if for only a second or two, the role of some ancient, landed nobleman, he was certain the Warrior would let him take the wheel without hesitation.

In order to conjure up the entirely unfamiliar air of courtliness he would need to pull it off, Noah imagined he was wearing a flowing robe and was seated on an elaborate throne. People were no more than supplicant dogs that begged at his feet, hanging on his every word. Noah convinced himself, if only for a fraction of second, that he was anointed by God himself.

Noah casually issued the command using his best entitled inner voice, "You will submit to me as you must."

There was a pause, and then the Warrior bowed his head and slowly offered up his sword. His image then grew obscure before finally disappearing altogether, as if it were a shadow consumed by the light of a new day.

"Ya ready?" Little P asked. Noah gave a curt nod. "Okay, kid, let's get to it then!"

By the time Noah's opponent launched the first savage punch, Noah's every nerve, every muscle, and every thought had been educated by decades of deadly fighting experience.

Right off, Pit Bull threw a wild haymaker at Noah's chin, intending to end the fight with a single strike. While powerful, Noah assessed as he watched it coming, this type of blow was also reckless because the sheer momentum of the swing would likely cause Pit Bull to be overextended and out of balance, thus vulnerable to a countermove. Just before the ham fist came in for a landing, Noah drew his head back. He could feel the wind as it narrowly missed his face. Sure enough, Pit Bull lost his footing and tumbled clumsily to the floor. Noah heard laughter from the crowd.

But he was back up more quickly than Noah had anticipated, and he caught Noah squarely in the corner of his mouth with a short right that sent Noah reeling to the ground. Blood was streaming from a long tear in his lip. He could taste the sandy grit from a broken tooth.

Noah coolly reevaluated the situation. His opponent, he now knew, was also highly trained, and much faster than his bulky build would suggest. As Noah climbed to his feet, he was already adjusting his strategy. Noah would close the distance and test his grappling skills.

When Pit Bull came again, instead of moving back, Noah shot in close, grabbed him around the torso under his arms and threw him over his right hip. Pit Bull landed hard on the concrete with Noah directly on top, straddling his body with his legs. Noah pounded his face with hammer fists and elbows until he was finally able to open a large cut on Pit Bull's forehead that split his left eyebrow in two. If he got to his feet again, the blood would run into his left eye, effectively blinding him to any blow thrown to that side of his body.

Once more, however, Noah discovered that Pit Bull was wilier than he had given him credit for. He managed to trap Noah's left arm and drag him to the floor. In that instant, the tables were turned. Pit Bull had climbed onto Noah's back and sunk in a deep choke hold with his right forearm. Using all his strength, Noah struck Pit Bull's arm with the heels of both hands, which loosened his hold just long enough for Noah to slide free. His escape was made all the easier by the viscous blood and sweat that now covered them both.

After they both stood, Pit Bull unleashed a right kick to Noah's ribs that he only managed to partially block. Noah ignored the pain and countered with a right hook that Pit Bull didn't see coming and that caught him on the temple. Though he stumbled, he did not fall. The roar from the crowd was deafening.

Pitt Bull snarled and charged forward once again. But his hands were hanging low, which meant his strength was beginning to fade. Noah slipped quickly to his right, into Pit Bull's obscured field of vision, then grabbed him and threw him violently once more over his right hip. Pit Bull hit the ground hard with a wet slap. He lay motionless, momentarily stunned and entirely defenseless. Allard Davey was screaming for a final, crushing stomp to his throat. Although Noah ordered the Warrior to stand down, he was not sure how long he could hold him off.

Just them, Pit Bull's eyes fluttered open to find Noah standing over him. He must have understood he was in big trouble, because he immediately tapped out. The crowd cheered, and somebody was holding up Noah's hand to signal victory.

Noah reached out to help Pit Bull up. The weary man grabbed hold, and Noah pulled him to his feet. To his surprise, Pitt Bull hugged him for a moment and smiled.

"You are tough," he said between breaths, "tough as hell."

Noah walked toward the door, and the stunned crowd parted to let him pass. That fat man found him. He took Noah's hand and slapped $1,000 in it.

"That ain't much," he said as he pointed to Noah's face, "but it should cover the stitches. Next time, we'll move you up the ladder, and you'll get a chance to make some real money."

Noah ignored him. He grabbed his clothes and his duffle bag and headed straight for his car.

Noah snuck quietly into the back door of his hotel. If he were spotted, dirty and bloody as he was, he would draw unwanted attention. He crept up the stairwell rather than taking the elevator. He glanced down the hall to be sure the coast was clear, then he scurried for the door to his room.

As soon as he was safely inside, the adrenaline began to subside. Noah felt the crushing weight of fatigue and throbbing pain. He tossed his bag onto the bed, stripped off his clothes, and limped into the bathroom. Noah was not entirely prepared for what he saw in the mirror. His right eye was bruised and swollen almost completely shut. A jaggedly torn lower lip hung limply at the right corner of his mouth and was still oozing blood down his chin. He also had a knot on the left side of his forehead that made it look as is if he were growing a horn. Noah reached up and gingerly prodded the rock-hard lump. Only then did he notice that his pinky finger was turned out at a ninety-degree angle and that bruises covered his torso, which could mean invisible yet serious damage to the organs underneath.

Noah could not have been more pleased.

It did not take but a sliver of a second to bring the Healer front and center. Noah steeled himself for the shockwave as Abreas spilled into his mind. Once again, Noah had to struggle to stay awake and aware as they both jostled for position in the space inside his brain that suddenly seemed so cramped and stifling. Noah could feel himself pressed tightly against Abreas, as if they were both wedged into a closet shoulder to shoulder. After a moment, Noah dared a sidelong glance. The Healer was apparently oblivious to Noah's presence. He was instead peering ahead with half-lidded eyes and a slight frown, ready to bring to bear his vast medical knowledge on any carnage he might find.

While Noah tried to think of another strange play that he could employ to trick the Healer into compliance, he noticed that Abreas appeared at the peak of his powers, as did all his other ancestors for that matter. As Noah looked on, it slowly dawned on him that Abreas could not really be inside with him, because he had long ago passed from this world. What Noah saw before him could have been no more than a symbol born from Noah's imagination to represent the entire collection of the Healer's memories, like art on an album cover. Noah did not have to scheme or beg for cooperation *because Abreas was already an integral, indivisible part of him.* The same was true for all of them, only Noah had not understood this obvious fact until that moment.

As if on cue, Abreas turned to Noah and gave a wide, almost victorious smile.

"Of course," Abreas whispered. "I *am* only through you."

Noah opened his eyes. He examined himself once more in the mirror, this time with the surety of a field-trained medical expert.

He instantly knew that his finger was not broken, only dislocated at the joint. This was easily remedied with a quick, though quite painful, tug that brought the finger back into line. Now, with two functioning hands, Noah set about assessing his battered body.

He felt gently around his right eye, prodding for any evidence of a fracture. He forced the eyelid open to get a better look at the eyeball itself. Blunt force trauma to the face and head were commonplace on the battlefield in the Healer's time, and he had tended to thousands of soldiers with similar injuries.

Noah's eyes were not bulging, and neither of them had shifted position. All these signs pointed to the lack of any badly broken or dislocated bones. He could move the eye in all directions, and he had no double vision, a good indication that there was no nerve damage. Though he was disfigured, he would heal nicely. A cool compress was all that he would need to reduce the swelling.

The lip was another story. The fat man was right. Noah would need stiches, and they would have to be small and very tightly grouped to minimize the scar. About ten or fifteen of them, Noah figured. But he would have to get back to that.

What most concerned Noah was internal bleeding. This was also a common occurrence in ancient times, and Abreas had a practiced hand in diagnosing it. If Noah had severe internal hemorrhaging, he would be in shock, vomiting, or coughing up blood, and his abdomen would likely be distended. Noah had none of those symptoms, but that did not mean he was out of danger from a slow bleed.

Noah laid down on the bed and instinctively began to poke and prod around his abdomen, searching for painful, hard pockets that might indicate where leaking blood had pooled. Aside from localized pain at the bruising sites, everything else seemed normal. Finally, he went back to the bathroom and forced out some urine, as Abreas often instructed his patients to do. Noah examined it closely. Though it had a slight pink hue, Noah was not concerned. He had taken several blows to his kidneys, and they were certainly bruised. A little blood in his urine, he knew, was fine and nothing to be worried about. He would also examine his stools when the time came to see if they were black, another obvious sign of internal bleeding. For the moment, it seemed there was no reason to visit an emergency room.

Noah turned his attention back to his torn lip. First, he filled the sink with warm tap water and stuck his face in it, gently massaging the wound to remove any foreign matter. He patted his face dry, then examined the cut closely in the mirror. The laceration extended upward from the right corner of his mouth for about three quarters of an inch, although it appeared more severe because the tension on the skin was pulling the wound wide open. The eye tooth underneath appeared to be only chipped, and no nerve was exposed.

Noah found the surgical medical kit in his duffel bag and unzipped it to examine the contents. Intuitively, as Abreas would have done, Noah found the smallest gauge curved needle, which, far different from the Healer's age, came pre-threaded. Noah returned to the mirror and immediately set to work. He maneuvered the forceps in one hand, and with the other, he threaded one stitch at the widest part of the cut so as to properly align the edges of the lip. He took a moment to register the eye-watering pain and decided he could bear it. Then, beginning on the inside of his mouth and working around to front, Noah sewed nineteen tiny stitches with almost mechanical precision, each placed about three millimeters part. The wound was perfectly closed.

Noah dropped the instruments in the sink and washed down four Advil with a swig of Wild Turkey. He laid back on the bed and folded his arms behind his head until the drugs and booze took effect. Once the pain was dulled, he found he could barely keep his eyes open. Though he was completely drained, he found strength enough to lament that he had still not found a way to test his ability to control the Leader, who was likely the most important and most powerful force at his command. He suddenly felt another pang of urgency, as if there were not enough time to prepare himself. But what did he fear, he thought, what was coming? The Rolodex still had no answer.

Noah yawned. It would have to wait until tomorrow, he decided. He needed a few hours of shut eye; there was time enough for that at least. He found the remote for the television and began scrolling through the channels. He stopped on a program called "The People's Press" only because he just could not summon the effort to hit the buttons any longer. J. T. James, the animated host, hawked survival gear and vitamins in between segments. Noah's arms soon dropped to the bed at his side, and he closed his eyes.

Just before a commercial break, the host dramatically teased the lead story of the night to keep his viewers tuned in. On some level of Noah's awareness, an alarm bell sounded. One of his many informants pled with him to pay attention. But Noah was already falling fast away into darkness, where words and warnings were nothing but hissing static.

Chapter 45

A S SOON AS he was clear, a seething J. T. James stormed off set in search of his producer. He soon found him at his desk rifling through some papers.

"What was that, Bill? You know I'm as good on the fly as anyone, but you should at least warn me *before* I see an entirely new script on the teleprompter."

William Jewell looked up sheepishly and removed his reading glasses. "I know, I know. But things just came together now, and this is too important to put off to another day. Besides, I knew you could handle the change up."

"And what is this story? People are disappearing all around the country? What does that mean? You know I like to shock the audience with a juicy story, but this sounds farfetched, even for us! We're already dealing with two lawsuits. You know how close the company is watching us! Why would you do this now?"

"I have it all here," the producer said excitedly as he stapled a packet of papers together. "I mean this is legit, J. T.; I did my due diligence on this and then some! I have been working on it quietly for almost a week." He stood up and walked over to his infamous television host, who immediately snatched the papers out of his hand and began to read.

"It seems you have a hardcore fan at the CDC," the producer began. "He agreed to be a confidential source. I know his name, but no one else here does. I checked his credentials and he does in fact work there in the public relations office. Anyway, this guy sent us some very interesting internal memos that have been going around his office. It seems that the CDC has been following a serious uptick in reports of EMF sensitivity."

J. T. Jones looked up with a puzzled expression. "What the hell is that?"

"Well," William Jewell explained, "it's like being allergic to electronic devices, or rather being allergic to the invisible electromagnetic waves that are generated by things like cell phones, computers, and virtually anything else that uses electricity."

"I've never heard of it."

"Neither did I, at least until I read the memos. But it is apparently something that has been studied at the CDC for a long time, almost twenty years now. It seems that some people are sensitive to this stuff, which means that it actually makes them sick. It gives them terrible headaches, nausea, that sort of thing. Some people in the CDC think it may even cause cancer and other more serious illnesses, although no one has ever proven it. Anyway, people have been complaining about this stuff a lot more lately. Quite literally, cases are up almost *four hundred* percent over the past three years. Although no one gave a total number of cases, I saw the words 'exponential increase' mentioned several times in the memos."

J. T. threw up his arms incredulously. "C'mon Bill. Some people feel bad when they use their cell phones? So what? You better get to the part about people missing, cause otherwise this story is about exciting as watching grass grow."

Bill Jewell shot him an annoyed look. "Somehow," he continued, "the CDC got word that there has been a corresponding increase in missing persons reports filed over the past three years as well, and those are also up exponentially."

J. T. folded his arms. "Now I'm listening."

"Again, actual numbers, even for the CDC, are hard to come by, due mostly to the fact that these missing persons reports don't get filed at a national level. A lot of the time, state and local police just bury their reports in a cabinet, because either the cops don't know about the national database or they have more pressing problems and simply don't have the time. Still, based on the work they have done, the CDC estimates that the number of people reported missing across the country has ballooned from 100,000 just three years ago to almost 500,000 today. And, get this, they believe that is a conservative estimate."

J. T.'s eyes widened. "Are you kidding me? At least half a million people gone and nothing but crickets in the news? Wait, . . . why isn't this story everywhere?" he asked suspiciously.

William Jewell smiled. "Because we got it first!" Then he shrugged. "And because maybe it just has not hit critical mass yet. But, hold on; it gets even better. The CDC has a working theory that the staggering amount of people who have gone missing recently are made up mostly of the same people who have been complaining about EMF sensitivity. In other words, these people who say that their phones and whatever else are making them sick are disappearing. Whether that means these people are killing themselves or running off or simply vanishing altogether, no one seems to want to guess."

"Christ, Bill, we have to have some of our consultants take a look at this! None of our usual crackpots this time—we need legitimate people!"

"I'm way ahead of you. I've been back and forth with a high-powered shrink at UCLA medical center. He's a Harvard-educated MD and psychologist, and he might be the foremost expert in the world on this EMF sensitivity stuff. Interestingly, the CDC has not been in touch with him, likely because they are trying to avoid panic, at least until they have more information. So, when I floated all this to him, it blew his mind."

Bill Jewell snatched the packet back from his flabbergasted host. He retrieved his glasses and flipped through the pages. "Here it is. . . . This guy says the CDC is on the right track, but they have only part of the answer. He believes that EMF sensitivity is just the tip of the iceberg, that it is the physical symptom of a much deeper psychological condition. The real problem, according to him, is that our society is beginning to experience a monumental paradigm shift."

J. T. stared at the ceiling and sighed. "Again, I have to ask, what the hell is that?"

"Don't worry, I asked him the same thing, and I wrote it all down." He cleared his throat and began to read. "It means to fundamentally change the way one sees and perceives the world. For example, at one time in history, humankind saw the world through a religious lens. This meant that we explained all events as a consequence of faith, or lack of it, in a divine power. If we didn't pray, God punished us. If we did, and did it in the right way, God rewarded us. Then came the rise of science, which gave us rational explanations for natural events. We began to see the world as something we could control and bend to serve our will." The producer looked at J. T. over the top of his glasses. "These most recent events, the shrink told me, might be the result of yet another shift in world view.

"The psychologist said that this paradigm shift, if it existed, was almost certainly an equal and opposite reaction to the stressors of modern life; like a stretched rubber band snapping back into its original shape. In this process, there would first be an overcorrection before a natural equilibrium was eventually achieved. He believed that the current trend was, in fact, that overcorrection. And it would get worse before it got better."

Bill began reading once more. "In only about one hundred and fifty years, which represents but a fraction of a second in the existence of our species, humans moved from a mostly rural, agrarian economy and lifestyle into the age of information and virtual reality. And while we are the smartest, most adaptable animal ever to exist on this planet, the exponential growth of technology that we perpetuated is outpacing our ability to cope, and we thus find ourselves even more alienated from the world around us than ever before."

Bill paused to let it sink in. "The doctor gave me a great example of that, too. He said not long ago he watched a video of man texting and walking along a sidewalk, so oblivious to his surroundings that he failed to notice a grizzly bear eating from a garbage can directly in front of him. It was not until he literally stumbled over the bear that he knew it was there. He thought it was pretty funny, but he believed the incident had a more significant meaning: We are out of balance and are at odds with our very nature.

"But here is the best part," he said as he returned to the papers. "And I quote, 'With the advent of cell phones and the internet, we spend our lives in front of screens trying to process massive amounts of mostly irrelevant information that prevents us from knowing any real peace. It is not inconceivable that people might begin to internalize the crisis, which manifests in the form of a severe EMF sensitivity. This is particularly troubling because it means that a person with this condition has a negative physical and emotional reaction not only to cell phones or computers, but virtually anything that runs on electricity. Unfortunately, this means the population could very quickly shift in one of the greatest migrations in human history. People might feel compelled to pack up and relocate to any place where the electronic human footprint is non-existent or at least substantially diminished.'"

"So let me get this straight," J. T. said. "People freak out, so they take a good old-fashioned vacation in the great outdoors. How long are they gone, how long until the 'rubber band' snaps back into place and they come home?"

"I asked the shrink about that, too. He said he doesn't know because something like this has never happened before. It could be a week, it could be a few years, or it could be never."

J. T. sat down on the edge of the desk and rubbed his eyes. "Wow. And when we break this story, then what? The stock market doesn't like this kind of thing."

"Yeah," Bill Jewell conceded. "I thought of that, and I agree. And there's more bad news, I'm afraid."

J. T. looked up. "Well?"

"I still have a contact at FEMA who was willing to talk to me on condition of anonymity. She said that while they have never created a disaster scenario to fit this, they ran the numbers on what they call a 'mass casualty event,' which gives us at least some idea about what might happen here." He took a deep breath. "My contact says that if thirty to forty percent of the population were taken out of circulation, the first thing that would happen, which you already know, is that the financial markets would collapse. This, of course, could lead to widespread panic and a rush on banks and other financial institutions. And we know where that goes, because that *has* happened before. But, of course, that's not the end of it.

"Federal, state, and local governments would have difficulty delivering services for lack of sufficient personnel. It would be the same with private businesses, which would experience supply and logistic interruptions because they would not have enough people to make the goods, drive the trucks, or work in the stores. And even if they did, because their stock had collapsed, they would not be able to pay their employees, who would, obviously, then walk off the job. All this would mean a decreased presence of authority and even a critical shortage of services, food, fuel, and most products that we take for granted."

"So why are we doing this, Bill? Why don't we just put this story back under the rock where we found it? We report the story, we start the panic, and the rest takes care of itself—a sort of self-fulfilling prophecy!"

Bill handed the papers back to J. T. "C'mon, J. T. You've seen the numbers. Outside of the lawyers, I'm not sure anyone is even paying attention anymore! You want to get back in the spotlight, right? You want to be a real journalist again, don't you? Anyway, if we don't break the story, somebody else will! So, are you ready?"

J. T nodded and stood up. He smoothed out his jacket and straightened his tie.

Bill Jewell checked his watch. "You're on in five."

Chapter 46

As Noah sipped coffee and gazed out on the busy street framed in the café window, his very general, uneasy feeling that something terrible was going to happen continued to sharpen to a fine point of certainty that something terrible was happening *right now.* But for the life of him, he could not figure out what it was.

He had been frantically draining the memories of anyone in the Rolodex who he thought could possibly give him any insight. All they could do was sound the sirens. Whatever the monster was that had descended on the land, it was silent and unseen. It was also likely unprecedented, at least from the point of view of his predecessors.

In his search for clues, Noah decided to turn his attention to the living, which is why he decided to observe and report from the lower east side of Manhattan for the past week. He took up his post every morning in a popular coffee shop at a rickety table by the front door where he could see and inspect everyone who walked in or who just happened to walk by. What better place could he find to assess the well-being of the masses?

Noah's long-held belief that society as a whole was critically stressed was quickly confirmed within the first few moments of his surveillance. Tired and stifled people rushed about, skipping all the pleasantries because there was simply not enough time before they had to chase the dollar in a glass bubble where the elements outside were nothing more than an inconvenience. Still, this was not exactly news. Yet the world was in its death throes. Noah could feel it in his bones. Why couldn't he see it?

Things started to make sense once Noah stopped watching and started to *listen.*

After the morning rush, the coffee shop was briefly desolate and quiet. One of the baristas stepped out to smoke a cigarette while the other took the opportunity to sweep the floors and restock shelves.

Noah was about to get up to use the bathroom when two women walked in. One seemed particularly upset. Her eyes were red, as if she had been crying, and she was wearing a long overcoat that could not quite conceal her pajamas. The other was clad in business attire: high heels, a blue dress, and a matching short jacket. Likely, she was on her way to work when she got a frantic call from a friend in need. They took a table in the back.

Noah settled into his chair once more and leaned his head back in the direction of the women so he could better hear them. He did his best to make himself invisible by pretending to casually scroll through text messages on his cell phone while they spoke.

"I'm sorry," the one in pajamas whispered between sniffles. "I just didn't know who else to call."

"I don't understand this, Kate," the other said in a low voice. "What did the police say?"

"Not much really, except that it was none of their business. But how could it not be? My husband is missing. Isn't that what they do?"

"What did you tell them?"

Kate sounded frustrated. "The same thing I told you on the phone: that he disappeared and that I haven't heard anything from him for almost two days!"

"But it's not as if he vanished, Kate," she said gently. "You said you spoke with him before he left."

"Spoke at him, you mean. I did all the talking. He mostly refused to even look at me." Kate coughed several times and blew her nose. Her voice began to rise. "I got so pissed off. I even smacked him across the face, just to get *something* from him."

"And?"

"And he looked at me like I was a complete stranger. There was no recognition that I'm his wife or that I shared a bed with him for the past four years! I mean, his eyes were just dead!"

The other woman put her finger to her lips to warn Kate that she was being too loud. "But it's not like you weren't having problems before," she said quietly. "You told me a couple of months ago that something wasn't right."

"I did not mean with our marriage. He was sick, that's what I said! He was complaining about how bad he felt, with the migraines and the buzzing in his ears, whatever that means. The doctors couldn't find anything anyway. I was starting to think it was all in his head. Any why not? He was working all the time, stressed out all the time." Kate leaned forward and threw up her hands. "Then it just stopped. Period. Two days ago, he stopped complaining. Actually, he stopped talking at all. I came home, and he had packed two bags full of his stuff. Like I said, I yelled at him, hit him, and then he was gone. Not a word about where he was going." Kate hung her head on the table and cried.

"Have you called him since he left? Have you called his parents, his friends? He has to have crashed somewhere."

Kate nodded. "I called everyone that I know. Nothing. He has not turned up anywhere, even at work. And I can't call him because he left his cell phone, his laptop, and his tablet sitting on the bed, almost as if to make a point. There is no way I can get in touch with him."

"Did you tell the police all this? Are you sure you told them everything? They could put out an APB, or whatever it's called. What did they say?"

Kate shook her head. "They told me they don't have time to chase down family members if they want to leave. No foul play they said, so no crime. Family squabbles are not their business. Come to think of it, the guy on the phone was rude, too, as if he were tired of hearing it all the time, as if I had not been the only one who reported something like this...."

Noah suddenly sat up. *You fool!* the voices seemed to say to Noah from the deep. *Don't you see? It's been happening right under your very nose!* Noah got up and slipped out the door unnoticed.

Chapter 47

NOAH SAT IN his car, waiting in the dark. He thought back, as he often did, to that day when he had set out to diagnose the world's fatal disease. It was similar to cancer, he had finally decided as he reclined his seat—each disillusioned person was a cell in civilized society gone rogue. It worked itself so subtly into healthy tissue that nobody knew what was happening until the damage was already done.

In fact, a couple of weeks ago, if you had stood in downtown Philadelphia or Chicago or a dozen other cities in the middle of the day, as Noah had done since he left New York, you would not be able to tell that anything unusual at all was happening. But this had been only the appearance of normalcy, Noah discovered, and it belied a quiet, desperate struggle, which became apparent if you started digging just a bit.

Under the guise of researching a novel, Noah began accessing police reports in various places of people gone missing over the past ten years. He found, incredibly, that most of them were filed in the last three years. The facts surrounding the vast majority of these cases were generally the same: people intentionally abandoning their families. Why it did not draw national attention until now was unclear. Noah suspected it was due to the fact that police were naturally hesitant to follow up on matters that did not involve any crime. As sad as each missing persons case was, they were simply not matters for the authorities, especially when there were so many crimes that required police attention.

Perhaps it was also because many people, who realized that the government would not help them, had taken it upon themselves to try and find their loved ones. Or maybe they were embarrassed for others to know and had kept it to themselves. Whatever the reason, it burst suddenly onto the scene as if it had reached an invisible tipping point. Now, it captivated the nation and the world.

Noah turned on the radio and scrolled through the stations until he found the first clear voice. The general consensus from news outlets these days was the same: people were disappearing without a trace in ever-increasing numbers all over the world. That is not to say they were dying or had vanished, as in some magic act, but they had quite literally walked away from everything, never to be heard from again.

As more facts came in, the female voice on the radio said, it seemed that the affected people had been carefully planning their exits in advance. Families had found clues: missing money used to buy survival supplies, cleaned out desks, and cryptic web posts that set meeting places, routes, and possible destinations for others to follow. And there was another common theme: curiously, none of them took anything electronic with them. Computers, cell phones, tablets—they were all left or locked in drawers or tossed into the garbage; they were cruel reminders that wherever the missing went, they had no intention of being found, even by those closest to them.

Whatever escape paths these refugees chose, they were careful to remain hidden. They were likely traveling alone or in groups at night, taking painstaking precautions to keep out of view. Noah remembered the woman with the trailer and her children with the colorful backpacks. What an idiot he had been, he chided himself. He was too wrapped up in himself to see. It was right there, and he had missed it.

Unfortunately, the radio voice reported, any hope for loved ones that the intense coverage the issue received in the press might prompt a mobilization of government resources to get to the bottom of it would not be realized in the near future. Instead of engaging state and local governments to find a solution, the Feds had precious little to say about it. It made sense, Noah considered. There was no loss of life and no property damage; what could the government do? Moreover, the reporter reminded her listeners, citizens had a constitutional right to move unfettered across state borders.

How many people were gone? No one knew for sure, the reporter said. There was so much empty air when it came to specifics. Some had taken off, and some had set out to find them. In her personal experience, the voice offered, most people she met knew at least a handful of others who, for lack of a better explanation, they did not see anymore. What were the figures? Nobody knew for certain, she said.

Where they were going, however, had recently become clearer. They were heading away from population centers, which meant that they were mostly walking inland from the coasts to rural areas where there was little or no access to electricity or utilities. Still, it could not be determined if they had a particular destination in mind. If, however, they intended to take up residence in harsh, empty places, what would they do for shelter, food, and medical care? We would just have to wait and see, she said. And if they did not come back, at least any time soon, what then?

The cause for the "mass exodus," as the reporter put it, was by far the deepest mystery, and yet, it was the most important question to answer. If we knew why this was happening, she said, then we could likely fix it before the damage was irreparable. Although it was too soon for science to offer any concrete explanations, a theory was beginning to emerge: a form of mass hysteria. But there was no shortage of crazy explanations floating around, which ran the gamut from the Rapture to an alien invasion. Every day, news outlets across the nation were inundated with calls from people, some well-meaning and some not, in support of various explanations. Then, with biting sarcasm, the radio voice mentioned that an unnamed, yet controversial conservative newscast host was clamoring that he had predicted the crisis six months ago, yet nobody had listened. The woman was quick to note that this same host would probably sell you his own mother if the price was right. Nevertheless, she reluctantly acknowledged, maybe he had stumbled onto something.

Noah turned the volume down and craned his neck to scan for movement outside. Still nothing. He leaned back in his seat and suddenly caught his breath. He had almost forgotten for a moment that he was no longer just an objective observer, and that his own family had become casualties of the crisis.

Noah's parents were, at least for the moment, out of reach. Just as the bad news broke, they had left for a bucket-list European vacation that ended in Russia with a cruise down the Volga. They were supposed to be home soon, but, last he talked to them, over a crackling cell phone connection a few days before, they were stuck in Moscow. Russia, like some other nations, was on lockdown until the government got a handle on the emergency. Though his parents said they were safe, Noah's thoughts ran wild. He imagined broken-down planes sitting on broken-down runways for lack of pilots or technicians, and he thought about his aging parents being huddled near a barrel fire begging for food. Still, he had no choice but to shake it off and hope for the best, because even Noah's outrageous abilities did not permit him to walk across the sea to rescue them.

Chapter 48

A PAIR OF HEADLIGHTS pierced the gray distance. Noah sat up and squinted for a better view. A car was moving slowly toward him. Noah was backed just off the road down a dirt lane, so he turned the key and flicked the high beams to be sure he was noticed. A few moments later, the other car turned off the road and stopped next to him, pointed in the opposite direction.

When the dust settled, and Noah finally got a good look, he became alarmed. He realized the car was a blacked-out Mustang GT with a throaty, menacing exhaust sound, certainly not the ubiquitous four-door sedan he had expected.

In his travels, Noah had heard rumors about roving bands of criminals searching for abandoned homes to loot, especially in rural areas like the one where Noah found himself at that moment, where police coverage was already stretched too thin. Some even said they had taken to blocking the roads in places and demanding a "toll" to pass.

The Mustang's heavily tinted window retracted slowly. Noah pulled a pistol out from beneath his seat and rested it on his lap. He held his breath.

"You should see the look on your face," Rick Hallman said, quietly laughing. "So, what do you think?"

Noah shook his head and threw up his arms. "Jesus Christ, Rick! You should have warned me you were driving something new, especially something like that. I can't even see into it. You know how things are now. I didn't know what to think!"

Rick suddenly looked chastened. "Yeah, ... maybe it was a bit much," he admitted. "I'm sorry, kid. I know it sounds strange, but I finally feel like things are getting back to normal, at least for me."

"Come in here and talk, Rick, I want to make sure we don't miss anything."

A moment later, Rick climbed into the passenger's seat of Noah's car. They both gazed into the night.

"What do you mean things are getting back to normal for you? How can that be when everything else is so fucked up?"

"My kids, Noah. I finally got my kids back. They know now that I had nothing to do with my wife leaving. It's plain as day: she took off with the rest. They are going to move home with me soon. We will look for her together."

"Well, this is as good a place as any to start," Noah said. "That's why I called you." He glanced at his watch. It was a little after three a.m. "We still have some time though, I think. If they're moving as slowly as the guy said, they probably won't get here until just after dawn."

"Good," Rick said. "So, you can fill in the details for me while we wait."

Noah folded his arms across his chest while he explained. "Yesterday, I was heading home from the city, and I stopped at a gas station off 95, near Ironton. I went inside to grab a cup of coffee, and I heard a mailman telling somebody that there was a group of them, he said fifty or so, heading west on 522. He said they weren't hiding but were walking in broad daylight and stopping at night. I checked the map, and 522 runs right into Pennsylvania, where we are now. If they camped last night, that means they will start again today, and they will pass right by here."

"That's weird," Rick said, "because everyone on the news says the opposite; that they move around after dark and hide during the day, just a few at a time. That's why they are so hard to find."

Noah nodded. "I know, I know. But maybe they don't care anymore. Things are getting so bad, maybe they know nobody will mess with them now."

"Speaking of things getting bad," Rick interjected, "have you had any problems getting gas or anything else?"

"Well, the grocery stores are starting to look a little bare; supply problems, they said. That makes sense I guess: people don't show up for work, so everything slows down. But gas—I have not had a problem getting it, but paying for it, yeah. Most places will take only cash. I don't know what that's about."

Rick shrugged. "Neither do I, but I can tell you that a lot of places, at least back toward home, don't even have gas. I went to four places before I found some. And when I did, I had to wait in line for almost an hour to fill up. That's when I regretted getting this car. It guzzles fuel."

Noah turned toward Rick. "Now that you mention it, what's the story with that? Are you having a midlife crisis or something? You picked a hell of time to regress."

Rick let out a waggish chuckle. "What can I say? I always wanted one. But with a wife and kids and bills, I just never had the money before."

"And you do now? Now that you retired, I mean? Aren't you on a fixed income or something?"

Rick seemed deflated. "Well, that's if I actually get my checks. They said due to the wild market fluctuations, there could be income 'interruptions.' Besides, the car doesn't technically belong to me. I guess you could say I borrowed it."

"You mean you stole it, didn't you?"

"C'mon Noah. These people, they left their cars behind for whatever reason. If you look, you can find them. Just pick one you like and keep an eye on it for a few days. If no one comes, you can assume it belonged to the ones that took off. If they don't want them anymore, why can't I put at least one of them to good use? This one here, the guy left the keys right on the front seat, almost as if he was asking a person to take it off his hands. What do you care anyway? It's like you're on the Titanic, and it's going down, and you're still worried about whether you're properly dressed for dinner."

Noah sighed and rubbed his temples. "I just feel like if we stop caring about this stuff anymore, then we won't ever be able to get back to where we were; we'll be too far gone to ever get home again."

Rick thought for a moment and then nodded with approval. "You're right, you know. There is certainly some truth in that. But how is it that you are the one saying it? Shouldn't I be telling you that, kid? By what strange turn of events have you suddenly become the old soul here? I feel pretty bad now, that's for sure. I'll tell you what. When we part ways here, I will take the car back and drop it off where I found it, okay?"

Noah yawned. He just then remembered he had not slept in more than twenty-four hours. "We'll call it even if you let me catch a little sleep," he said with a smile. "But you have to keep watch and wake me up when you see something, *anything*. You got it?"

"As long as I don't have to be shamed by the likes of you anymore, consider it done."

Almost instantly, Noah drifted off.

Chapter 49

A HARD SHOVE BROUGHT Noah abruptly back to consciousness. "Hop to it, kid! C'mon, it's time to get up! You were right; they're headed our way!"

Noah jumped so hard he hit his head on the roof of the car. He looked over at Rick, who was staring, transfixed, through the windshield. Noah followed his astonished gaze. In the purple half-light of dawn, Noah could make out solemn-looking figures emerging from the distance.

After what seemed like an eternity, they finally began to filter by slowly, in no apparent hurry. Many of them were pulling trailers or pushing make-shift carts or wheelbarrows that were piled high with food and clothes. Some were riding bicycles. A bleary-eyed child was sitting on his father's shoulders, likely just roused from sleep.

They were young and old, black and white, and every color in between. They rarely seemed to speak out loud. Instead, they mostly exchanged what Noah could only describe as knowing glances, as if everyone was on the same page and there was no need to say anything more.

Other than the fact that the group seemed to collectively slow to wait for stragglers, Noah could not discern any leader or hierarchy, let alone their purpose, with the exception that they seemed to have brought everything they might need for an extended stay outdoors. There was something about them, about their quiet familiarity, which suggested they knew exactly what they were doing and where they were going.

After the last of them passed by, Noah finally found his voice again.

"Could you see well enough, Rick? Was your wife there?"

Rick lowered his head in an expression of defeat and stared at the floor. "No, . . . she's not there. What were the chances of that anyway, right? It's been a while; she probably got to where she was going by now, wherever that is."

Noah quietly opened his door and stepped out of the car.

"What are you doing?" Rick demanded, struggling to keep his voice low.

Noah leaned his head into the car. "I'm going to try and talk to them," he whispered.

Rick pointed at Noah. "If you're trying to be quiet, then you have the same scary feeling I do about them; they are not to be messed with! Whatever you do, do not get them riled up."

Noah nodded, then turned and walked to the road. They had their backs to him, still giving no indication they were aware of his presence. He felt his heart pounding. So why should he be afraid? They seemed peaceful enough.

But Rick was right. The harsh chorus of warnings sounded by his dead relatives at that moment told him so. They had seen refugees on the move before. They knew how quickly they could turn violent if you blocked their path. But what were they fleeing from, and where were they going? Noah still could not fathom a reason people might abandon civilization for the wilderness, especially on the cusp of winter. He decided he would risk their wrath to get some answers.

"Wait," he said softly, trying not to startle anyone. No response. Perhaps they did not hear him or were ignoring him altogether. He edged a little closer to the group, being sure not to get too far from the car, in case he had to bolt. "Wait!" he said again, this time in a loud, commanding voice. A woman looked back and put her finger to her lips. She was perhaps in her late forties, dressed in a long wool overcoat and carrying a backpack. She hurried back toward Noah while the rest pressed on.

"Shut up, you fool!" she hissed through clenched teeth. "Just leave them be if you know what's good for you."

Noah stared at her in disbelief for a moment. "What's happening?" he finally asked.

"They won't talk to you," the woman said flatly. "You're one of *them*. So, you can forget about that. I should know. I'm one of *them* too. Even my own family hasn't said more than two words to me for the past three days. It's like they don't even know I'm here."

Noah shook his head. "I don't get it."

The woman shrugged her shoulders. "I got up one morning and found my husband and my two daughters packing, like they were going camping or something. They had already turned the power off and had thrown all the cell phones into a toilet. When I asked them what they were doing, my husband said that they had to go, that they had to get away until their heads weren't foggy anymore, whatever that means. I swear, they were like zombies. I said, 'What about work? What about school?' But they blew me off. Then I heard the news. This is going on everywhere."

"So, you're just walking? Walking where? You've got to get help, do something!"

"I'm doing the only thing I can. I'm going wherever they're going. If they know where that is, they haven't told me. I get the sense they'll know when they get there. You tell me then. What else am I supposed to do? I mean, this is my *family*, some of my neighbors, too. If I'm not with them, then where am I? There are others like me and you here, with their own families. We've been talking, and we're hoping that once we get far enough away, this will all sort itself out, and we can come back home before it's too late.

"Besides," the woman warned, "I heard people say something about looting, which seems right to me. Empty houses full of valuable stuff: that invites all kinds of trouble. Not enough cops to deal with all that, the way I see it. That's why I was afraid to wait it out at home. At least here, there's safety in numbers, and I can keep an eye on them. The ones that stayed behind, it's them I'm worried about now. I hope they make it."

The woman glanced over her shoulder. Her group was almost out of sight, around a bend in the road.

The woman exhaled slowly, leaned forward, and put her hands on her knees, as if suddenly exhausted. "I've got to catch up," she said, trying to convince herself. "I've got no choice. I'm just not used to so much walking." Then she stood up and pointed at Noah's car in the brush. "And don't start that *thing* up until we're a good distance away. You might get torn apart. It makes a noise, something you and I can't hear, but it drives them crazy. That's why there's no phones, radios, or anything else electronic. It makes them crazy . . . and angry."

"I still don't understand. What are they running from?"

"Everything," she said.

"But why? Because of a noise? That doesn't make any sense."

The woman threw up her arms. "Who knows? There's a lot of stuff on the news. Take your pick. As far as I know, the experts can't do any better. All I can say is that I think they're sick. I think they're sick of it all, and they want to start again fresh. It doesn't make any sense, I know, but that's the best I've got. I can only hope they get it out of their system soon."

Noah opened his mouth to speak once more, but the woman was already walking away down the road. She looked back toward Noah for a moment. "I'm sorry, but I've got to catch up, because they sure won't wait for me. Just worry about your own family, that's all you can do."

Noah numbly walked back to the car and slid into the drivers' seat. He glanced over at Rick to tell him what had happened, but he was nodding to indicate that he had heard everything already.

Noah thought back to what the woman had said. *Family.* That word stabbed Noah's heart like a spear. He fumbled through his pockets for his cell phone. It was turned off. He cursed under his breath while he waited for it to power up. Still no message. Noah tried his parents' number, but the call failed. Finally, on the fourth try, it went right to voicemail. He tossed the phone onto the dashboard.

"Any word from them?"

Noah let out a long breath and shook his head. "I guess I shouldn't be surprised. The coverage has gone spotty. Maybe, like me, they're trying, but they just can't get through."

"So, what's next for you then?"

That is the question. What do I do now? He had no real answer, no plan, nothing on his to-do list. He suddenly felt more lost and hopeless than ever before. Then it occurred to him that the least he could do was get to his parents' house. He could circle the wagons there and keep an eye on their stuff until he figured out what to do next.

"I think right now I should pick up supplies, go to my parents' place, and hole up for a while." Noah shrugged. "Not much else I can do. What about you?"

"Back home to wait for my kids. We'll come up with a plan, a way to find my wife, I guess."

"I wish you luck, my friend," Noah said sincerely. "I really do. And if you need something, let me know. Other than that, I'll keep in touch when I can."

"Same here," Rick said as he opened the door and climbed out of the car.

Chapter 50

THOUGH HE CHANCED getting mired in rush-hour traffic, Noah decided to head straight through Philadelphia to get to his parents' house because it cut twenty miles off the trip. As he got closer to the city on I-95, it appeared his gamble would pay off, as there were fewer cars than usual. At one point, two ambulances followed by a state police car passed him with lights and sirens on, rushing toward the looming skyline. Noah rolled down the window. It was not long before he caught the scent of acrid smoke, and he could just make out a gray haze hovering over the city center. The alarm bells started clanging in his head. Noah found his cell phone and tried Rick to find out if he knew anything, but the call kept dropping. Noah made an abrupt U-turn at an emergency cut through and got off at the last exit he had passed.

He was soon on a two-lane road that meandered lazily through farmsteads and patches of forest. Realizing that he had no idea where he was, Noah pulled over so he could work out a new route. He did not bother with his phone this time, but he grabbed a map he kept in the glove compartment, which he then spread out on the hood of his car.

Noah glanced around while he got his bearings, then he pored over the map. It was clear that he was on Route 60, headed north around the city. After about thirty miles, it looked as if he could pick up Route 512 East again, which he knew eventually ran near the house. While this circuitous route took him about an hour or so out of his way on back roads, if there was trouble downtown, it seemed less risky.

Once back in the warm, sunbathed car, Noah felt profoundly tired, to the point where he knew that all he had to do was lean his head back, and he would drift off. That seemed to be the way of things for him now, to find sleep in short bursts whenever he felt it coming on, be it day or night. Perhaps his body knew better than he did when it was safe to nod off. Perhaps his ancestors took watch when Noah could not.

8—ᴛ

Noah stirred slowly then glanced at his watch for a long moment until his eyes could focus. *Wow!* It would be dark in a couple of hours, he realized with a pang of urgency. Something told him to get as close to his destination as he could before that happened. A moment later, he got back on the road and hit the gas hard to try and make up some time.

A short time later, Noah approached a stop sign at a crossroads, where a rusty pickup truck was parked off to the side of the road in the stubble of a cornfield. At first, Noah thought the truck was abandoned or broken-down, but as he got within a few feet of the stop sign, the doors of the truck were suddenly flung open, and two male figures emerged. One of them was shouldering an assault-type rifle, and the other had a handgun holstered at his hip. Noah immediately retrieved his own pistol from under his seat and let it rest in his lap.

Noah thought about whipping the car around and taking off back the way he came, but he seriously doubted he could get out of range of a high-powered, high-capacity rifle quickly enough to avoid having his car, and likely his own body, shot full of holes. Besides, if they were intent on killing him, Noah concluded, they could have taken him out already, likely before he had even suspected any danger.

Noah inched his way forward until the one with rifle stepped out into the road and blocked his path. The other man remained partially concealed on the far side of the truck, where he would have cover in case things went sideways. No doubt his gun was drawn and at the low ready.

After Noah was forced to halt, the man with the rifle walked casually around to Noah's side of the car and motioned for him to roll down his window. At the same time, Noah slowly tucked the pistol under his right butt cheek, where it was hidden but easily accessible in case he needed it.

Noah hit the button. As the window descended, the man slid the rifle off his shoulder and held it across his body. He was wearing a faded T-shirt and jeans. A pack of cigarettes was stuffed in the shirt pocket on his chest. The deep wrinkles in the man's scruffy, sun-worn face suggested he was in his early sixties. Yet, he had the lean and chiseled physique of a much younger man. Given the circumstances, Noah thought it likely that he was a local farmer who had been kept unnaturally fit by hard physical labor.

"Pardon us," the man said as he leaned over and looked around the inside of Noah's car, "but these are strange times." Then he stepped back. "By authority of the Glannon Sheriff's Department," he said, as if reciting from a form, "you must state your business here."

Noah stared at the man curiously. "You sure don't look like a cop. Aren't you supposed to be in uniform?"

The man shrugged. "Like I said, these are strange times. But since you asked, the ones like me, who've been in the forces, we've been deputized by the sheriff on account of the fact there are not enough cops to go around. Not enough badges either, so you'll just have to take my word for it."

Noah nodded. "Fine. As far as what I'm doing here, I'm just trying to get home."

"And where's that?"

"Hamden."

"You armed?"

Noah swallowed hard then lied. "No."

"Why not?"

Noah stared quizzically at the man once more.

"We've had some problems. People coming out here from the city and running cars off the road and breakin' into houses. They don't seem to care now whether someone's home or not. They think we're easy prey. But you tend to know who they are right off. They shoot first and ask questions later. So, you should have a gun, too, just in case."

Noah nodded silently. After a moment he asked, "So, where did all the cops go?"

"Some took off with the rest of them. A lot of the others got called out to help in the city. First it was looters, now its food and gas riots. We always took care of our own, more or less, so it just seemed natural for the sheriff to give us the order."

"What about the people leaving? Have you seen some of them?"

"Not at first, but now we see them all the time." The man shrugged. "Maybe that's because there's a lot of them lately. They don't bother anyone though, so nobody bothers with them. Even the punks stay away from them, on account of there being so many. You don't poke the sleeping bear, right?"

Noah heard the crackle of a two-way radio. The man reached into his back pocket to retrieve it, then turned and walked away while he spoke out of earshot. After a brief conversation, he made his way back to Noah's car.

"We've got some other problems to deal with, so I won't keep you no more. You seem like a nice enough fella, so I say you're good to go. If you get stopped again before you get to Hamden, give them my name: Bob Attenbach. Tell them I vouch for you. But beyond that, I can't help you. So, you gotta pay attention; you got it?"

"Got it," Noah said as he put the car in gear. He headed straight through the intersection as the two men jumped in the pickup truck and sped off in the opposite direction.

Chapter 51

AS THE LANDSCAPE began to wash out in the last of the day's light, Noah strained to see into the ever-shrinking distance. He thought he should just about be on top of it by now, and he began to wonder if he had made a wrong turn somewhere. Finally, as he rounded an uphill curve, the sign for Route 512/Hamden suddenly materialized.

"Now we're in business," Noah said to himself as he let out a pent-up breath.

He allowed himself to relax and to not constantly imagine that he was in someone's crosshairs. After all, he was in familiar surroundings once more. Only five or six more miles, and he would be there, right on schedule.

However, no sooner had Noah put his attention back to the road than he found his way blocked by several downed tree limbs. He hit the brakes and came to a screeching halt with only a few feet to spare. Then, out of the corner of his eye, Noah caught movement in his rear-view mirror. He turned his head just in time to see a car pull out of a shadow and across the road behind him.

The trap had been sprung.

Immediately, Noah reached for his pistol, but his hand found nothing. He glanced down only to realize that the gun, along with everything else on the seat, had been flung onto the floor when he had jammed on the brakes. He felt his pocket; at least he had his phone. A shot rang out. The back window shattered. Noah jumped hard, then dared a look. Several heads appeared behind him, on the other side of the car. They were taking aim once more.

Noah knew there was not time enough to root around the car until he found his gun. He sized up the tree limbs. If he hit them hard and fast, he thought, it was possible that his momentum could carry him over the top and that he could get away.

Noah ducked down below the dashboard as another shot ripped off and instantly turned the windshield into a dense network of spiderweb cracks.

Noah threw the car in reverse and gunned the engine. He hit the car behind him hard on one of the wheels, blowing out the attacker's tire with a pronounced crack. Then he dropped the transmission into drive and pushed the accelerator to the floor. He slammed into the tree limbs, and the front of his car popped high into the air. When it came crashing back to the ground, Noah realized he was clear. But he was also out of control.

Noah was careening off the road at full speed. He tried his best to straighten the car out, but the right wheels had already dropped off the pavement into a weed-choked drainage ditch that ran along the road. A moment later, the car turned on its side and came to a dead stop, slotted tightly into the culvert.

His head was spinning, but somehow Noah managed to unbuckle his seat belt. He tumbled down out of his seat and landed hard on the passenger side door, which was now the bottom of the car. Already, he could hear shouting, and it was getting closer. Noah immediately began to search for a way out.

He pressed his hand against the shattered windshield; it bowed out easily. He threw an elbow against it several times. It partially popped out at the roofline, leaving him just enough room to crawl through. Noah put his head in first, then frantically pushed with his legs and forced his shoulders through, completely oblivious to the jagged edges that were tearing at his skin. Suddenly, he was birthed from the wreck and free. By the time he got to his feet, they were almost at his car.

For a fraction of a second, Noah thought about making a stand, but he knew that even Allard Davey was not bullet proof, so he decided to run instead. Noah quickly assessed his options. Taking off down the road was out—he would be an easy target the whole way. But to his right, no more than fifty feet away, across a ribbon of open grassland, there was dark-filled forest that stretched as far as Noah could see.

The problem was that he would be completely exposed until he got to the cover of the trees. Unless he was quick and elusive, it would be like shooting fish in a barrel.

Noah would need some help.

He dove into the Rolodex. An instant later, Noah bolted across the grass. But this was no panicked, disorganized flight. Using a blend of Jonathan Begrew's stealth and Alice Raines' fleet-footedness, Noah knew now exactly what to do. He made sure to move quickly and keep low to the ground so as to reduce the chance of them seeing him right off, especially in the failing light, and to make himself the smallest target possible when they finally did. He also sprinted in a seemingly unpredictable, zig-zag pattern, which was specifically designed to ensure that he dashed from shadow to shadow. This would help to further obscure him and prevent any of his pursuers from drawing a bead on him.

And it worked perfectly.

Noah was already into the forest before he heard the shot, which crashed harmlessly into the thick undergrowth behind him. Noah took in his new surroundings. Although the world outside was painted in burnt orange and purple, deep night had already filled the forest. Noah knew he would be invisible to them, at least for the moment, so he paused to catch his breath and consider his next move.

When he looked back, Noah could make out three featureless, dark figures backlit against the receding horizon. They were still coming, stumbling forward and cursing. Noah turned and made his way deeper into the forest, this time at a more leisurely pace. By the time his pursuers could coordinate their efforts, he reasoned, he would already be long gone.

Noah soon happened on a narrow, well-worn deer path that meandered in the general direction of where he wanted to go, so he followed it, if for no other reason than he did not have to waste energy blazing his own trail. Perhaps a quarter mile later, the trail disappeared just ahead into what Noah first thought was a small clearing, but as he came upon it, he realized it was a road, the very same old, abandoned farm road that ran alongside his parents' property!

But as Noah bounded heedlessly out from under the canopy of trees into the gray twilight, he saw something that stole his breath.

He had run right into the head of a large column of now very startled people, and he had to pull up hard to avoid colliding with them. To make matters worse, Noah realized that he had unwittingly blocked their path, the very thing he had been warned against. The alarms were sounding in his head, but it was too little too late.

They surrounded Noah with surprising swiftness, silently gauging the threat. He guessed there were at least a hundred, maybe more. He knew he would be quickly overwhelmed if it came to it. Finally, one of them, a man in his sixties who was wearing a greasy baseball hat and sporting a scruffy beard stepped forward and glared at Noah. His narrowed, glistening eyes conveyed an equal mixture of desperation, exhaustion, and anger. It was like he was waiting for Noah to make one wrong move, even to look at him the wrong way, so they would have a reason, any reason, to tear him apart. Noah bowed his head and retreated inward.

The gracious Lady of Old Town welcomed him into her arms and whispered in his ear.

When he looked on the angry man once more, Noah's eyes were aglow with wisdom, and he had a confident, radiating smile, the kind that drew people in and lifted the weight of the world from their shoulders.

Noah slowly held up his hands, palms forward to show he meant no harm.

"I am a friend," he said calmly, his smile never wavering, "and we are more alike than you know."

The man stopped. He tilted his head, and his face took on a bemused expression. He opened his mouth as if to speak, but just then, the noise of feet clumsily trampling dried leaves drifted out of the forest from behind Noah. It drew closer, followed by the faint sound of heaving breaths.

"That fucker is around here somewhere," a voice grunted. "Just up there," a different one said. "I think I see somebody!"

Without turning, Noah pointed over his shoulder toward the commotion.

"I am sorry, but they are not."

The man grunted and stepped forward. He placed himself between Noah and his pursuers.

"Then you should go," he said.

Noah felt hands on his shoulders pulling him backward. He was brusquely passed along toward the rear of the group until they all stood between him and the ones intent on harming him. Noah could not see anything through the wall of bodies, but he could hear it all.

"Back off you freaks," an angry voice growled. "Back off!" The group suddenly surged forward, almost in perfect unison. A single shot pierced the air. It was followed almost immediately by terrible screams. Then there was no sound at all except the shuffling forward of determined feet.

Chapter 52

HIS PARENTS' HOUSE sat back from the road at the end of a long gravel driveway. The nearest neighbor was about a quarter mile away, separated by a band of thick woods, several pastures, and a winding brook. When Noah finally arrived, he found the house completely dark and virtually indistinguishable from the starless night that was now draped over the land like a blackout curtain. Although, the absence of light made it easy to mark the campfires of his new "friends" dotting the distance.

Noah considered that he was a long way from help if he needed it, so he approached the house as quietly and lightly as he could, so as not to alert any trespassers. Noah walked first to the front door and slowly turned the knob. It was locked. He jogged down the driveway to the back door. Again, it was locked. He peeked in through the garage windows. The glass was dirty, so he wiped the window with his shirt. Noah could make out the shapes of both of their cars. He looked for the house key under a mat by the back door. It was gone.

Noah backed up a step then pushed off and threw his right shoulder against the door. It flung open into the wall.

He stood perfectly still for several moments and just listened for any response or movement within. Nothing.

"It's me, Noah!" he yelled loudly enough to be heard by anyone in the house. "Is anybody home? . . . Hello?" He waited patiently once more for several minutes. Only silence filled the air. He walked in.

He tried the lights, but they did not even flicker. He knew they kept a flashlight in the kitchen drawer. He found it, but the batteries were dead. However, there was a lighter and some candles. First, he checked the back door for damage. While the frame was splintered near the doorknob, the slider bolt on the inside was still intact. Noah forced the frame into place and pulled hard on the door to be sure it was secure.

Noah slowly made his way through the house by candlelight. Every bed was made. Nothing appeared out of place. His father's gun cabinet in the basement was undisturbed. He went back to the kitchen. There was food in the refrigerator, and it was cold. The power could not have been out long. The pantry was full, and much to Noah's delight, so was the bar.

Noah grabbed a fresh bottle of Jack Daniels. He walked out into the living room and sat down on the couch. As the adrenaline surge subsided, Noah began to feel the sting of his cuts and the lead weight of exhaustion. He took several long swills and stared into the dark. Inevitably, his thoughts drifted back to his parents. He was suddenly overcome with emotion.

Noah was certain that he was to blame for their fate. Had he told them everything from the beginning, it might have gone differently. He might have convinced them to stay close to home where he could have watched over them, where he could have protected them. Though he had never before given them reason to believe that he could do much of anything, at least anything useful, this time it could have been different. But they were on the other side of the planet now, out of touch, and perhaps out of time. If the trend toward disorder kept up, he might have to row a boat across the Bering Sea to get them. How long could they last? How much could they endure?

There was no denying that he was a blunt instrument, which explained why he had not understood the part he was meant to play until it was far too late. Despite everything he could do, Noah had done nothing at all. He allowed the two people he could have saved to wander where Noah, at least for the moment, could not go. As for everyone else, what could one man do, even one like him? He was about as useful as a match in a raging monsoon. Noah decided that survival stories were not so interesting if you were actually in them.

After the bottle was half-empty, Noah found his way to the gun cabinet. He was swaying as if he were on a storm-tossed ship, and he had to lean against the wall to keep from doing a face plant. He reached for the cabinet but stopped himself. He tried to imagine what it would be like if he put a gun to his head and pulled the trigger. Did the sound beat the bullet to the brain, or was it just a silent shove into darkness?

He had been in this place before, balancing on the slippery edge of self-destruction, and yet again, despite having every reason to finish the job, he could not manage it.

"Coward!" he growled.

Or was it something else?

Noah plopped down on the floor, his head between his knees. He searched his mind, but his thoughts were jumbled and spinning, as if he were falling from a great height. A wave of nausea followed. He threw up on his lap, but he was too drunk to care. He leaned back and passed out.

It turned out that Noah was not alone in the dark after all. The presence was comforting at first, like hands gently massaging his shoulders. A reassuring voice filled his mind. It came as a soft whisper from somewhere behind him: "Don't be a fool. You are truly great, better than I ever was," Noah thought it said. "Think of the things we could do now." Noah wanted to turn to see the face, but the hands and the sweet voice made him turn into mush. Soon he could feel arms enveloping him, gently rocking him while they drew him closer to the sound. The voice was all around him now, coming from every direction, but it took on a more menacing tone. "There is nothing beyond the veil. That is the only great truth. So, there is no reason not to make use of our . . . talents." It was the way the voice emphasized the word *talents* that snapped Noah to attention. He was certain he had heard such boasting before. For all the charisma and cunning possessed by the beast, he could not conceal his tell: hubris.

Noah forced his eyes open, expecting the nightmare to evaporate, but the Darkest Heart was not so easily flung aside. Noah could feel the tentacles slithering deeper into his brain, trying to wrest control from him. To Noah's utter shock, his hand moved when not commanded. His body lurched forward in a clumsy attempt to rise, even though Noah wanted to curl up into a ball. He could have even sworn that he heard himself laughing. If he did not do something soon, Noah realized he would have a front row seat to a real-life horror show.

In a daring move, Noah surrendered, as if letting go of the rope in a tug of war. Using the last shred of his will, he turned his eyes inward. The moment Allard Davey crashed through the door, spoiling for a fight, the evil thing slithered back into a deep crevice. But that did not mean that it ceased to exist, Noah knew. It was always there, though not always seen, forever probing for a weakness, for the right time to work its ambush.

Once Noah got the Warrior safely stowed away once more, he shook the cobwebs from his brain and slowly found his feet. How long had he been out? He checked his watch, but that did not help. Perhaps a couple of hours, he guessed. Though his legs were still shaky, he managed to climb the stairs. He knocked off his shoes and stumbled to the couch in the living room. He fished his wallet from his back pocket before he peeled off his wet jeans and threw them across the room. He was about to set the wallet on the coffee table but stopped in mid-motion. He found himself studying his wallet intensely. He felt the weight of it in his hand and tried to remember what was in it. He thought for a moment. There were three credit cards, some random business cards he had collected, cash and, of course, his driver's license; all relics of another time it seemed,. But he was missing something.

Noah could have just looked through it, but that seemed so tedious, and since he was now in the vise grip of a wicked hangover, he just did not have the strength. "Think," he whispered to himself. It was on the tip of his tongue. "C'mon, think!" Noah hit himself on the forehead with the heel of his hand. A memory was jarred loose. There was a small piece of paper with a number on it. It had been slipped into his hand, and he, in turn, had slipped it into a small pocket in his wallet for safekeeping.

Noah caught a glimpse of his future.

He grabbed his cell phone and prayed it would work.

Chapter 53

CHERYL WYATT STOOD entranced at the window in the living room. Another group was making its way quietly past the house. The power had been out for the last two hours, but the darkness cloaked her and made her feel safe. It wasn't that they had ever threatened her, but they were bound by some common purpose that Cheryl simply could not wrap her head around. After all, what reckless urge could drive them from warm, safe homes? And what strange compulsion could bring them there, to a forgotten jumble of buildings at the edge of the yawning wilderness?

When the first few began trickling into town, Cheryl tried to talk to them to find out what was happening. But she was mostly ignored or met with annoyed and sometimes angry expressions, which suggested that if she had to ask, then there was no point in an explanation. And now there were so many. Cheryl felt all the more intimidated by their increasing numbers. She had learned to suppress the ever-present urge to rush outside and plead with them for answers.

To make matters worse, power and utilities were increasingly on the fritz. There were blackouts every day now for a few hours, and the cable had gone out completely. Cheryl got most of her news from an old battery-powered radio with a snapped-off antenna. The only thing she could pick up consistently was a Christian AM station in Olympia, of all places. Science and fact were rarely mentioned. It was mostly talk about the wrath of God and the end of times. Certainly, there was a more rational explanation, she thought. Then again, what did it matter? What could she possibly do about it anyway? Like everyone else, all she could do was hope that the world woke up from this nightmare before everything was lost.

Just then, the lamps in the living room flickered to life and bathed the yard outside in pale yellow light. The group instantly receded further into the dark on the other side of the street in perfect unison, as if the light might fry them. It reminded her of a school of fish attempting to avoid a predator. Cheryl darted across the room and hit the light switch. She was once more made invisible by the night.

Cheryl forced herself away after a few moments and walked down the hall to check on her father. He was sleeping, breathing heavily. On the nightstand next to him were three brown plastic bottles of his medication. She made a quick inventory. There was a statin medication, blood pressure medication, and heart medication. He had about a two-week supply left of each one. He could do without the statin, and perhaps even without the blood pressure pills, Cheryl considered, but he would fill up with fluids and drown without his heart medication. If this was really the end of times, Cheryl knew she would soon be breaking into pharmacies to get what her father needed. She shuddered to think of all the sick people who relied on medication. They would be the first to go. And what about people in hospitals that needed machines to survive?

Cheryl could resist the urge no longer, so she again took up her post at the window in the living room, but she found the street empty once more.

At least she did not have to guess where they were going.

A few days before, Cheryl had gotten up the courage to follow some of them, from a safe distance, of course. She threw on a warm coat, grabbed her cell phone and a bottle of water, and set out far behind them. She tiptoed in the shadows, stealing glances from around corners and behind trees when she thought it was safe. She had the hair-raising sensation that they would not tolerate anyone who got between them and their destination, wherever that might be.

The first thing Cheryl noticed was that they seemed to be made up of all races and ages, and they all looked weary and underfed. Clearly, the journey had been long and had taken a greater bite out of some of the older and more infirm members who fell behind at times. But the rest always slowed their pace until everyone caught up. When the children lingered, they were scooped up by adults and carried or set down upon makeshift carts. And all those that were able were hoisting heavy backpacks. Strangely though, she did not see one cell phone or flashlight or any other way to light the dark.

Cheryl also found it odd that they barely said anything to each other. Even when they did, she could not hear it because they spoke so softly, as if any loud noise might cause an avalanche. It also seemed that they had no real need to talk because each one of them intuitively understood where they were headed. That may have explained why there was no obvious leader of the pack. No one pointed the way or passed on instructions or encouraged them to push on. They just kept trudging along toward the horizon.

Once they got outside of town, they crossed the highway into the woods and made their way for almost a mile along the Sauk River. As there was plenty of cover, Cheryl slinked along in their footsteps. About two hours later, just as Cheryl began to think it was time to get back home, they began to slow, as if nearing the end. They disappeared over a low rise down to where the river carved a snake through the trees. Cheryl crawled to the edge. They were unpacking their gear, setting up tents and gas stoves, and even greeting and shaking hands with some of the others that had arrived before them. Perhaps there were a couple dozen who were already there.

Two nights later, Cheryl returned to find that their numbers had at least doubled, and they were still coming from several directions. They were cooking or doing laundry in the river. Some were huddled around small campfires, sitting in folding chairs or on coolers. They seemed perfectly content, as if they were out for a family camping trip.

If a person was going to make a go of it in the wilderness, Cheryl decided as she watched them, then Darryville made perfect sense. There was plenty of wood for fire and shelter, and the lush, fog-shrouded forest was home to all types of game, from elk and black-tailed deer to black bears and cougars. Not to mention that the Sauk River was teeming with trophy-sized trout, along with king, silver, and blackmouth salmon. And, due mostly to the wet, temperate climate, you could grow almost anything.

But winter was another matter altogether. Though the temperature rarely dropped below twenty-five degrees, the land was perpetually socked in by a curtain of fog and rain, which made it almost impossible to get a fire going. It also made it difficult to orient yourself if you got lost, which was so easy to do unless you had spent most of your life there. In another cruel twist, the rain turned any hard surface under-foot slippery and treacherous. Sometimes storms brought wet, heavy snow that would flatten anything but the sturdiest shelters like tissue paper. And, as anyone who spent time in the mountains in winter will tell you, you were always soaked to the bone, which made hypother-mia a constant worry, especially since it tended to sneak up on you like a stabber in the dark.

And the cornucopia of animals and edible plants that was almost always within an arm's reach most of the year belied the sudden absence of it in the winter. You had to travel longer and farther to find the calories you needed to survive, assuming you knew where to look, which exposed you for greater periods of time to the elements and increased the risk of injury and death. Sometimes, even the best mountaineers were swallowed by the vastness in winter and never seen again.

But these people were going to be cannon fodder. And it would hap-pen soon.

To start with, they were mostly city and suburb dwellers according to the radio, so it was likely that none of them had any real survival experience. And with winter looming and their food in short supply, it would not be long before starvation and disease stalked their camp. But even more pressing was the unseen danger inherent in the very place where they had set up shop. No doubt they chose it because it was a wide, flat expanse of land directly adjacent to the river. Although they did not know it, they were in a flood plain. And as any resident of Darryville can attest to, the Sauk River can swell quite rapidly in winter and jump its banks with little warning. If they were caught unaware, it would be a disaster. Even if they managed to escape in time, they would almost certainly lose precious food and gear, which would only accelerate their deaths at the hands of more subtle killers.

8—

Cheryl felt her eyelids growing heavy. She shut the curtains and sat down. She rested her head against the back of the armchair. How long had it been since she had slept more than a few hours? She could not remember.

She closed her eyes, and the face of Noah Batson appeared on the back of her eyelids. Was it all just coincidence that the world had stumbled so soon after he had appeared and claimed his mysterious prize? And why had she given him her number? And why hadn't he called her? She had thought a lot about him since then, but she did not understand the reason for it. Maybe it was just good entertainment, a way to occupy her mind and distract her from her woes. Cheryl had created several elaborate backstories that explained everything. Perhaps he was a long-lost heir to a vast fortune and had finally found proof of his birth. Maybe he was on the run from the law and something in that box could prove his innocence. He could even have been a time traveler retrieving a memento he had left for safekeeping long ago.

Whatever the explanation, Cheryl could not escape the feeling that their lives would somehow converge.

Cheryl suddenly felt the urge to check her phone. It took her a moment to dig it out of her back pocket. She kept it turned off the rest of the time to conserve juice. Not that it mattered, she thought. She had not had a call in days, as almost everyone else she knew had either drank the Kool-Aid or set out in search of the ones who had.

This time was different.

Cheryl stared at the screen and froze. Three missed calls in the past several hours. She did not recognize the number, not even the area code. Just as she began to scroll through her contacts for a clue as to who it might be, the phone rang and startled her. She had almost forgotten her ring tone, the Indiana Jones theme. It was the same strange number.

"Hello?"

"Is this Cheryl?" The voice sounded groggy and distant.

"Yes, who is this?" she asked, though, somehow, she already knew. "Wait, the guy from the bank, Noah, right?"

Noah cleared his throat. "I'm sorry it took me so long to call."

Cheryl suddenly felt the weight of it all and unleased an expletive-laced narrative about everything that had happened since they had met, about the power, the radio, her ailing father, and the doomed people gathering outside of town. He could not get a word in edgewise.

"Did you have something to do with this?" Cheryl finally asked, as silly as that question seemed. But these were crazy times, and she did not take it back.

A long silence. She thought she had dropped the call.

"Noah?"

"I'll be there with you as soon as I can," he finally said. "I think I know what to do now. I think I can help." Noah paused once again. "I mean, . . . this sounds crazy, I know, but of course it's up to you."

Cheryl had so many questions rattling around inside her brain that she could not decide in what order to start. But, after a beat or two, her mind became oddly clear, as if something else grand were at work, as if the fates themselves had plucked her thread to remind her that she had only to feel her way through this moment to know that she really had no choice about what to do or say next.

"Just hurry," she found herself saying with irrational conviction.

Chapter 54

AFTER WATCHING THE Prius for several days, Noah was convinced that nobody was coming back for it. He tried the handle, and the door opened. The keys were lying on the passenger side floor along with a dead cellphone. He climbed in and hit the start button. It had about a quarter tank. That was more than enough, at least for now. Noah rifled through the glove box. The car was registered to Carolyn Folmsby. He found himself muttering an apology to her as he adjusted the seat then pulled away.

Back at the house, Noah inventoried the load of supplies he had bought, borrowed, or even stole, over the past month and dumped in the living room. There were MREs, a med kit, blankets, a tent, toiletries, water and water filters, his father's Savage .308 rifle with 200 rounds of ammunition, a Sig-Sauer P226 (which also belonged to his father) and 250 rounds of ammunition. He had antibiotics and medicine that Cheryl had said her father needed, warm clothes, an extra pair of boots, flashlights, a tarp, and a sleeping bag. He would be lucky to get all of it into such a small car, he thought, but he needed a hybrid. The fuel shortages made it likely that he would have to drive for hundreds of miles between fill ups.

Noah knew well the journey would be a crucible. He would likely be beset by bad weather and neglected, snow-covered roads and, of course, other people. But he had thousands of invisible travelers with him, at least one of whom would be uniquely equipped to solve virtually any problem he might encounter along the way. Yet, there was one above all the others on whom Noah would rely heavily.

Francesca, the Lady of Old Town, was his constant companion these days, always close at hand. Sometimes she was a warm, tingling current just beneath his skin or a reassuring presence in the dark every time he closed his eyes. Noah even saw her dreams play while he slept, as if he had a front row seat behind her eyes. She was lending him her confidence, strength, and boundless optimism because Noah would need her most if he was going to help everyone else.

A loud knock on the door woke Noah from his daydream. He snuck a peek from between the drawn blinds, just to be certain, then smiled. He shook Rick's hand as he ushered him inside.

"Wow!" Rick said as he glanced around the living room. "You really are gonna do it!"

Noah nodded. "For sure; I'm going."

Rick held out his arms with his palms turned up. "All this for a woman you met one time? What if you get all the way out there and you find out you don't even like her?"

"It's hard to explain, Rick. I just feel it in my bones; that's where I need to be right now. Anyway, isn't that how every great story starts: following after a woman you barely know?"

"To each his own," Rick said with a shrug. "I just think there has to be an easier way to do it. I heard on the news that the airlines are going to start flying cross-country again. That makes sense because they also said that more supply chains were coming back online every day and that the shortages were easing up. If you wait long enough, you'll be able to just get on a plane like everyone else and go see her like a normal person."

Noah waved him off. "They've actually been saying that for a while, and I can almost guarantee you that nothing will change in the next couple of months. In the meantime, I can wait here for my parents, or I can go out there and wait with her. What's the difference?"

Of course, that was only part of the reason Noah was leaving, a very small part, in fact. How could he really explain to Rick that the voices of the dead inside him were in perfect harmony on this point: Noah must set off now if he was going to help mend this world.

Rick plopped down on the couch. "You're probably right. I'm just trying to give you an excuse to stick around longer." Rick took a deep breath and suddenly looked as if he had remembered something. "Hey, aren't you going to offer your guest a drink?"

"Hold on," Noah said and walked out of the room. A moment later, he appeared with a bottle of bourbon and two glasses.

Rick grimaced. "Old Crow? Are you trying to kill me?"

Noah laughed. "Sorry, I drank all the good stuff already."

Noah poured a finger of bourbon in each glass and handed one to Rick, who immediately downed it.

"Jeez," Rick said in a hoarse voice, "that really is rot gut."

Noah followed suit. He coughed several times. "You're right."

Rick stared quietly down into his empty glass for a moment. "All kidding aside, Noah, do you know what you're doing? The cops, the National Guard—they're a skeleton crew, and they're barely keeping a lid on things. You won't have much help out there."

"I understand, but except for you, I've got no one here, no reason to stick around, especially since you *promised* to keep an eye on the house while I'm gone."

Rick leaned back on the couch and laced his fingers behind his head.

"I'm a darn fool," he said contritely. "I didn't think that one through. You had one reason written in the 'stay' column, and you crossed it off as soon as I said yes. Here I thought I was helping a friend, but what I was really doing was sending him out into a world turned upside down."

Noah smiled. "I appreciate the sentiment, but I'm the one who should feel guilty. You've got a lot on your plate, and I just gave you more to worry about. . . . By the way, how *is* your wife?"

"Pretty good actually; better than the last time I talked to you anyway. She put on some weight; she looks better. I guess she looks and mostly acts like her old self. She is still squirrely about some things though. When some electronics are powered up, she complains about noise and headaches, but even that is starting to fade."

"Does she remember anything yet?"

"Not really, only that she wanted to come home. She still doesn't know where she was or what she was doing before I found her sitting on the porch like a dirty bag lady. She describes it like waking up after a crazy, vivid dream that you can't picture anymore. She said it drives her nuts sometimes, because it's always on the tip of her tongue." Rick shrugged. "Honestly, I could care less. Me and the kids are just happy to have her back."

Noah opened his mouth to speak, but Rick suddenly jumped up from the couch and cut him off.

"Noah! I forgot to tell you something. I heard on the radio last night. It's not just Karen; other people are coming home, too! It's not a whole lot, at least yet, but reports are coming in that people are beginning to come back!"

"I guess that makes sense," Noah thought out loud, "some people returning to their senses. I wish it were that easy, but things are so fucked up that even if everyone comes home right now, I don't think the world will ever be quite the same. It sucks, but it stands to reason that some, or even most of them, will not ever want to be found. That means a lot of people will still be off the books for a long time. And with winter on us, my guess is a lot of them will soon be corpses."

Rick suddenly looked at Noah solemnly. "I don't want you to be one of them, kid."

Noah laughed. "Don't worry, old man; I don't think my story ends just yet." He grabbed the bottle of Old Crow and, much to Rick's chagrin, poured a generous portion into each of their glasses. Noah held his up. "A toast then, to the future. May each of us have one."

They touched glasses and tossed them back. Once they had both stopped retching, Noah saw Rick to the door. Like always, Noah promised to stay in touch when he could. Rick reiterated his oath to keep the house on lock down. After a back-slapping hug, Rick climbed into his car and drove off.

Noah immediately set to work.

By the time he had shoehorned everything into the car, it was already late afternoon. He called Cheryl and told her he would get on the road first thing in the morning. She said that they were still coming every day. She told him that he should be careful but that he should get there as soon as he can. Then she said she *missed* him. Rather than ask her how she could pine for a man she had met only once, Noah told her he missed her, too. Strange, he thought, when he hung up the phone, that he should feel the same way. While Noah could imagine any number of reasons why that should not be the case, he could not square himself with any of them. All he could do was shrug, for he was as inexplicably and inescapably drawn to her as he was to the place where he would find her. Perhaps, he considered, the answer was in the Rolodex, but if it was, he could not put his finger on it. Then again, although it seemed impossible, maybe his ancestors had some ideas for themselves that Noah could never know.

Chapter 54

St. Joe National Forest, near William, Idaho

NOAH GLANCED UP to the opaque, afternoon sky. Light snow began falling. He decided it was a good time to stop and reorient himself.

Noah unshouldered his rifle, then his backpack. He looked back across the vast meadow from which he came. He guessed it was close to ten miles since he had left his car. Noah fetched his binoculars and aimed them ahead into the distance. The trail wound across the meadow for another half mile or so before it disappeared into a spinney of Douglas fir trees that stood at rapt attention. How much farther? If what the guy at the gas station had said was accurate, Noah had a mile or two to go.

After a long pull of water and a power bar, Noah gathered his things and set off again. Once he had cleared the dense ribbon of trees, Noah found himself back in open country. But the snow was falling harder now, making it difficult to spy the terrain that lay beyond. Still, he did not need to see the St. Joe River to know that he was getting close.

Noah kneeled down. The fresh snow made the webbed prints pop. Unless they were scouting new territory, Noah's invisible guides had told him that beavers rarely travel far from home. It was not long before he could hear the sound of rushing water. Just as he got within sight of the river, the trail made a soft left, running parallel to the water but against its sparkling current.

That path took him through a copse of pine trees, up a long but lazy incline, and finally onto a yawning, tabletop meadow. Noah stopped to catch his breath. He squinted and shaded his eyes against the pelting snow as he scanned the distance. He caught a flash of unnatural blue, then bright red. Noah walked closer. Soon, there was no mistaking the multicolored clutter of tents set up at the far end of the clearing.

Once Noah got within earshot, he began shouting "Hello!" at the top of his lungs to give warning and to be sure he could be heard above the wind. He also held his hands high above his head to show he was no threat. No one responded.

Noah slowly moved forward until, unchallenged, he stood in the shadow of the camp. It was only then that he could see with enough detail to understand that their situation appeared to be far more serious than rumor had suggested.

Noah quickly counted at least thirty small dome-type tents of various colors, which he guessed could have sheltered two to three people in each. They were arranged in rough circles around several stone fire rings that were cold and blanketed with a fresh coat of snow. Some of the tents appeared to be sagging or had collapsed entirely under the weight of an older snowfall, indicating that they had been abandoned for some time. And there was garbage strewn about everywhere: empty cans, empty water bottles, and spent food wrappers. It was as if the occupants had neither the inclination nor, as seemed more likely, the energy to carry off waste to a safe distance.

Noah cupped his hands and let a yell rip, "Hello! Is anyone here?"

An orange tent a few feet away shuddered slightly, shedding its fluffy snowcap. Noah walked toward it as a zipper was slowly undone.

A weak voice called back, but Noah could not make out the words. A hooded head with sunken eyes emerged from the dark opening. Noah could not tell if it was a man or a woman. They started to cough. Noah kneeled down. The person retreated inside and made way for him to enter. Noah poked his head inside and was immediately met with the stench of urine and feces. It was all he could do to keep from puking.

"Food . . . just a little food if you have it," they said in a hoarse, halting voice.

Noah set down his things outside the tent and fished a power bar out of his pack. He tore off the wrapper and handed it over. They pulled their hood off with a dirty hand, revealing a greasy clump of long, tangled hair. "They" were a woman, Noah decided, though her age was impossible to determine. She frantically ate the power bar in small bites, like a rat nibbling at a hunk of cheese.

"I'm Susan," she said when she was done. "Do you have more?"

Noah retrieved another power bar and tore it in half. "Not too much at one time now; you'll get sick." He placed a piece in her outstretched hand. She immediately tore into it.

"I'm not going to hurt you," Noah offered.

The woman stopped eating and looked up at him. "I got that much."

"Good," Noah said. "You feel better now?"

She nodded. "A little."

"How many of you are there?"

"Now? About twenty or so."

"How many did you start with?"

"Fifty-three."

"What happened to the rest?"

"Some went back home; some died."

"Died? What happened?"

"We only had a little food left, and that ran out a couple of weeks ago." She shrugged. "We buried them off in the woods."

"But there's game everywhere: whitetail deer, mule deer—enough meat to feed an army!"

"We tried, believe me. We could see the deer everywhere, but any-time someone went to hunt them, they were nowhere to be found. All we could get were some rabbits, squirrels, and a couple of fish, and that was just not enough."

"Why didn't you just get smart and leave?"

Susan shook her head. "I'm not going back to that madness, not ever."

"Would you rather starve to death?"

She shrugged. "If you felt like you were being water-boarded every waking minute of every day, what would you do? For me, I'd rather be dead than live in a torture chamber for the rest of my life."

"I can't say that I understand, but at least I can help. Do you think you can gather up the rest of your people? I'll start a fire while you do that, then I'll see about getting food. That way you can all keep warm till I get back. Do you understand?"

Susan nodded, then started to sob. "I guess we didn't know how hard this was going to be, especially for the kids. . . . Most just weren't strong enough."

"Well," Noah said, "maybe it does not have to be that way anymore."

Chapter 55

NOAH PUT THE three-hundred-plus-pound mule deer in his crosshairs. He let out his breath and steadily pulled through the trigger until the shot rang out. The deer bucked, then jumped, then bolted off madly across the meadow. But it would not get far, Noah knew. It was hit through both lungs and probably its heart as well. And it would be easy to track its crimson blood trail against the new white snow.

Noah jumped up from behind his makeshift blind of twigs and grass and raced off after it. He soon found the deer, not more than twenty-five yards from where it was stricken. It died in stride, plowing its antlers into the ground with enough force to turn up the black soil below.

Noah could not help but be awestruck by his borrowed hunting skills. Locating, tracking, and killing the beautiful creature was but a flick of the wrist for someone who could tap into the knowledge of the many trackers, trappers, and woodsmen like Jonathan Begrew who had come before. Noah glanced around for a moment. In fact, where the hapless others saw only barren trees, water, soil, and stone, Noah's experienced eyes could see that there was everything that one could need for shelter, food, and warmth a mere arm's length from where he stood. And that was when a vague idea became as crisp and sharp as the deep night frost: He could teach them, and they would pass that on long after Noah was gone. Maybe he could even find a place for them all, a sort of promised land for the disaffected, where he could keep watch over them until they could fend for themselves.

More pressing, however, was the immediate need for food, so Noah put his bigger thoughts aside and squatted down to set about field dressing his kill, which Noah was sure would yield at least one hundred pounds of food, not to mention all the other inedible parts that could be put to practical use. It would be too heavy to haul out in one piece though, so he would carry out as much meat as he could after hiding the rest high up in the tree until he could come back for it later.

Just as Noah put knife to flesh, he caught something in the snow just a few feet beyond his prize. It was a strange track, about four inches wide, one unfamiliar even to Noah. He examined it intensely, letting his fingertips sense its shape and measure its depth. The ridges were delicate and soft, lightly made, though certainly fresh. Although incomplete, it was clear it was a paw print consisting of a pad and four toes. Noah expanded his search area, and he found another, then another. They trailed off to a tree line that lay about fifty yards beyond. He suddenly had a bad feeling. Noah tapped into the Rolodex.

A woman by the name of Ida Aple came to mind. She was, oddly enough, a prostitute-turned-trapper in Montana in the late 1800s who had made a good living in the beaver pelt trade before settling down with a dentist in Helena. She had crossed paths with mountain lions, who more than once had ambushed and shredded her pack animals; thus, she had learned to spot their tracks. When she did, she took the long way around no matter how many miles out of the way it took her. But if the prints were fresh, she knew, it was likely already too late to avoid violence. And because you could rarely see them coming, she was yelling to Noah to get out of there as fast as he could.

Noah's heart stopped—he could feel the killer slinking in from his blind spot, about to make a charge, about to turn predator into prey. Noah looked quickly to his rifle, but it seemed miles away. Then he realized he still had his blood-stained knife in his hand.

He swiveled his head in time to see dagger teeth and deadly claws all aimed toward his throat.

Chapter 56

R ICK HALLMAN WAS scrolling through television channels merely for the sake of it. Lately, the news was mostly good; a return to normalcy was imminent. He was happy to hear that from any angle, whether it was Fox or MSNBC or any station in between. Rick was perfectly content to point and click and bathe in the optimism like the first sunny day of spring, until he caught a familiar face and froze in his tracks.

"I'll be damned," Rick whispered.

Although the man on the screen had a full beard and a long, angry-looking scar that ran down his right cheek, there was no doubt in Rick's mind who it was: Noah Batson. Rick had not heard anything from Noah in almost a year, and he had for a while now counted him among the dead or those who were still missing. Yet there he was, surrounded by microphones and cameras, standing in a vast meadow that lay like a lush carpet at the foot of misty forests and mountain peaks that pierced the low-hanging sky in the distance. Several reporters were asking questions all at the same time.

"Please," Noah Batson said in commanding voice, "one at a time now." The set grew quiet. Noah pointed at someone off screen. "You sir, the one with the blue coat, go ahead."

A voice spoke up. "What's your message? What do want people to know?"

Noah closed his eyes and rubbed his forehead for a moment, as if to think of what he would say. When he stared into the camera once more, he was somehow a different person than he had been just a second or two before. The face was the same, but there was suddenly a rich depth to his eyes, as if they were a set of fathomless blue sinkholes that you could not tear yourself away from.

"They say things are getting back to normal, but for all of you still out there," Noah finally said, "I know it's not over. But you don't have to be alone, cold, or hungry anymore." Noah pointed over his right shoulder. "You see what's behind me? That's almost two million square acres of wilderness, a tract of land about half the size of the state of Delaware. For the past eight months now, we have been working with federal, state, and local governments to secure permission for this venture." Noah held up a packet of papers in front of the camera. "Yesterday, all the approvals came through. This represents a promise for a promise. We promise to take care of you, and the government promises to leave us be on this land, a place where we will forever be off the grid."

Another reporter started to speak, but Noah held up a pausing finger. "So, you must get the word out, anyway you can. Come one, come all. You don't have to bring anything. We have food, we can provide medical care, and we will give you shelter. And when the time is right, we will get word to your loved ones to at least let them know you are safe."

Noah pointed at someone off camera once more, presumably the reporter he hushed. "Go ahead now," he said.

"That could mean a lot of people. How could you possibly care for them?"

Noah nodded, acknowledging that it is was a fair question. "Let's just say that . . . *we* possess just about every skill a person might need to survive."

⏀—⚓

Cheryl zipped her coat up to fend off the chill and then scrambled quickly up the short but steep slope. Strangely winded, she had to pause for several moments to catch her breath at the top. *That's new,* she thought as she thrust her hands into her pockets and made her way carefully along the narrow trail in the predawn darkness. About a half hour later, Cheryl arrived at her destination, which was nothing more than a flat, weather-worn slab of stone that jutted out from the top of the hill like a neglected diving platform. It provided a sweeping view of the ever-growing settlement just below and the Sauk River beyond that, which seemed to be set on fire by the orange light of new sun that had just begun to rise into the sky.

Cheryl could make out a figure wrapped in a blanket sitting on the rock staring out toward the cold skyline.

"I had an idea I would find you here," Cheryl said as she walked over and sat beside him. "You didn't think I knew about this place, did you?" Noah turned to her and smiled, then threw the blanket over her shoulders and pulled her close.

"You shouldn't be here," Noah chided her softly. "You could have slipped and fallen. . . . Still, I'm glad you found me."

"I woke up, and you were gone. I started worrying about, well, *everything,* then I couldn't get back to sleep. . . . I'm just so emotional these days."

Noah nodded. "I think that's normal for a person . . . in your condition."

Cheryl playfully punched Noah in the shoulder. "It's not an illness you know. . . . But seriously, why can't *you* sleep? The press conference is over now; the stress is gone, right? I would have thought you would be out like a light."

"The more I think about it," Noah said, "the more I realize that getting up in front of the cameras was the easy part. It's what comes after that that really bothers me now. Be careful what you wish for, right? What I mean is that once the word gets out, they will come from everywhere. Then what? It's been easy so far because there just aren't that many of us now. I have to admit, for the first time, I feel a little overwhelmed."

Cheryl gently set her head on Noah's shoulder. "I understand, but look at what you can do." Noah followed her eyes to the collection of sturdy cabins nestled in the crook of the hill below. Smoke was already rising from their chimneys as fires were stoked for breakfast. "You taught them everything they needed to know, and they will pass that on to the new ones. If it's five hundred, fifty thousand, or even five hundred thousand, what does it really matter? The seeds are already planted, I guess you could say. It doesn't have to fall just on you."

"They will always look to me though, even if it is only to speak for them."

Cheryl turned and kissed Noah on his cheek, then took his hand and pressed it to her belly. "Only until our daughter is old enough to take over," she said softly.

Noah reared his head back and laughed. "You think we're having a girl, do you?"

Cheryl nodded. "I know it; I just had a dream about it. A name even popped into my head: Francesca! I'm not sure where I got that from, but doesn't it have a proud ring to it? Like it belongs to an inspired lady from a long time ago?"

About the Author

For the past twenty years, Christopher Shipman has been a criminal defense lawyer living and working in Eastern Pennsylvania. During that time he has tried more than fifty cases in both state and federal courts, including capital homicide matters, and he has lectured to both students and peers on various topics concerning crime and punishment. But he has long harbored a desire to blaze a more creative path and to write a thought provoking novel that provides a unique and fascinating take on the age old question of who we really are.

www.ingramcontent.com/pod-product-compliance
Lightning Source LLC
Chambersburg PA
CBHW070344090426
42733CB00009B/1282